Gendered Freedoms

Southern Dissent

Florida A&M University, Tallahassee
Florida Atlantic University, Boca Raton
Florida Gulf Coast University, Ft. Myers
Florida International University, Miami
Florida State University, Tallahassee
University of Central Florida, Orlando
University of Florida, Gainesville
University of North Florida, Jacksonville
University of South Florida, Tampa
University of West Florida, Pensacola

Southern Dissent Series

Edited by Stanley Harrold and Randall M. Miller

Gendered Freedoms

Race, Rights, and the Politics of Household
in the Delta, 1861–1875

Nancy Bercaw

Foreword by Stanley Harrold
and Randall M. Miller, Series Editors

University Press of Florida

Gainesville · Tallahassee · Tampa · Boca Raton

Pensacola · Orlando · Miami · Jacksonville · Ft. Myers

08 07 06 05 04 03   6 5 4 3 2 1

Library of Congress Cataloging-in-Publication Data
Bercaw, Nancy.
Gendered freedoms: race, rights, and the politics of household in the Delta,
1861–1875 / Nancy Bercaw; foreword by Stanley Harrold
and Randall M. Miller, series editors.
p. cm.— (Southern dissent)
Includes bibliographic references and index.
ISBN 0-8130-2591-5 (acid-free paper)
1. Delta (Miss.: Region)—Race relations. 2. Delta (Miss.: Region)—Social
conditions—19th century. 3. Plantation life—Mississippi—Delta (Region)
4. Households—Mississippi—Delta (Region)—History—19th century.
5. Whites—Mississippi—Delta (Region)—Social conditions—19th century.
6. African Americans—Mississippi—Delta (Region)—Social conditions—19th
century. 7. Sex role—Mississippi—Delta (Region)—History—19th century.
8. United States—History—Civil War, 1861–1865—Social aspects. 9. United
States—History—Civil War, 1861–1865—Influence. 10. Reconstruction—
Mississippi—Delta (Region) I. Title. II. Series.
F347.M6 B47 2003
305.896'07307624'09034—dc21   2002040906

The University Press of Florida is the scholarly publishing agency for the State
University System of Florida, comprising Florida A&M University, Florida Atlantic
University, Florida Gulf Coast University, Florida International University, Florida
State University, University of Central Florida, University of Florida, University
of North Florida, University of South Florida, and University of West Florida.

University Press of Florida
15 Northwest 15th Street
Gainesville, FL 32611–2079
http://www.upf.com

For

Esther Fuller Allison, Woodson Woods Bercaw, Jr.,

Sue Allison, Scott David Kreeger,

and Reva Allison Kreeger

Contents

Figures

Tables

Foreword

*A*MERICANS REGARD the Civil War as the most divisive event in their country's history. It pitted North against South, antislavery against proslavery, a modernizing culture against a traditional one. Union and Confederate armies confronted each other during four years of brutal warfare, most of which took place in the South. The determination of southern whites to maintain slavery and an extreme form of white supremacy had led in 1861 to secession and war. Very conscious of this motivation and seeking to weaken it, President Abraham Lincoln initially declined to make the abolition of slavery a United States war aim. He feared that precipitate action against slavery would alienate southern whites who might otherwise stand by the Union. Enslaved African-Americans by their actions helped convert Lincoln and other northerners to the belief that the North must fight not only to save the Union but to abolish slavery as well. Lincoln's Preliminary Emancipation Proclamation of September 1862 and the Final Emancipation Proclamation of January 1863 were the products of this conversion.

As soon as the war began, many enslaved African-Americans left their masters and headed for the Union lines. Even before emancipation became an official northern war aim, the Union army enlisted black men to fight against those who claimed them as property. The war, which caused southern white men to depart their plantations and join the Confederate army, also gave some black men an opportunity to take control of plantations. Some black families turned to subsistence farming. These actions precipitated confrontations on the southern home front that, as Union forces penetrated ever more deeply into the Confederacy, became increasingly complicated for black and white southerners.

Historians since the 1860s have been aware of how divisive the war was and how much was at stake. Some portray it as an economic, social, and political turning point that set the United States on the path toward a more prosperous, democratic, and inclusive future. Others contend that it initiated unbridled capitalism, cultural uniformity, and centralized government. Only recently have historians begun to probe the war's impact on how noncombatants perceived themselves, their family relationships, their community standing, and their gender, class, and racial identities. Studies of these issues indicate that the war not only divided the country against itself but divided personalities as well. It shaped not only national development but how Americans thought of themselves as individuals. Recently, too, historians have focused on southern households to better understand the impact of the war on the people of that region. Especially important have been studies of how ordinary black and white southerners struggled over dismantling slavery and reconstructing southern society.

In *Gendered Freedoms: Race, Rights and the Politics of Household in the Delta, 1861–1875*, Nancy Bercaw places the story of war, abolition, and reconstruction in a context of households as centers of human identity. She shows that two types of households—plantation households and black households—shaped Civil War–era struggles between white planters and their former slaves. In turn the struggles reshaped the households. Before the war, white men ruled plantation households that included the masters' families, slaves, and dependent whites. Black households were subordinate to the plantation households. During the war, with masters away and the slave system unraveling, white women assumed masculine roles within plantation households. Meanwhile black men expanded their authority within their households and radically reshaped plantation households. This put black women in the difficult position of seeking to support the aspirations of black men while maintaining their own standing.

Through the lens of households, Bercaw shows black and white southerners acting during the Civil War and its aftermath to redefine their cultures' most fundamental assumptions. White women found themselves dissenting from traditional southern notions of race, class, and gender. White men, distracted by the loss of power they suffered as a result of the war, used violent means to reassert their masculinity. African-Americans, determined to make the land serve their households, entered politics to protect their new freedom while simultaneously dissenting from the victorious North's individualism. Competing notions of household and contested notions of gender, Bercaw shows, fundamentally shaped the politics of Reconstruction in the Mississippi Delta. Very likely they did so in much of the rest of the South as well.

Bercaw has produced an insightful book that will provoke a thoughtful response from readers. It is a book full of interesting people struggling to comprehend themselves and their radically changing world. A worthy addition to the Southern Dissent series, *Gendered Freedoms* shows that the divisiveness reflected in and enhanced by the Civil War went well beyond the military, political, and economic to strike directly at people's most fundamental conceptions of themselves.

Stanley Harrold and Randall M. Miller
Series Editors

Acknowledgments

$\mathcal{M}$ANY FRIENDS, families, and institutions helped me to complete this project by offering friendship, guidance, and financial support. I did not always take their advice willingly, but I am grateful nonetheless.

I thank my families. To Scott Kreeger, for understanding so much, doing so much, and bringing a weird, manic joy to the work of writing—thank you for making life so rich. I thank Reva Allison Kreeger for sweet gladness; Esther Fuller Allison, Nancy Scott Bercaw, Sue Allison, and Woodson Woods Bercaw for faith, perception, courage, and support; Pete Daniel for showing me by example; the commune, Elizabeth Feder and Mark Johnson, for keeping me sane and very amused; my Mississippi cousins, Martha, Barbie, Susie, Beth, and Amy Bercaw for their spontaneity and companionship; Kim Wallace for always making unforeseen connections; and Winston C. McDowell for honesty, criticism, and encouragement.

Many friends and colleagues have done more than their fair share on this project, especially Laura Edwards, Drew Faust, and Ted Ownby, who (along with Scott) read this more than once and sometimes a lot more than twice too. I thank Randy Finley, Noralee Frankel, Laurie Green, Jerma Jackson, and Anthony Kaye for making me see things differently. Aileen Ajootian, Amy Bentley, Beverly Bond, Beth Boyd, Kirsten Dellinger, Robbie Ethridge, Brett Gary, John Gennari, Thavolia Glymph, Ken Goings, Sue Grayzel, Erica Hess, Nancy Hewitt, Evelyn Brooks Higginbotham, Jed Levin, Laurie McLary, Gail Murray, Jonathan Prude, Joe Reidy, Julie Saville, Stephanie Shaw, Sheila Skemp, Barbara Ellen Smith, and Nan Woodruff read and commented on various portions of the manuscript, and I am grateful for their insights. I cannot adequately express my gratitude to Kevin McCarthy for his incisive reading, and I remain especially indebted to Alice Hull Lachausse, Jeffrey Fuller, Tracie Milam, and William Morris, who worked with me and covered my blind spots.

A Rockefeller Foundation Grant, the Mellon Foundation, the Smithsonian

Institution, Oberlin College, the Department of American Civilization at the University of Pennsylvania, Bob Haws, the Department of History, the College of Liberal Arts, and the Graduate School at the University of Mississippi gave me the invaluable gift of time to research and write.

I must credit University Press of Florida editor in chief Meredith Morris-Babb's encouragement, project editor Jacqueline Kinghorn Brown's patience, copy editor Ann Marlowe's acumen, and series editors Stan Harrold and Randall Miller's persistence for the final product.

And finally, I thank Nellie, Cecil, Sam, and Ruth for their dear friendship.

Introduction

Framing Dissent: Household(s) in Black and White

ON MARCH 10, 1870, Delta planter James Lusk Alcorn stood before Mississippi's legislative assembly as the state's first governor elected by a black majority. On this momentous day, Alcorn attempted to bridge the past and the present. To do so, he called on the most powerful institution he knew—the "family." He did not speak of political parties or of the 60,167 African-American men who helped elect him to office.[1] Nor did he speak of other pressing public concerns—Mississippi's relation to the nation, the state's crumbling economy, or its changing legal structure. Instead, to locate a sense of order and stability within the turbulence caused by emancipation, war, and Union occupation, Alcorn placed the domestic institution of family at the center of his speech. "Where the State government had been called on in the past, to discharge its functions in reference to but one man," Alcorn reasoned, "it is called on now to discharge them in reference to each individual of that man's 'family'—of twenty or five hundred [former slaves]."[2]

The "family" Alcorn referred to in this speech was the plantation household. Like many planters, Alcorn assumed that slavery was a domestic institution and that enslaved African-Americans were "members" of each planter's "family." Emancipation suddenly replaced each plantation household with up to five hundred black households. The problem of freedom, from Alcorn's perspective, was this exponential growth in the number of households. Suddenly the state represented thousands of new citizens—African-American men who had established mastery over their own households. Searching for unity, he assumed that households would continue to function as the foundation of domestic and political authority. Dependents, in his mind, remained sequestered within their homes while the heads of their households—men, whether black or white—assumed full rights of citizenship.

Alcorn mistakenly assumed that emancipation was a question of quantity, not quality. The abolition of slavery had simply created more households—hundreds of miniature versions of the same institution. What Alcorn overlooked was the fact that not all new citizens accepted his construction of the household and its concomitant borders between private and public. Attempting to locate the familiar, Alcorn glossed over the evidence that households varied not only in number but also in kind.

In his inaugural speech, Alcorn assumed that all Mississippians defined the household, and the power it accorded them, on his terms. They did not. Not everyone conceded authority to the head of the household. In the Delta, southerners—white, black, male, and female—understood the household as the foundation of their rights. Yet they disputed both what constituted a household and which "rights and obligations" it upheld.

This study examines the centrality of the household, in its various contested forms, in grounding southern dissent from 1861 to 1875 in the Yazoo-Mississippi Delta. Attention to competing understandings of the household reminds us that people frame dissent in direct relation to what oppresses them. They do not—and in many ways they cannot—create a new world out of whole cloth. Instead they take bits and pieces of the past to create a future.

In the antebellum Delta, the household represented the political, economic, and personal force of slavery. Why then would a former slave declare in 1866, "The Marriage Covenant is at the foundation of our rights"?[3] Marriage, and the household more broadly, served to naturalize and legitimize inequalities. Why would former slaves adopt the language of the household at the very moment of emancipation? On the one hand, the household represented the seat of power. Consequently, former slaves and former slaveholders expressed dissent by calling on the legitimizing force of the household to defend their vision of their rights. On the other hand, when southerners called on the household to defend their sense of justice—as Alcorn did in his inaugural address—it became clear that they did not share the same understanding of either the ideologies or the structures of a household. Although slaveholders included slaves in their definition of the household, slaves understood the household in more expansive terms and constructed a competing understanding of power and authority. The experience of slavery, therefore, gave each southerner his or her own individual perspective on how domestic relations undergirded political and economic rights.

Emancipation tore apart these competing understandings of the household.

As plantation slavery dissolved, African-American and white southern households collapsed. Without them, the location of power and authority became scrambled and confused. To set their world to rights, black men, white women, black women, and white men worked to reconstruct a politics of household on new ground.

Competing Constructions of the Household in the Antebellum Delta

Like most members of the planter elite, Alcorn connected the word *family* with the enormous power of the plantation *household*. When white men spoke of *family* in the antebellum South, they referred to much more than just immediate blood kin. They included everyone residing on their plantation or farm who fell under the authority of the head of the household. On a plantation, this would include the planter's wife, his children, miscellaneous relatives, and enslaved black families. On smaller farms, the household might consist of just a farmer, his wife, and children. Households varied by region, class, and a person's stage in the life cycle. Despite these differences, law and custom granted each white male head of household the rights of mastery over all his "family" members. By defining the household in these terms, planters consciously argued that slavery was the logical extension of the family, where wives, children, and slaves fell into a rough hierarchy below husbands, fathers, and masters. Slavery, they argued, was a domestic relation. The household, therefore, referred to more than a type of family structure. Instead, each antebellum household served as a physical representation of southern power relations.[4]

The ideologies of household extended these domestic relations out to the public sphere, marking the free and the unfree. Southern laws denied white women, African-Americans, and hired hands full legal rights and privileges, not because of their gender, race, or class per se, but because they lived as dependents in another man's household. As dependent people, they were considered subject to manipulation by their husbands and masters. They could not be trusted. The household, therefore, set most white men apart from other people. They alone were free in a landscape dominated by their dependents— wives, children, and slaves. This measure of independence awarded white men citizenship and the right to vote.

Yet a man's independence was qualified. His authority did not spring from his whiteness, his manhood, or his individualism alone. Instead a man's political privileges rested on his ability to head a household. Only then was he considered free from the corrupting influence of others. Legal and political privileges, therefore, stemmed from the domestic relations of household rather than a white man's gender and race alone.

Without whiteness and manhood, however, a person had few legal rights. The state naturalized household hierarchies and extended them to people's bodies. Across the nation, governments denied women and African-Americans full political privileges because of their gender and race. A woman, black or white, could head a household and manage a plantation, but she could not vote. A free black, male or female, could own and operate a business and still have few legal rights. The state associated blackness and womanhood with dependency and in consequence denied all women and African-Americans full citizenship. Their bodies—their "blackness" or their womanhood—excluded them from the public sphere.

The ideologies of household, therefore, performed several tasks at once. The household served to justify slavery, allocate political rights, and naturalize gender and racial hierarchies.[5] The household acted as the point of negotiation between the citizen and the state, slaveholders and slaves, and men and women.

Under this antebellum system, enslaved African-Americans had none of the privileges of the household. As dependents, they had no domestic or public rights. They could not marry, testify in court, trade goods, or move freely across the public landscape. Although represented by their masters, slaves legally had no public self.[6]

Emancipation changed all that. Suddenly African-American men and women, freed from the shackles of the plantation household, could assume mastery over their own households. They became, at least in Alcorn's eyes, independent. Therefore, they deserved political rights. The household, in his mind, was the cornerstone for freedom. By linking rights to the household, Alcorn disrupted the neat dichotomy between Old South and New South and between slave-labor and free-labor societies.[7] He carried the past into the present.

Alcorn was not alone in using the past to gain a firm foothold in the new political landscape. The household, after all, was as much an ideology as a specific household structure. As an ideology, the household took on many meanings at once. No two people had experienced the past in the same way. The chaos of war and Reconstruction provided an opening for redefining the household and its privileges.[8]

Living under the constraints of plantation slavery and the legal codes it generated, African-Americans had formed alternative visions of the rights and privileges of the household. On one level, slaves upheld the theoretical model of the plantation "family" to negotiate with slaveholders. They appealed, as "members" of the plantation household, to keep their own families together, reduce workloads, fire overseers, or win free time to work gardens, attend religious services, and care for their children.[9] The conditions of slavery forced African-Americans to recognize the slaveholders' definition of the plantation household.

Yet, during slavery, African-Americans constructed their own families within the plantation household. They defined their households on their own terms within their own communities. Of course, planters encouraged slaves to marry, and most did. However, it was not necessary to be husband and wife to form a family. In the Mississippi Delta, African-Americans formed households with one another without regard to gender, age, or even kinship. Isabella Harris lived and raised a child with her mother-in-law, Charity Smith. Brothers Cary and Pleasant Adams lived together their entire lives. As Cary testified, "we went into the service together, served together, and were discharged together and have lived together ever since." Likewise, Daniel Bell was taken in by his uncle Samuel Spencer, forming an all-male household that lasted throughout the Civil War.[10]

African-American family structures, then, were more varied and diverse than the definition of the household upheld by the planter class. Granted, slave families existed within the confines of the plantation household where a master could, and usually did, claim sole authority over each man, woman, and child residing on his plantation. Yet, within these constraints, the slave households pointed to alternative constructions of power and authority based on domestic relations. In white southern households a man, by virtue of being the head of his household, presumed a unilateral flow of authority descending from himself to his wife, children, and slaves in a rough hierarchical order. Slave households, however, did not reflect this understanding of power stemming from one individual. Unlike their white counterparts, African-American men could not assume authority over their households by virtue of their manhood, their rights of property, or the legal sanction of their marriages.[11]

Slave households provided an alternative understanding of power that was based less on manhood, property, and individual authority than on a complex interweaving of relationships mediated by the community. Within specific families, gender did not always dictate who was in charge. Women teamed up with other women, men hooked up with men, and husbands and wives sometimes lived apart, on separate plantations with individual homes and personal property. Relationships might be hierarchical, but it was not always clear that men would be the dominant partner.[12] Authority could not be claimed, but had to be negotiated instead.

African-Americans invested their communities with an active role in mediating relationships, displacing individual authority. For southern whites, the law served to protect a man's right to property, and the courts regulated marriage relationships. Without these protections, African-Americans accorded the community the right to certify marriage and property rights. An enslaved woman might marry her sweetheart before a preacher or a master, but as former slave testimonies make clear, a marriage ceremony did not constitute a marriage. In order to be considered husband and wife, a couple needed to act married over a period of time, and the community needed to call the woman by her husband's name.[13] Like marriage, property ownership was a social act. According to southern laws, slaves could not legally own property. Yet many slaves managed to acquire possessions ranging from cash to livestock. Exactly who owned what, therefore, could not be determined by law. Instead, a person had to demonstrate effective ownership. As historian Dylan Penningroth argues, African-American men and women called on their communities to establish proof of ownership. How a person acquired an object was less important than acts that demonstrated ownership over time. Neighbors testified as to how the person had used the property and when. And they described who had witnessed these acts. Marriage, authority, and property rights had to be performed to be earned, and witnessed by one's community.[14]

African-American households, therefore, modeled a complex understanding of authority based on both relationships and performance. The basis for an individual's authority varied from place to place, as community standards and customs differed. Despite the variety, however, one factor remained static: African-American households posed a challenge to planters' neat assertion that patriarchy, invested in white men as the heads of their household, was natural or inevitable.

For African-Americans, the household held two meanings simultaneously. As slaves, they were forced to recognize the very real power of their masters' plantation households, but at the same time they constructed competing structures and definitions of the household—and of authority—within these plantation communities. The plantation household and the slaves' households existed, and were experienced, simultaneously. Individuals learned the competing lessons of power and authority from both. Yet within the black and the white communities alike, one fact remained undisputed: Domestic relations served as the basis for public power; the household, regardless of form, was the foundation for political action.

The Civil War and emancipation shattered the plantation household, separating master from slave and husband from wife. Households scattered as Union and Confederate armies launched a series of attempts to control the Delta's waterways. None of these households would ever take the same form again. White households, in the wake of emancipation, lost the foundation of their authority, while black households faced the glare of legal marriage. The customary relations—between men and women, black and white, independent and dependent—were irrevocably altered.

Three questions center this study:

First, in the absence of the plantation household, how did southerners, black and white, male and female, reconstruct the social basis for personal and political authority? The plantation household had secured social order before the war, investing the head of the household with economic, political, and social authority. How were power relations contested and reconfigured when the plantation household collapsed?

Second, how did the disintegration of the household affect individuals' sense of their own identity? Without the plantation household, the antebellum understanding of manhood, womanhood, blackness, and whiteness eroded. Where did personal power reside in the absence of mastery?

Finally, how did the domestic relations of household affect political consciousness? A person's very sense of self was constituted in the domestic hierarchies of the household. This process was a social act, shaping an individual's sense of what was right and just. The household relationships, therefore, provided an important foundation for political action or inaction. How did black men, white women, white men, and black women transfer the lessons taught in their households out into the world to defend their particular vision of freedom?

The Yazoo-Mississippi Delta

The Delta proved an unusual testing ground for early expressions of freedom in both black and white communities. The region is significant for several reasons. First, the Delta provides a counterpoint to recent scholarship on the Civil War and emancipation. Most studies focus on communities along the eastern seaboard—Georgia, the Carolinas, Virginia, Maryland, and Delaware—where slavery was well established for several generations prior to the Civil War.[15] By contrast, the Delta was a frontier society. At the time of the Civil War, the region had been open to American settlement for only twenty-nine years—roughly one generation. People imported the practices of the household, in all its varied forms, from the more settled regions of the South. Second, the Delta, like the South Carolina lowcountry, had a large slave majority. African-Americans represented a full 76 percent of the total population in the Delta and, in four of the nine principal counties, more than 87 percent. To travel along the Mississippi before the war, Frederick Law Olmsted commented, "was like travelling through Angola." African-Americans cleared and settled the Delta. Unlike in South Carolina, however, the slave communities in the Delta had shallow roots. An extremely high mortality rate and the active slave trade grimly shaped African-American communities. By 1861, few African-Americans born in the Delta reached adulthood. Freedom took on new form in the absence of long-standing customary rights and traditions.[16] Finally, the Delta had an unusual Civil War history. Large-scale emancipation occurred in the Delta in 1862, before the Union had a stable presence in the region. Former slaves freed themselves and established their visions of freedom with limited interference by Union troops. The Delta, therefore, provides a unique example of emancipation as defined by freedpeople themselves.

The Delta—more accurately referred to as the Yazoo-Mississippi Delta—is a vast alluvial plain formed by the floodwaters of the Yazoo, Mississippi, Sunflower, and Tallahatchie Rivers. Bordered by river bluffs a hundred miles inland, the Delta resembles a large egg nestled between Memphis to the north and Vicksburg to the south (see figures 1 and 2). Each spring the melting snows of the Midwest flow down the Mississippi River and deposit layer upon layer of rich topsoil across the Delta's massive floodplain. No amount of erosion can strip the soil of its wealth. Before the Civil War, and for a good generation after, the Delta was a vast swamp of "cypress, water oak, sweet gum and pecan trees [that hid] . . . the sun from the virtually impenetrable cane and brush." Every year the rivers that crisscrossed the region rose to create a vast lake, teeming with wildlife.[17]

At the time of the Civil War, the Delta was perhaps the rawest region of the Cotton Belt. Until 1832, the Delta was Indian territory reserved for the Choctaw and Chickasaw nations. White men had traded, hunted, and squatted in the Delta, but its rich soil belonged to Native Americans. It was a rough life. "Log

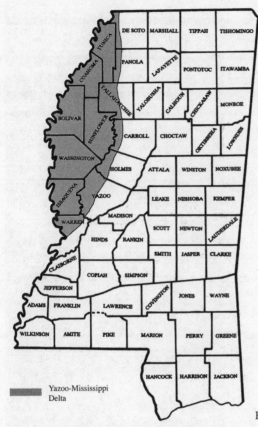

Fig. 1. Mississippi counties in 1860.

cabins afforded almost the only shelter," wrote Colonel James R. Creecy in 1834, "and perhaps, in a whole day's ride through an open wilderness, you would not meet with more than two of these."[18]

By 1832, the United States had forced Native Americans off the land. In these dense watery forests, plantations stood like islands in the wilderness. People reported that a farmer could drop a cotton seed in the rich earth and sprout a seven-foot plant. In less than seventy years the swamps were drained, the forests cut, and cotton spread across a flat treeless plain.[19] The Delta had come to resemble the midwestern plains of its birth. Today, the landscape is a man-made creation built with the sweat and blood of African-American laborers.

The severe physical environment created an unusual social geography. Only very wealthy planters and enterprising lumbermen bought land in the Delta. Few yeomen farmers were willing to risk their families' lives trying to clear and

Fig. 2. The Yazoo-Mississippi Delta, ca. 1860.

drain the thick Delta swamps. Instead, planters sent more than a hundred thousand slaves into the Delta to bring it into cotton production. Settling along the riverbanks, slaveholders purchased vast plantations. In Issaquena County, bordering both the Mississippi and the Yazoo Rivers, the average plantation exceeded five hundred acres in 1860. Across the Delta, 71 percent of all settlers owned more than a hundred acres, and 24 percent held more than five hundred.

This stood in marked contrast to the neighboring hill country, where only 19 percent owned a hundred acres and fewer than 2 percent owned more than five hundred. Moreover, of the 3,383 white families living in the Delta, 79 percent owned slaves in 1860, when only 23 percent of those living in the hills were slaveholders. Large plantations, wealthy planters, and a pronounced slave majority dominated the region.[20]

Absentee ownership marked the Delta. Because life in the dense swamps was extremely precarious, anyone who could afford to leave did so. More than 35 percent of all landholders in the Delta lived elsewhere.[21] For those who stayed, malaria was the most common killer. Fevers became a part of daily life, recorded like the weather. "I don't know what is to become of me," wrote Amanda Worthington, "I have so many chills and afraid they will *undermine my constitution* before long."[22] To avoid illness, planters and their families often left the Delta for months at a time, hiring others to manage their affairs. Bazil Kiger maintained his family for most of the year in Washington, D.C., and visited his plantation in northern Warren County once a year. Every summer he wrote doleful letters to his wife Caroline, explaining, "I sometimes think that was I able I would never spend a summer in the South . . . [but] tis indispensable that most of my time should be spent here. . . . my Interests are suffering in my absence." To manage vast plantations in absentia, planters kept up copious correspondence with their overseers, including detailed instructions. "Reduce the width of the Cotton rows in fresh land to 5½ feet," commanded Francis Leake. "Run 4 furrows to form the planting ridge, if time will admit."[23]

Absentee ownership created a rough and isolated life for most whites in the Delta. Many "big houses" were crude log structures built for shelter alone. Whites who stayed in the Delta faced extreme isolation. "Mrs Rhodes has a lovely time indeed the poor creature," commented William Gale. "Since the first week she has not seen the 'skin' of a white woman and most of the time the weather has been so wretched she could not put her foot out of the house. I really feel pity for women whose situation in life compels them to live in such a manner." Annie Jacobs recalled that her mother "never liked the Delta. She loved society, gayety, visiting among friends. . . . Old traditions, the unwritten laws of a settled social prestige of the past could not be pursued in the new environment where the first consideration must be the fight with elemental powers." Jacobs remarked that "nobody cared so much about family as the character, strength or ability of their new neighbors." Some found this liberating. Edwin Bolton gambled his life for profit, saying he "can be respected [in the

Delta] in a Log cabin and be happy without splendor." Yet he paid a price. "I do not want to stay here next year if I can avoid it I am fearful for my health ... but rather than sacrifice the property I am willing to stay."[24]

Despite (or perhaps because of) this transient population, the planter class clung to the ideologies of the household. With few churches, few schools, and only occasional circuit-riding judges, slavery represented the one common social institution in the area. Order, planters maintained, rested in their command, even from afar. Absent white men and women kept close track of the slave communities, inquiring into individuals' health and family life. Many women, like Ellen Hyland, made an effort to spend Christmas on the plantation to oversee slave marriages and allocate "gifts." The ritual of paternalism continued unabated even if it meant traveling hundreds of miles each year with children in tow.[25]

Searching for white southerners and finding so few, many historians argue that the Delta had little antebellum history. After all, only 3,383 white families lived in the Delta in 1860. Yet these historians overlook the 70,000 African-Americans who lived in the Delta and worked the land. While most white southerners came and went, black southerners settled the Delta. As Janie Matthews remarked, it is a "flourishing country which abounds with *Negroes*."[26]

The Delta had one of the largest African-American populations in the Old South, rivaling the southern Louisiana sugar fields or the South Carolina rice district. To amass their great wealth, Delta planters forced tens of thousands of African-Americans into the swamps to bring the land under submission. The harshness of life in the Delta became legendary in slave communities across the South, symbolized by the simple phrase "sold down the river." This was not an empty threat, but literally referred to the horrors slaves experienced in the Delta swamps. For most slaves, the brutality began with the slave trade. Stripped from their families and communities, hauled halfway across the country, locked up in "slave yards," and sold at auction, these black southerners found themselves at work in dense malarial swamps. James Henry Clay remembered being sold twice from the same slave yard in Natchez. Both times he was sent back to the Delta.[27]

Once in the Delta, slaves faced hard labor in a deadly environment. Before cotton could be cultivated, the dense swamps needed to be drained and cleared. The work never ceased. The planting season began in late February or early March. All summer, men and women plowed the fields, sowed cotton and corn, and tended the crops. Picking season began in September and did not wind down until Christmas. Then, during the cold winter months after the corn was harvested and the cotton ginned, planters sent slaves to the swamps to clear more land. Men timbered while "women and boys" cut cane.[28] The wood had to be cut while the rivers were high so the logs could be floated down to market. This forced slaves knee-deep in water during the coldest month of the year. The combination of the hard work and disease killed many black southerners.

Death, disease, and slave sales shattered families and communities. Unlike those along the South Carolina coast, African-Americans communities in the Delta faced constant rebuilding.[29] Black southerners created new families. After being sold from her mother, Emiline Farley lived with her uncle Gabriel Davis "all my life before the war." Likewise, Daniel Bell was taken in by his uncle Samuel Spencer. When Courtney Burton's husband died before her son's birth, Edward and Frances Hickman stepped in and helped her raise Philip. Frances nursed him while Edward taught Philip to pick cotton and plow. Marriage also cemented family bonds. Martha Willis lived with her father-in-law after her husband was sent to another plantation.[30] Life was too precarious to try to go it alone. This rich evidence of African-Americans' alternative constructions of household complicates our current understanding of southern social relations.

Thus the Delta provides new insights into the plantation South. Most historians searching for large, well-developed, more culturally autonomous slave communities turn to the South Carolina lowcountry. They reason that, in the lowcountry, the large black majority and vast plantations provided slaves with greater isolation from white southerners. Under these circumstances, African-Americans on large plantations were better able to create a separate culture than those on small farms. Consequently, for many southern historians, the South Carolina lowcountry serves as a benchmark for understanding African-American perspectives on slave culture, emancipation, and Reconstruction. The Delta shared many of the characteristics of the lowcountry but differed in one— longevity. Life was short in the Delta, and consequently slave communities constantly changed.

How did African-American communities define rights, obligations, and the meaning of freedom in this environment? What were the problems of freedom on the southern frontier? The Delta's unique Civil War history provides unusual evidence for addressing these questions. Unlike most areas of the Union-occupied South, the Delta experienced almost one full year of emancipation without Union oversight. In the spring of 1862, the massive Vicksburg campaign hemmed in the Delta on three sides. With Union troops to the north and the west and Confederate forces to the south, slavery hemorrhaged as African-Americans ran for the Union lines. However, the Delta's dense swamps protected both blacks and whites from invading armies.[31] In this strange no-man's-land, southerners confronted the first year of freedom in relative isolation. The Delta's southerners defined freedom on their own terms, affording uncommon insight into their particular expressions of liberty.

Moreover, a community study provides the specific context necessary to explore identity relationally. Race, class, and gender conventions varied with the plantation, crop, and region. By selecting a single area for study, one can more closely establish precisely what those practices were in the Delta. A community provides access to names which, when encountered often enough, can be fleshed out into people who reveal complex and often contradictory motives for their actions. Planter-class men and women have always been relatively easy to research. Many of their letters, diaries, and plantation journals are neatly preserved in regional archives. It is much harder to establish the subjective experiences of black men and women. The Delta's rich Civil War history, however, provides rare access to the intimate lives of African-American men and women immediately following the war. More than twenty thousand black men (55 percent of the African-American male population) qualified to serve in the United States military in the Delta. Heavy recruitment by Union troops in the area guaranteed that most served at least some time in a United States uniform. Aware of their rights, these men and their wives applied for U.S. military pensions after the war. The Union soldiers' widows' applications paint detailed portraits of the Delta's African-American communities. To receive a pension for her husband's service, a wife had to prove that she was married to the soldier during the war. Because slaves could not legally marry, pension examiners interviewed the applicants' neighbors, relatives, and friends to certify the marriage. These applications contain the voices of hundreds of African-Americans recounting their lives from the 1830s through the turn of the century. When combined with complaints filed with the Freedmen's Bureau and claims for property filed with the Southern Claims Commission, these sources record the voices of entire communities and indicate a complex web of relations that knit Delta society together. They enable us to better understand how power was repeatedly constructed and contested throughout the period.

In a community study, individual families, as much as the household itself, will be under investigation. Despite Alcorn's insistence that all households were fundamentally alike, white and black southerners often lived in families that did not resemble the archetype. For purposes of clarification, therefore, the term *households* (plural) will refer to individual black and white families, while the term *household* (singular) will be reserved to refer to the plantation household as an expression of public order. Of course, the borders between individual households and the plantation household were porous at best. The household and individual families existed in relation to each other; they were intimately related and, in many ways, formed in direct reference to each other. Indeed, the force of the plantation household—the term's usefulness as an ideology or an expression of the social order—rested in this constant slippage between "the household" as a lived experience and as a social construction of power relations. Yet the distinction between *households* and the *household* permits a better understanding of how individuals negotiated and translated domestic hierarchies.

The clearest articulations of southerners' competing interpretations of household occurred in the first years of the war. Part I, "The Unfettered Self: Dismantling the Plantation Household," examines the impact of the Civil War on individual identity. During these years, the full complexities of households, black and white, rose to the surface. War tested each relationship, providing us a glimpse into daily domestic life usually considered too mundane to record. Under the strains of invasion in 1862, what many southerners always perceived to be "natural" began to break down. The "freeing" of dependents (white women, children, and black southerners) caused a series of slippages between race, class, and gender. Was a master without slaves still fully a man? Moreover, what did whiteness mean in the absence of slavery? And was a freedman free without mastery over his household? Did independence strip a freedwoman of her womanhood? Emancipation threw everything open to question, testing each southerner's most intimate identity. Black and white southerners quickly learned that neither race nor gender is easily grasped outside the boundaries of the culture in question. Yet as the physical plantation household vanished, its ideological constructions lingered on in twisted and mutable forms.

Part II, "Forced Intimacies: Reconstructing Households in the Postwar Delta," moves the study from a discussion of individual identities to a social contestation of rights. As white and black men returned home after the war, southerners faced each other as a community for the first time since emancipation. Broadening the study from individuals to society, the succeeding chapters explore how hotly contested domestic relationships grounded the complex renegotiation of labor and politics. These chapters explore how the reconstruction of households informed the way people challenged and reframed their perceptions of rights and obligations.

The ideologies and practices of household remained alive long after the war. Freed from the suffocating grasp of slavery, men and women, rich and poor, black and white, voiced their understanding of freedom in terms of the household—the one institution that they held in common even as they interpreted its meaning and its structure on vastly different terms. In letters, diaries, newspapers, interviews, affidavits, and depositions, southerners, black and white, defined their understanding of human relations. They adamantly and persistently disagreed about the nature of manhood and womanhood, blackness and whiteness, and dependency and freedom.[32] By emphasizing their experiences as either man, woman, black, white, worker, employer, or farmer, they defended their vision of a just society. The complexities and contradictions of these meanings of household enrich an understanding of how ordinary people, caught up in the turmoil of everyday life, constantly use the most intimate institutions to carve out a place for themselves where they can act with authority and demand a recognition of their rights.

I

The Unfettered Self

Dismantling the Plantation Household

WAR AND EMANCIPATION shattered the plantation household, as first white men, then black men, and finally entire slave communities set off to wage war. Gone were the masters. Gone were the slaves. And gone were any easy assumptions that power correlated with whiteness, masculinity, or class position. The force of the older laws no longer prevailed. In this strange new world, men and women, white and black, grasped for anything knowable and familiar. How did southerners find their place in a world without slavery? How did each locate and assert his or her unique understanding of authority in a world turned upside down? How did their self-conception affect their vision of a free society?

Part I, "The Unfettered Self: Dismantling the Plantation Household," examines the impact of emancipation on individual identities. In a slave society, people were brutally categorized as either powerful or powerless. The dissolution of slavery, however, complicated such neat assertions. Suddenly planter-class women were both empowered and subordinate, African-American women at once both strong and vulnerable, African-American men both nurturing and destructive, and white men both righteous and ashamed. In this spectral no-man's-land, exactly who held authority and on what terms was by no means apparent. Familiar ideologies of race, class, and gender became confused, scrambled. People thrashed about, seeking the most powerful weapons they knew.

In the Delta, the conditions of war created an odd phenomenon—plantation slavery dissolved, but no single coherent social structure rose up to take its place. Emancipation forced people to look inward, not to society, to locate a sense of self. Moreover, the war placed African-American men and women, plantation mistresses, and planter men in relative isolation from one another. Examining each group individually—first African-American men and women, then white elite women, and finally planter-class men—the first three chapters explore their members' responses to the collapse of slavery. Striving to reconstruct personal and group authority, each discovered that emancipation was not completely emancipatory. A person's habits, beliefs, customs, and actions, learned over a lifetime, refracted the world she or he once knew.

Part I, therefore, emphasizes the personal over the social. As war ruptured Delta society, each individual or group was, at least in some ways, more free to express a unique form of dissent—dissent against slavery, the Confederacy, emancipation, or the Union. In framing their opposition, southerners were forced to confront just who they were in the absence of the other. Who was a mistress without a husband, or a master without slaves? And, as one man poignantly wrote, "what kind of free is free" if you are torn from your family and working for another white man? At root, each chapter asks how the ideologies of household informed individuals' most intimate sense of self and, in turn, shaped their understanding of the body politic.

1

❧

The Foundation of Our Rights?

Emancipation, Marriage, and African-American Households

*I*N THE WINTER of 1864, the United States Third Colored Calvary rode onto the Basin plantation in Washington County and ordered the white overseer, William Wallace, to assemble all the slaves. Standing before more than two hundred men, women, and children, the African-American soldiers "told them they were all free and all who were in favor of going away were to step forward." Everyone stepped forward. Wallace panicked. "[T]here was nobody there but me and my wife," he remembered, "but I could not persuade them to stay." En masse, the former slaves turned around and walked away. The sudden shock of emancipation was too much for Mrs. Wallace. She fainted—or, in Wallace's words, "dropped down flat"—knocked unconscious by events she could not reconcile.[1] William Wallace called out, "You are going away and have left me nothing." One man returned to hand him a piece of meat, and then rejoined the others. In a single afternoon, a busy plantation was transformed into a ghost town. The silence created by their absence must have been awful.

The moment of emancipation on the Basin plantation dramatically juxtaposed at least two competing definitions of the household. The Wallaces watched in disbelief as what they had assumed was their household walked away without so much as a backward glance. The former slaves, however, were not walking away from what they defined as their household. They left with family and friends—as a neighborhood—carrying their households with them.

Emancipation exposed how fragile the plantation household had been. As the African-Americans on the Basin plantation demonstrated, they never accepted white southerners' definitions of the plantation household. Their loyalties lay elsewhere. Small wonder that Mrs. Wallace fainted. She could not face the demise of her world and the sudden reversal of dependencies—her husband begging for food and, even worse, begging not to be left alone. Leaving the plantation, African-Americans abandoned the Wallaces and forced them to confront the remains of their world in the eerie isolation of the Delta swamps.

The Wallaces, like most white southerners, defined the household in relation to slavery. The head of household was the owner of the land and slaves—in this case Alexander Bullet, Wallace's employer, who managed the Basin, Longwood, and Glenora plantations from his home in Louisville, Kentucky. Bullet, as the head of household, claimed mastery over his wife, children, six hundred enslaved African-Americans, and even to a degree the Wallaces themselves. Slaveholders recognized individual slave households, in part, by permitting informal marriages. But southern law and southern slaveholders denied legal marriage to slaves. This tied each individual African-American to the direct and immediate control of the household head and allowed slaveholders to buy and sell slaves without any consideration of family bonds.

How did black southerners in the Delta contest the meaning of the household? Moreover, how did competing meanings of the household ground dissent—dissent from white southerners and Yankees and dissent within the black communities themselves?

The black southerners on the Basin plantation dramatically demonstrated what the household was not. The household, from their perspective, was not bounded by the borders of the plantation or the will of a white man. The Wallaces were not "family" by kinship or community. The Wallaces deserved an act of simple human kindness: they would not starve. Yet as the freedmen and women carried away horses, cows, chickens, and hogs, they made sure that the Wallaces would not reap the full fruits of the former slaves' labor.

We know how African-Americans rejected white southerners' definition of household, but we know less about how they defined household for themselves. Antebellum records provide a mere glimpse into the basic structure of the Delta's slave households. We know that slave households were extremely fragile. Hard labor, deadly living conditions, and frequent sales tore families apart. As a consequence, highly flexible family forms developed. Kinship and marriage served as the basis for many families, as uncles teamed up with nephews, cousins shared homes, and women moved in with their in-laws. However, many family members also shared less traditional ties. Older couples took in orphans, single women lived with other women, and men and women "took up" without marriage ceremonies.[2]

Individual households, however, did not exist in a vacuum. The slaves on the

Basin plantation did not leave in family groups; they left as an entire community or, as historian Anthony Kaye argues, as a neighborhood.[3] By leaving as a group, the African-Americans on the Basin plantation demonstrated an important facet in slaves' understandings of their own families. Their households did not stand apart from one another, but were intimately interwoven into the social fabric of friends and neighbors.

Neighbors played an important role in slave households, witnessing marriages, adoptions, and acquisitions of property. In a society where slaves had no formal legal rights, neighbors sanctioned, disputed, or debated social claims and, thereby, helped to establish accepted patterns of behavior.[4] According to Kaye, a neighborhood might consist of the adjoining plantations or, on some of the vast Delta plantations, the home place itself. Personal contact determined what constituted a neighbor or a neighborhood. A neighbor was well known. A neighbor knew your history—who you had married, who your children were, and where you had come from. Beyond the neighborhood were strangers. Regardless of whether they were black or white, free or slave, strangers were not to be trusted. Herein lies the critical distinction between neighborhood and community. As Kaye argues, the term "slave community" implies a common bond between all slaves based on the condition of slavery alone. Yet the capricious nature of slaveholders' power—a master's ability to punish or reward according to his own rules or, more accurately, his whims—meant that slaves experienced slavery differently from place to place. To withstand the often erratic use of force, slaves counted on those they knew—on personalities they could attempt to predict. A stranger threatened this delicate effort to balance slaveholders' power.[5]

The household, therefore, served as the first foundation for organizing Delta slaves' perception of their social and economic rights. Yet those rights depended on the approbation of neighbors. No one could stand alone, and no family lived detached from the neighborhood. So when the freedpeople on the Basin plantation left, they left together, carrying their connections—their historical memories of justice—with them.

Between 1862 and 1865 the war tore many neighborhoods and households apart. The reaction of the freedpeople on the Basin plantation was only one of many responses. Some freedpeople chose to travel with family, while others went with friends, leaving family behind. Entire plantation neighborhoods left together, as the Basin slaves did, while others split apart. Several factors influenced these decisions. Within the slave neighborhoods themselves, gender, age, children, and social ties pushed or pulled people apart.[6] The timing of emancipation also played a role.

Emancipation arrived in the Delta in two stages. The first, initiated by slaves, occurred in 1862. The second wave of emancipation occurred in 1863, after President Lincoln pronounced the Emancipation Proclamation. The two separate moments of emancipation differed in kind and character. The first, as a largely grassroots movement, reflected Delta African-Americans' definitions of freedom. Running from the plantations or simply refusing to work, slaves declared themselves free. After the Emancipation Proclamation, however, Union forces tried to direct emancipation. The army initiated recruitment drives into the Delta, sorting and classifying freedpeople as either army material, worker, or dependent. Moreover, the meaning of freedom often became actively contested as Yankees and black southerners met face to face.

Despite the significant differences between the two periods of emancipation, one pattern remained firm—more women than men chose to stay home. For the most part, the first African-Americans to confront free labor on the Delta's plantations were women.[7]

This chapter explores African-Americans' changing understanding of household during the Civil War years 1862–65. As historian Laura Edwards has argued, during Reconstruction "marriage lay at the very center of the postemancipation political structure."[8] With legalized marriages, former slaves became masters of their own households (see figure 3). Marriage marked black men's independence and buttressed their claims to full political participation: namely, the right to vote. As Corporal Murray, an African-American soldier, declared, "The Marriage Covenant is at the foundation of our rights."[9]

Yet marriage—the bond between husband and wife—was not the only foundation of slave households. How did African-Americans come to accept marriage, as opposed to other forms of domestic relationships, as the foundation of rights? A closer examination of the war years in the Delta provides insight into how black southerners began to reconceptualize the relationship between household and rights, both within and without the bonds of marriage.

The first half of the chapter examines the first wave of emancipation—the critical year 1862, when African-Americans freed themselves. During this year, the United States government had little, if any, organized presence in the Delta. As a consequence, 1862 provides a rare glimpse into how African-Americans defined freedom for themselves. While young men ran for freedom, crossing

Fig. 3. Most African-Americans recognized the family as the foundation of their rights. Yet many questioned whether marriage made a family. Instead they accepted a wide variety of household types. ("Wedding at Diamond Plantation, ca. 1863." Courtesy of The Old Court House Museum, Vicksburg, Mississippi.)

Confederate territory into Union encampments, most African-Americans claimed freedom at home. Building on the dense webs that linked family and neighborhood, freedpeople maintained the habits of household developed during slavery. They did not perceive their households as discrete, isolated social units, but as integrally enmeshed in the neighborhood's social fabric.

The second half of the chapter turns to the next wave of emancipation. After Lincoln issued the Emancipation Proclamation, Union troops began concentrating on the Delta. They hoped to recruit African-American men into the United States Army and place women, children, and older men on plantations, under the supervision of mostly white employers. In effect, a large proportion of the Delta's African-Americans suddenly fell within the purview of United States government agents, who had precise opinions about marriage. Family, from the northern perspective, was grounded in the law, not the neighborhood. To counter wage labor and military regulations, African-American men and women turned to what was familiar—their households. Yet their definitions of what constituted a household and which rights it secured varied by gender, age, and whether they found themselves in a military camp or on a leased plantation.

Looking first at the leased plantation system and then at military service and life in camps, the analysis turns to African-Americans' competing expressions of household.

African-American households, in short, changed dramatically during the war years. They changed in structure and altered their expressions of power and authority. As war, personal decisions, and Union policies separated men from women, parents from children, and families from neighborhoods, the social meaning of household changed. With emancipation, African-American households—like the plantation household itself—were loosed from their moorings. Households had to be rebuilt on new ground.

We Shall Free Ourselves: Emancipation, 1862

In the summer of 1862, Federal troops approached the Mississippi Delta and altered the landscape forever. Plantation households scattered as planters fled from the advancing Union troops. Some ran for Alabama, some for Texas, while others stayed at home. Most attempted to take their slaves with them or send them off to Confederate strongholds. Planters met stiff resistance. "I am the only one of my acquaintance," wrote Jonathan Pearce, "who had not . . . attempted to . . . move [my slaves]." He continued, "[E]veryone who did so lost nearly if not all of the men and many of the women and children."[10] Taking advantage of the chaos, slaves dropped any pretense of labor.

The Delta stood between the Union and the occupation of Vicksburg. In the spring of 1862, Ulysses S. Grant's Army of the Tennessee captured Memphis and readied itself to advance on Vicksburg to the south. Vicksburg, however, offered plenty of natural defenses. The city lay high on a bluff above the Mississippi, making a river attack from the west difficult, if not impossible. And the Delta protected the city from the north, its thick cypress swamps and shallow winding rivers producing an almost impenetrable thicket that harbored Confederate sympathizers, local militias, and homegrown guerrilla troops. Grant planned to overcome these obstacles by squeezing Vicksburg in a two-pronged attack along the Delta's two natural borders—the Mississippi River on the west and the hills to the east (see figure 4). In the effort to capture Vicksburg, the Delta would be pinched between two flanks of the U.S. army.[11]

As Federal forces approached, slavery ruptured. Running for army camps or establishing independent communities on plantations abandoned by whites, slaves declared themselves free.

The first declaration of freedom exposed differences within the Delta's black

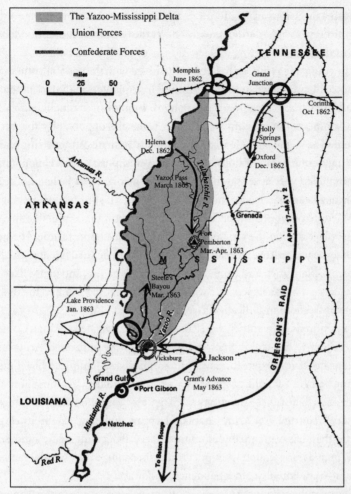

Fig. 4. In the winters of 1862 and 1863, Union forces surrounded the Delta from the north and the west. Slaves took the opportunity to free themselves and run to Union encampments.

communities, revealing a gendered construction of liberty. Young men broke away from the plantation community and ran for the Union camps while women, children, and the elderly remained on the plantations. The young men laid claim to their bodies and to the right of self-determination, forcefully denying slaveholders' rights of mastery. Upending the plantation household, they also appear to have walked away from their own households. Nevertheless, most African-Americans laid claim to the land. They located the meaning of emancipation in the land, the crop, and the community.

Both expressions of freedom rejected slavery and, with it, white southern definitions of the plantation household. Yet the two definitions grounded their dissent in often competing understandings of black households.

The young men who ran to freedom gambled with the possibility they would never see their families and friends again.[12] Irate planters made it clear that they would punish any loved ones left behind. Moreover, if caught, slaves faced imprisonment, punishment, or sale. Yet when the opportunity for freedom presented itself, men like George Parker did not hesitate. Parker, living on Leota Landing on the banks of the Mississippi River, slipped onto a Union gunboat one night. His wife never saw him again. On the night that he left, George and Maria had been married for more than five years. Maybe Maria chose not to go with George. Maybe he simply left her. We only know for certain that she "staid on the place during the war" despite the numerous opportunities she herself would have had to leave. Perhaps Maria and George defined freedom on different terms. Many men and women faced this same choice, and many, like Maria and George, went their separate ways. They experienced war and the first moments of freedom in radically different contexts.[13]

As hundreds of freedmen defied the odds and navigated through Confederate territory to the Union lines, many Yankees were impressed. According to popular belief in the North, slavery infantilized and feminized black men by placing them in a childlike dependency upon slaveholders. Yet the actions of the young men belied these stereotypes. "[They are] very shrewd in escaping their masters," reported U.S. Army Chaplain J. Grant, and they "exhibit intelligence greater than has been attributed to their race." By defying white southerners, black men demonstrated what northerners recognized as essential masculine virtues—individualism, independence, and bravery.[14]

The seeming autonomy of these young men, however, is tempered by a closer examination of the sources. Most did not travel alone. Instead they traveled with their "comrades." Sometimes these comrades were family members. Other times they were simply best friends. Living "up in the swamps" on the Cashmire place, Turner Holts and John Ben decided to make the break for freedom. As Holts recalled, "I knew [John] all my life. I first knew him in Crawford Co. Ga. where we had the same owner. He was my mother's brother. He was older than I was." In 1859 their owner moved both men from Georgia to Louisiana, then up the Yazoo River to Sunflower County, Mississippi. In 1862 they took matters into their own hands. Traveling some sixty miles through Confederate territory, they made it into the Union camps and declared themselves free.[15]

These relationships between men lasted throughout the war and long after. Men carried their best friends—a piece of their old neighborhood—with them wherever they went. In a common refrain, Kinchen Cook reported: "We had the same owner before the war & lived on the same place & we enlisted at the same time in the same Co. & have lived close after the war."[16] Often these men lived on separate farms, even in separate states, but they used the rivers and roads to stay in close contact. Gus Bell and William Brooks became best friends during slavery despite the fact that "I worked the upper [plantation] & [William] worked the lower one but we often seen one another once or twice a week."[17] They enlisted together, fought together, and returned home together, and they kept in touch long after the war. These male relationships represented an intimate bond that defied boundaries. Separate plantations, separate families, and various wives appear to have made no dent in these men's friendships.[18]

Escape, moreover, was only possible with the aid of neighborhoods along the way. Turner Holts and John Ben traveled for days through miles of swamp to get to the Mississippi. They, like many others, must have received assistance from strangers who fed, sheltered, and guided them through unfamiliar neighbor-

Fig. 5. Young African-American men were the first slaves to run for freedom in 1862. (Engraving by W. L. Sheppard. Courtesy of Photographs and Prints Division, Schomburg Center for Research in Black Culture, New York Public Library, Astor, Lenox, and Tilden Foundations.)

hoods (see figure 5). Perhaps Holts and Ben had friends living on these plantations, or perhaps the long-held distinctions between neighbor and stranger
began to break down in the face of impending emancipation. The problem
became so endemic that planters could exercise little control on their own
plantations. Unable to master the situation, Howard W. Wilkinson asked the
governor for help halting the "negroes in numbers [that] are constantly coming
here from the interior & are harbored by ours until the means of escape to the
Fed's is afforded them."[19]

So while the Union troops perceived the actions of the young African-
American men as evidence of possessive individualism—as expressions of autonomy and independence—the men themselves grabbed liberty with their
best friends. These male friendships represented a bond as close, if not closer,
than family itself.

For every African-American who left the plantation, hundreds remained
behind. By the summer of 1862, slavery no longer functioned on many plantations. One did not have to run away to claim liberty. Freedom could be won
at home, with or without the slaveholder present. Taking advantage of the
planter's precarious position, the slaves on Jonathan Pearce's plantation forced
him to negotiate. They refused to leave the plantation. According to Pearce,
"they have made up their minds to stay at home." Any attempt to move them,
he claimed, would produce "such a state of insubordination as will render it
doubtful if I can again controul them at all without the severst measurs."[20]
Facing a similar situation, one African-American community in Marshall
County struck a deal with the planter, George Gorman. From 1862 forward,
they would work for themselves and pay Gorman half the cotton crop as rent.
Gorman was lucky. When slaveholders refused to negotiate, African-Americans
simply laid claim to the land.[21]

First, the land offered security. Ada Burton, like Maria Parker, chose to stay
on the plantation when Peter, her husband of ten years, left to join the army.
Like many women who remained on the land, Ada had young children to feed
and raise. It was a practical decision. Perhaps unwilling to gamble with the
complete unknown, Ada chose to stay where she knew she could provide for
her children. Ada's actions after the war, however, suggest that more than
security kept her at home. For close to forty years, she and Peter remained
committed to their marriage. Yet they lived together for only a handful of those
years. Peter, an active Republican Party member, could not stay in the South,
and Ada would not leave. Peter wrote to her from St. Louis, and then Kansas,

sending her money to join him, but Ada never did. Land, community, and family kept her home.[22]

Second, the land—or, more accurately, the cotton—offered the chance to reap a tidy profit. Freedpeople did not avoid the commodity market in 1862. Instead they hoped that they, not the planters, might profit from their own labor. In the Delta, many former slaves had gained experience in the cotton market. During slavery, black southerners took advantage of the Delta planters' persistent search for higher and higher profits and crop yields by negotiating the right to sell cotton grown on their own time.[23] Using this knowledge in 1862, they aggressively entered the unregulated cotton market and made substantial incomes. Many secured enough in one year to pay their passage north and finance their future.[24]

African-Americans' interest in the cotton trade surprised Union officers. Rear Admiral David D. Porter remarked, "I have scarcely ever yet met with a Negro who has not been able to support himself, they are naturally astute at making money, and when they are not it is an exception to the rule." He continued, "Many of them have been allowed to trade and resere [sic] their profits to themselves, and they all have money, more or less, when they come to us."[25] Yet in 1862 the U.S. government had still not developed a firm position in relation to the self-declared freedpeople. The government would recognize southern blacks only as contraband of war. In the Delta, this policy proved to be no policy at all. Driving into the richest cotton region of the South, U.S. forces were overwhelmed by freedpeople, cotton speculators, and cotton pouring into their camps. Improvising, each officer charted a course between greed, duty, and morality with mixed success.[26] In this unstructured environment, freedpeople laid claims to land and commodities.

Household and neighborhood were crucial to freedpeople's financial success in 1862. The links between family and neighbors remained strong. Most often, freedpeople continued to work the crop by neighborhood. Together they followed the gendered pattern of labor developed during slavery. Men ginned, pressed, dug drainage ditches, and wove the baskets for the picked cotton, while women and children shelled corn, repaired fences, and cut down the cornstalks after harvesting. Together, men and women plowed, chopped, and picked the cotton.[27]

The sale of cotton provides insight into neighborhood and household gender hierarchies. When the cotton was ready for market, most communities would nominate two or three men to go into town or a military camp to negotiate the sale. The proceeds were then divided up by family. Sam Washington remembered: "There were 20 Bales raised by the colored folks on their own ground that year. . . . The cotton was sold in the lump, and the money divided equally among us fifty four." He continued, "I got for me, and my boy $53.00."[28] Whether Sam lived alone with his son or had a wife and daughters is unclear. Women rarely appeared in the records of cotton sales.

Perhaps women owned no cotton or perhaps they simply counted on men to sell it for them. During slavery, men had dominated the record books, selling all of the wood and 75 percent of the corn. Women raised and sold corn, but little else. Moreover, only men had held formal accounts to purchase goods on credit. Although women had bought tobacco on occasion, no ledger pages were devoted to their accounts.[29] With emancipation, the pattern established during slavery repeated itself. Men's customary rights to the crop seemed to have been upheld—at least on the surface.

Some war records, however, disrupt this neat assertion of men's rights. Immediately following the war, black communities filed claims for lost crops that indicate that they recognized both male and female heads of household as having a legitimate claim to the property. This was clearly the case on the upper Tallahatchie River. On June 15, 1865, John M. Dangold, a white citizen "in good standing" with the Union, boarded the steamboat *Free Stone* to file a complaint on behalf of his black neighbors. In the petition, twenty women and seventeen men claimed that they lost twenty-six bales of cotton during the Vicksburg campaign and asked for "liberal compensation" for having "picked by hand, & with arduous labor, separated the decayed and decaying cotton, conveyed to the nearest Gin, repacked, rebaled & repressed" the cotton. Of those twenty women, ten worked with men as members of a household, while the other ten worked either with their children or in all-female households. Each of them, however, had her name recorded in full as rightful owner of the crop and of her labor.[30] Still, Dangold justified the claim using a language of manhood: "they are men of colores of African descent, who have been recognized . . . as *free* . . . and as freed-men are labouring for the support and benefit of their families." By assuming that only men had the right to property, Dangold reflected northern beliefs that dependents—wives, children, and former slaves—owned almost nothing in their own right unless specified in a legal document. Perhaps these beliefs prevented most African-American women from selling cotton in their own names in 1862.[31]

By August of 1862, Union officers began to crack down on what they saw as a usurpation of property. The U.S. government decided that African-American men, too, held no rights to the crop. New policies defined all African-Americans, regardless of whether they were slave or free, male or female, as "dependent people" with no legal right to property. In the Delta, Union commander Frederick Steele enunciated this new policy. As former slaves, Steele argued, black southerners legally owned no property. The land, cotton, and timber belonged only to whites who, in turn, could be classified as either loyal or disloyal. Steele permitted white loyalists to keep their property, while seizing rebel property as contraband goods. Significantly, not just slave status but also black skin exempted an individual from legal trade. Even if black southerners could establish a legal claim to the crop, Steele's policy refused them any right to trade the cotton themselves.[32]

Revoking their rights of property, the Union army imposed dependency on all freedpeople remaining on plantations. Without a crop, African-Americans could not support themselves. By 1863 the U.S. government began to formalize policies that would place this "dependent" race back under the control of white men.

Gendering Freedom: Northern Policies after the Emancipation Proclamation, 1863–65

In January 1863 the Emancipation Proclamation freed all slaves "in states still in rebellion." Thus slaves in Mississippi were "thenceforward, and forever free." In their camps along the Mississippi River, Union forces observed what they considered to be a gendered response to emancipation in the black community and drew conclusions that would shape U.S. government policy toward freedpeople for the duration of the war.

In March 1863, U.S. Secretary of War Edwin M. Stanton ordered Adjutant General Lorenzo Thomas to the Mississippi Valley to investigate the possibility of recruiting former slaves into the military. Thomas quickly developed a two-pronged approach.

First, he approved the recruitment of all able-bodied black men into the armed forces. Second, he established a system of leased plantations on land abandoned by white slaveholders. Under the leased plantation system, venture capitalists rented confiscated rebel property from the United States government and hired former slaves to work the crop for wages.[33]

In many ways, Lorenzo Thomas's two-part plan—to enlist black men into the military and to put black women to work on leased plantations—was a direct response to freedpeople's actions in 1862. The decision to recruit black men into the military recognized, at least in part, the young black men's definition of freedom. In U.S. army uniforms, the young men further demonstrated the valiance and bravery they had exhibited in early 1862, when they crossed Confederate lines and entered Union camps.[34] In contrast, the military classified those remaining on the plantations primarily as dependents. Many Union officials perceived freedpeople's decision to remain on the land as a reflection of a cautious and submissive nature.

By April 1863, Thomas's plan took effect in the Delta. Union troops swept the Mississippi River plantations, confiscating the land and property. Soldiers then sorted freedpeople into either potential soldiers or agricultural workers. The officers forcibly recruited many young men into the army while encouraging women, children, and the old and disabled to stay at home and work for wages.[35] "It was done in this way," remembered Isaac McLean. "The force—I can't say how many, of Federal Soldiers came to Mr. Irish place, about two or three o'clock in the afternoon—they were mounted—and came right on into the field where the hands were working—some plowing and some hoeing. The man in command of the squad then said, Boys put down your hoes & stop plowing—you are all free,—He said Boys, you have got to come with us." Dropping their plowlines and unhitching their mules, the men rode off with the plantation stock, following the Union squad.[36]

With the simple announcement "you are all free," life on the plantations changed dramatically. Families were often separated and entire neighborhoods torn apart. Freedwoman Ailsey Tyler testified that "her former home was broken up by the war" and that after forty years she had not met up with anyone she knew during the days of slavery.[37]

When possible, freedpeople tried to decide for themselves whether they should stay or leave the plantation. As William Wallace discovered on the Basin plantation, the entire slave community could pack up their possessions and simply leave. On other plantations, however, many chose to stay. On the Sessions plantation, African-Americans as a group decided who should stay and who should leave. When Union troops neared the plantation, five young men rode off to meet them, returning a few days later with news and information about the Yankees. All work ceased for a week as people discussed and planned the best course of action. Then, several weeks later as the Union forces withdrew, fifteen men, women, and children chose to travel with them. According to James Oliver Hazard Perry Sessions, these were his best hands. Unwilling to be separated from their families, the young and strong traveled together into the unknown.[38]

Left behind, women were scarcely dependent or helpless. A. W. Harlan, agent of the U.S. government, reported that a recruiting officer came through his region "and carried away twenty of the Best men [on the plantation] leaveing some families without any men to assist them. Some of those women thus left alone with little children seemed discouraged whilst others were quite cheerful." An amazed Agent Harlan continued, "I will give a single instance one Martha Thompson eighteen years old had a small Babe when asked where her husband was replied that he ran away the first chance and joined the union army . . . I enquired how she made a liveing she replied that she left her baby with a neighbor and then went and piled cord wood."[39] Martha Thompson, like other African-American women who called on the resources of their neighborhoods, assumed mastery over herself and went to work.

Union officers welcomed freedwomen's willingness to work. More troubling was the fact that, in 1862, these "dependents" laid claim to the land and the crop. Union officers feared that this would disrupt cotton production and establish a precedent for the redistribution of property.[40] The leased plantation system placed so-called dependents back within the secure confines of a radically restructured plantation household. Separating the men from the women and the fit from the unfit, the government imposed a gendered experience of war and free labor.

Avoiding Wage Work: Households on Leased Plantations

The leased plantation system took effect in the spring of 1863. African-Americans learned that all former Confederate property—land, houses, livestock, and crops—now belonged to the United States government. The land they had worked independently since 1862 was going up for rent. The Federal government permitted freedpeople to retain their personal possessions, but even these claims could be quickly contested because, under slavery, slaves had no legal rights to own property. Suddenly, freedpeople had no stake in the crop. Men were promised ten dollars a month, and women seven, but their rights ended there. The gains made in 1862 rapidly eroded as an estimated eight thousand women, children, and older people in the Delta confronted free labor for the first time.

Union policies were contradictory at best, creating a wage labor system that fell decidedly short of full freedom. According to Thomas, military service and the structure of wage labor would provide training camps for independent manhood, grounded on the twin pillars of political and economic freedom. There was only one problem. The African-Americans still working on the plantation were not men but mostly women and children. One year into the program an estimated 45,000 of the 60,000 freedpeople employed under the free labor system worked in the Mississippi River valley. Of those 45,000, approximately 31,000 (or 69 percent) of those laboring on plantations during the war were women.[41] Perceptions of African-American womanhood, therefore, shaped southern wage labor systems long after the close of the war.

When they confronted the plantation household, northerners faced what they perceived as a gender inversion. The army, caught in a bizarre web of contradictory gender, racial, and class ideologies, attempted to teach black *women* to be free and independent working*men*. As African-Americans, as women, as former slaves, and as skilled field workers, freedwomen could not be easily located within northern ideologies of gender and free labor. From the northern perspective, southern black women appeared to be both male and female, worker and dependent, strong and helpless. Could the nation build a system of free soil, free labor, and free men out of a work force of women? Northern categories of manhood and womanhood, black and white, free and dependent became scrambled and confused.

Brigadier General James S. Wadsworth recognized the dilemma of constructing independent manhood with a work force of dependents. His testimony before the American Freedmen's Inquiry Commission reflected the conflicting attitudes toward freedpeople that shaped Union policy. Only men could head households, but Wadsworth feared that, as former slaves, freedmen were incapable of manly independence. "When these people first come to the depots," he commented, "you must take them, like children, get them on the plantations, and make the bargain for them, no matter whether it be for seven or ten dollars a month." He continued, "They are only too docile.... It is because of that docility, that we must exercise a certain guardianship over them and suspend reconstruction until we have thoroughly emancipated them, and got the idea of freedom into their heads."[42] Under this system, freedpeople were not free to sell their own labor. Others sold it for them. The wage labor system was treated as a halfway house between slavery and freedom.

To complicate matters further, Wadsworth then contradicted himself. He suggested that freedmen needed to be granted independence, which in Wadsworth's eyes would "inaugurate at once the regeneration of the African Race, restore the productiveness of the Country, make the people of the South homogeneous with those of the North, and give to the nation a Peace which will be lasting."[43] This could be accomplished, he believed, if they were permitted to lease land. "I would take one of those great estates . . . and divide it into ten, twenty, or fifty lots," he said, and then emphasized, "wherever there was a whole family at home—husband, wife, and children, (because you could not put a woman on a lot; she must go work the plantation for wages,) and I would say to the man—'Here are ten acres, you may have these ten acres for $10 an acre, payable in ten years.'"[44] Blacks may have been seen as dependent; laborers may have been seen as dependent; but, with the critical component of manhood, this could be overcome.

Having saved money from the previous crop year, some freedpeople attempted to lease the plantations themselves. Chaplain J. S. Herrick, Superintendent of Freedmen in Helena, wrote on their behalf, asking that this land be reserved for black lessees. Less than one month later, the government leased these plantations to white men from Wisconsin and Iowa. Some freedpeople did manage to secure leases to small tracts of land in the area. In 1864, twelve black men leased an average of 271 acres. White lessees, in comparison, rented an average of 761 acres.[45] Black women, however, leased no land at all. A woman "must go work the plantation for wages."

Freedom was minimal at best on the leased plantations. Regardless of how one defined liberty, the leased plantation system fell short. From the southern African-American perspective, the leased plantation system did not represent freedom because it ignored the rights of the producers to the fruits of their labors. The government stripped away black claims to land and other forms of property, forcing African-Americans to work for wages. From a northern perspective, wage work represented freedom, but only under certain conditions— few of which were met by the leased plantation system. According to theory, workers' freedom was secured by an open market. Workers could bargain for high wages and change employers at will. Free labor advocates argued that a worker's ability to control his labor—his ability to determine who he sold his labor to, for how long, and for how much—placed him on equal terms with his employer. Yet the leased plantation system violated most of these rights. Women, children, and the elderly were forced to move to plantations, their wages were fixed by the government, and everyone was forced to contract for one full year. The result was a "free labor" system noticeably less free for southern workers than for their northern counterparts.[46] The Union restricted women's mobility, told them who to work for, and decided the terms of their labor.

Acting as quasi–labor agents for lessees, the Superintendents of Freedmen tried to force freedpeople back to plantations. They targeted women in particular because, in the words of General S. A. Hurlbut, "women & children [are] incapable of army labor.... [They are] a weight and encumbrance." Despite the fact that women performed many essential tasks for the military—chopping wood, nursing, cooking, and laundering—generals wanted them sent away from their camps. General William Tecumseh Sherman flatly stated, "we give employment to men.... we never harbor women or children."[47] Again and again the solution to the "woman problem" was to send them back to the plantation. In a period of three months, the Superintendent of Freedmen sent 12,700 freedpeople from Vicksburg alone to work for lessees.[48]

Once on the plantation, freedpeople discovered that the Union could not protect them. "I regret to state that in no case have I found a strict compliance with the terms of their contracts on the parts of Lessees of plantations," wrote an inspecting officer; "and in too many," he continued, "an utter disregard of even the commonest principles of humanity and the rights of individuals.... Generally the negro has been treated by those employing him, as a mere brute." Brigadier General John Hawkins reported, "All the bargain is on the side of the white man and at the end of the year the Negro has less money than was usual with him when he was a slave." Hawkins concluded: "he has been worse fed and worse treated, the only difference perhaps in his favor being that he has not been flogged, though killing may be resorted to." To reform the system, Hawkins recommended that the full rights of contract be upheld. "In fact," he wrote, "I want no laws for the negro as if he were a child.... under this guise of protection we rob him of every right." For Hawkins, full legal protection would put wage labor back on the right track.[49]

Freedpeople did not wait for legal protection. Employing the resources of a fluid and flexible household structure, women expanded their freedoms just enough to terrify planter and Yankee alike. They withdrew from the production of cotton. This was a dramatic reversal from their first response to freedom in 1862, when they acted as careful stewards of the land. With neighborhoods dismantled and scattered, African-Americans turned to their households for support and to create a measure of autonomy.

The black families on the Adams place in Yazoo County provide a glimpse into the relationship between family structure and independence on the plantations. In 1865, five families lived on the Adams plantation. Of the five, women headed two, one was a nuclear family, one consisted of only men, and one consisted of an older single man. Using similar strategies, each family, regardless of its size and composition, worked to establish as much independence as possible.

Each family on the Adams plantation devised a system where some family members would work for wages, thereby guaranteeing that everyone could remain at home. Meanwhile other family members turned their energies to gardens and livestock, hoping to provide income free from the oversight of the lessee. In one female-headed household, Manese Swayze, age thirty-two, went to work for wages. Her mother, Hannah, worked in the garden, raised livestock, and helped care for Manese's three young children. Like the Swayzes, the two brothers George and Jackson Collins divided their labor between field and garden. Jackson, at age thirty-two, was disabled and could no longer perform heavy labor. He relied on his younger brother George to work the fields while he took care of the household duties. The third family, the McClanes, stayed on the plantation as a nuclear family with their five children. William at age forty-five no longer worked in the fields. Instead the family counted on Susan, seventeen, and Hannah, fourteen, to perform most of the field labor. Their mother, Maria, worked in the fields on occasion, as did their brother William, but by and large the family counted on the young women for wages.

Even for those living alone, the neighborhood offered a safety net. During the war, two single people decided to stay on the Adams place: Charles Moore, age fifty-one, and Elizabeth Hendrel, a mother with two young children. Charles escaped the draft because of his age and chose to stay on the land, while Elizabeth doubtless preferred to remain where she knew people rather than venture into the cities to find work with her babies in tow. Both Charles and Elizabeth must have relied on others to help them cook, clean, garden, and hunt while they contributed labor in the fields. They counted on the fluid boundaries between family and community.

Hannah McClane's name alone suggests the close ties between neighborhood and household. Two Hannahs lived on the Adams place: Hannah McClane, age fourteen, and Hannah Swayze, who, at fifty-four, ranked as the oldest person on the plantation. The relationship between these two families remains unclear, but conceivably the McClanes named their daughter after the elder Hannah. Perhaps Hannah Swayze helped out the McClanes as kin, or perhaps she held such a position of importance on the plantation that the

McClanes wanted to honor her and solicit her support. As historian Larry Hudson suggests, slave households often worked to establish ties with other families to ensure help in hard times. Family members depended upon one another to carve out a degree of autonomy and expanded this pattern of dependence beyond their own households.[50]

Men as well as women reduced the number of hours that they labored for the plantation. Some freedpeople, mostly the old and disabled, did not work the crop at all. Others simply worked whenever they chose to. "Many well able to work are idle," reported Major Julian Bryant. "What crops there are, on these places, are due solely to the exertions of a few individuals. . . . A portion of the negroes are earning a good living by the sale of vegetables, by day's work, and by cutting wood."[51] Building on established gendered divisions of labor, men and women went to the fields only when their skills were required. Men (and some women) plowed, while women (and some men) hoed, and children were called in for harvesting. Freedpeople's steady work in their gardens reflected their focus on gaining self-sufficiency. They concentrated on the tasks with the greatest guarantee of return and avoided jobs over which they had less control or those that required a long-term investment. Freedpeople resisted repairing fences, clearing land, draining swamps, and building houses. In general, they refused to care for and maintain property not belonging to them.[52]

In painstaking negotiations with lessees, freedpeople made it clear that they controlled exactly when they would work. A northern lessee, Isaac Shoemaker, agonized that "it will take many years to get [freedpeople] systematized." Having rented a plantation and hired a work force, he found that by "3 P.M. all hands off fishing—that is the men; while the women are washing clothes." He concluded that they were "governed by whim; and pay no attention to any promise made you." Another lessee, A. G. Swain, estimated that only 35 of 112 freedpeople living on his plantation worked the crop.[53]

Withdrawing from the crop, freedpeople set to work expanding their independent production. A recurring contest centered on livestock. Having raised the livestock and worked many of them for "some twenty years," men like Isaac McLean "knew nearly all the mules by name." As far as freedpeople were concerned, the animals belonged to them. In fact, one Allen Walker filed a formal complaint with the Freedmen's Bureau after the war, demanding that three cows, which he had kept and fed, be returned to him.[54] By maintaining hogs, chickens, cows, and mules, freedpeople could feed their families without depending on cash wages. Shoemaker regretted permitting anyone to keep livestock on his plantation, as he believed that it led to "the temptation to steal my corn." Moreover, he complained that "you can't let an animal get out of your sight or someone may steal him."[55] Freedpeople claimed both the livestock and the corn as their own.

Freedpeople were remarkably successful in establishing an alternative economy on the plantations.[56] Government agent T. P. Anderson reported that near the mouth of the Yazoo, 1,200 worked the crop while 3,500 worked for themselves raising "small patches of corn and potatoes." This pattern repeated itself across the Delta. In 1864, Federal agents estimated that only 25 percent of the people living on the plantations worked the crop. Moreover, this practice had expanded into a right. In labor contracts, freedpeople forced lessees to permit them to enlarge their garden plots in order to raise fruits, vegetables, and livestock. And they did not stop there. African-Americans also won the right to grow their own cotton. Step by step, African-Americans attempted to win back the economic independence they had experienced in 1862.[57] Freedpeople won these concessions by building upon fluid household structures. Without the strength of an entire neighborhood, African-Americans began to use the household as the foundation of rights.

Many freedpeople, however, decided to vote with their feet. They left the plantations. The conditions of labor and constant guerrilla attacks made life on the land too difficult and dangerous. The dense Delta swamps harbored guerrilla troops and bands of outlaws who freely roamed the Delta, looting plantations at will. Despite constant effort, neither the Union nor the Confederacy could control these men. As a result, the Delta plantations faced repeated assaults by each group—guerrillas, bandits, Union troops, and Confederate militias. On January 4, 1864, Acting Assistant Secretary of War Charles Dana testified before the American Freedmen's Inquiry Commission: "The Valley of the Mississippi is a pretty bad place. It is a place where robbers and marauders can easily hide." Lessee M. D. Landon explained that "it is a hard thing to cope with the three hundred rebels continually harassing the plantations. . . . Almost every evening I have a fight with men trying to steal my mules." Mules were not the only target. In the fall, when the cotton bolls opened, guerrillas routinely swept down, burning the crop, the gins, and the living quarters. "The negroes," reported inspector Julian Bryant, are "captured [sold into slavery] or driven from the plantations and scattered." Rear Admiral David D. Porter was more direct and linked the violence to the lessees themselves. "The people who enter the business," he reported, "are greedy adventurers, who have no interest beyond getting one crop.... They treat the Negroes brutally." Moreover, he claimed that "they enter into an agreement with the former owner" for protection. "In short time," Porter concluded, "the former [owner] takes chief control. ... [They] come back and burn the Plantation kill half the Negroes and carries off the rest in irons to Texas."[58]

On Deer Creek, in Warren County, freedpeople fought back. A "citizen" reported that twenty-three armed black men killed eleven white civilians.[59] Others used the threat of rebel troops to try to negotiate with lessees. Susannah Morris was one of the few workers lessee Isaac Shoemaker bothered to record by name. Arriving at the plantation alone, Susannah showed initiative at first. She was in the fields early and worked steadily. After one week, however, Shoemaker reported, "Susannah gives much trouble and dissatisfaction among the hands." Three days later, Shoemaker fired her "for intolerable lying, mischief making and laziness. She is a bad woman and possessed of the D___L." Susannah, however, refused to leave. She settled into the quarters and continued to raise hell. Shoemaker, asserting his right of property, had to force her out of her home physically. Susannah, using her last weapon, threatened to "burn some of the cabins" and "bring the rebels in."[60] Unfortunately for all concerned, her threat was realized. The rebels swept down and destroyed the plantation.

The Union troops, however, wreaked havoc as well. Madison Sharp, a private in the United States Colored Troops, recalled his mixed feelings as he marched onto his former plantation in the uniform of a Union soldier. On the one hand, he joyfully remembered confronting the overseer and declaring that his friends and neighbors were "set free by the War." On the other, he was sickened by the destruction. He flatly stated he "did not like to help." Piece by piece, he and his comrades dismantled the slave quarters for the wood and confiscated the food and livestock.[61] As part of the army, he freed his former mates, but he also helped destroy his home and theirs.

To escape these dangers and to avoid wage work, many men, women, and children left the plantations for the towns and cities. Others tried to hook up with their menfolk, rebuilding households near Union troops in cities such as Vicksburg, Goodrich's Landing, or Helena. The Union command, aghast at the steady exodus, made it quite clear that families were not welcome.

Rights or Freedom? Marriage, Households, and Life in Camp

Households became the center of an unresolved struggle between the army and its soldiers. Boldly heading in two directions at once, the army sent mixed messages. Commanding officers saw families as cumbersome, troublesome camp followers. No army, officers reasoned, could function with such a large domestic population following its forces. Army chaplains, however, believed that families (as defined by the marriage relation alone) taught responsibility. Each official interpretation of the "African-American family" ignored the alternative households established during slavery. In the struggle to defend their families, freedpeople's understanding of the household shifted, and rights were redefined.

Like many men, Philip Burton expected his family to stay with him when he enlisted in the Union army.[62] In fact, all three left the plantation together. Philip, his mother Courtney Burton, and his adopted sister Harriet Phillips traveled with the Union troops from their Issaquena County plantation down to Goodrich's Landing. Once there, the Burton household faced the first level of military sorting. Philip, along with other able-bodied men between the ages of eighteen and forty-five, was officially mustered into the Forty-seventh U.S. Colored Infantry. Officers sent Harriet, Courtney, and the other civilians to the contraband camp. In the contraband camps, the officers sorted and classified people yet again. The army tried to hire the healthy, but few made the cut. Major General S. A. Hurlbut estimated that of the five thousand freedpeople living in his camp, "say from two thirds to three fourths are women & children incapable of army labor." These, he suggested, should be sent to plantations.[63] Of course, most had just come from plantations.

When the army forced their families to leave, the soldiers protested. Many men repeatedly complained that they had been tricked into joining the army with the promise that their families could remain with them. Lieutenant Robert Campbell acknowledged that when they recruited new soldiers, "we told them as we did all others that they would be most likely kept along the river to guard the plantations where their families would be at work." However, this pledge was rarely fulfilled. "When I left my family," wrote James Herney, "I promised them I would come home on furloe in August last I lost two of my children I asked for a leaf of absence and was refused. . . . Thare has ben a grate meny of my felow soldiers who throgh grief and anziety about their families have pined away and died." Some soldiers took action. When Union officers in Memphis attempted to ship wives and families to plantations "down river," they faced mutiny. "The husbands swear their families shall not be moved to the Island," an officer reported, "and in some instances have come out under arms to prevent it."[64]

Within the Union army, military chaplains and officers of black regiments often tried to defend African-American "families" and keep married couples together. They argued that marriage served as a "civilizing" influence, teaching black southerners proper family relationships.[65] From the northern perspective, marriage alone defined "family." The flexible, fluid household structures developed during slavery did not qualify. Families needed to be legitimized by marriage and center on the relationship between a husband and wife. The ties between fathers and daughters-in-law, aunts and nephews, grandfathers and grandsons, simply did not look like a family to the chaplains. And in their eyes "hooking up" and "sweethearting" were dangerous transgressions. Drawing a line between "legitimate" and "illegitimate" relationships, many northerners simply could not understand black households.[66]

Therefore, despite their differences, commanding officers, chaplains, and officers in black regiments alike classified many African-American families as degenerate. Colonel F. W. Lister reported, "The immorality developed after last pay day required a strong effort to repress it. [L]arge herds of colored prostitutes flocked to Bridgeport from both ends of the line." Yet as George Buck Hanon, a soldier under Lister's command, explained, "men's wifes comes here to see them and he will not allow them to come into they lines. . . . After comg over hundred miles [to see him] a colard man think jest as much of his wife as a white man dus of his."[67] These women were, for the most part, not prostitutes, but wives and sweethearts attempting to reestablish their households by finding their men in the Union army. A relationship was no less real because it was not legal. Obligations did not rest upon marriage alone.[68]

African-Americans developed several strategies to defend their households. Women, by and large, built upon and expanded alternative household structures to remove themselves from military command. Soldiers, however, had less flexibility. Many turned to marriage to keep sweethearts and children close by.

Freedwomen carved out a measure of autonomy by moving out of contraband camps and building "freedmen's towns." Squatting on abandoned land near Vicksburg, women constructed homes out of tents, spare lumber, and tin sheeting. The army was a critical, if unwilling, partner in the erection of these towns. Soldiers, risking court-martial, helped women "carry off rations . . . axes, shovels, spades, and picks, wherever they can be found, to use in building and maintaining these households." With the towns located as close to camp as possible, food, clothing, and supplies passed back and forth between soldiers and their families. "The influence of these women over the members of my regiment is such, that I have great difficulty in keeping my men in camp nights," complained John Foley.[69]

Courtney Burton's and Harriet Phillips's experience provides a glimpse into how women maintained themselves. Burton and her adopted daughter Harriet lived for one year in a contraband camp near Goodrich's Landing. However, the moment the army posted Courtney's son Philip to Vicksburg, she packed up her daughter and left. In Vicksburg, Courtney and Harriet avoided the camps, deciding to settle in town. Using Philip's connections, they rented a house. Each family member then contributed what he or she could, building on skills and contacts. Philip used his army wages to pay the rent. Courtney used the house to take in laundry and bake pies and cakes. Harriet then sold the cakes by using Philip's connections in camp. Her youth helped sales, while Philip's presence assured her a degree of respect.[70] Much like the freedpeople on the leased plantations, women built upon flexible household structures to divorce themselves from direct supervision.

Yet these households did not function as discrete, isolated social units. They survived in large part by creating or renewing friendships. Ellen Ben was a teenager in 1863. When Vicksburg fell to Union forces, she left the plantation for the city. Not knowing anyone, she began working for a freedwoman, Mrs. Bland. "[S]he used to make cakes," Ben recalled, "and send her daughter and me to sell them to the soldiers. . . . In that way, I got acquainted with John Ben." By age seventeen, she was married. These new connections helped keep freedpeople afloat. When Dorcas Anderson arrived in Vicksburg, she, like Ellen Ben, did not know a soul. Anderson had married Peter Moore during slavery, and they had three children together. In 1862 the Confederates impressed her husband and took him to "Yellow Bush on the Tallahatchie River where they were making breastworks to keep the Yankees coming down the river." In a matter of months, Peter Moore was dead of pneumonia from "working in the mud and water." Anderson recalled the day that "they hauled him back to the Wilson plantation. . . . [T]hey hauled him back and heaps more too." Over the next year, all three of her children died. Alone, she traveled from Yazoo County to Vicksburg. In Vicksburg, she found a roommate, rented a house, and shared expenses and work. There she met and married Isaac Anderson. As plantation neighborhoods shattered during the war, women relied on new neighbors to make ends meet.[71]

In camps and towns, neighborhoods merged and blended. People learned the intimate histories of lives on far-flung plantations. Haynes Sharkey testified that he "became acquainted with Jane Matthews in Vicksburg, Miss during the war. Her mother was washing clothes at headquarters and she was a girl going among the regiment.... She looked like a baby doll to me," he remembered, and she had never had a husband. He could recite her family history in great detail, repeating all her kin connections from memory even though he had never met most of the people he discussed. Living in what Hester Speed referred to as "the colored folks correll," people told stories and established a common history.[72]

These connections created an extensive network, drawing people from the plantations to the city. In Washington County, Mary Jane Clear followed her first husband, Ed Kelley, when he joined the Union army. A comrade remembered that "all the women were put off the boat at Hawes Harris' landing & the men were carried off to Lake Providence to enlist." Almost immediately, Union officers hired Clear out to a lessee. Mary Jane, however, finally made her way to Vicksburg. "Ed's mother sent for me to come to Vicksburg," she remembered, "and when she was sick I waited on her until she died." In a common response to wage labor, women used kin connections to leave the plantations for the cities. Susan Bradford joined her father; Martha Willis joined her father-in-law; Minerva Divine went to be with her Uncle Nathan. Just as during slavery, one did not have to be married to form a household. Meeting up with kin, neighbors, and even strangers, freedpeople formed flexible households in order to carve out a measure of autonomy from both the military and lessees.[73]

Needless to say, these actions frustrated both military commanders and the Superintendents of Freedmen. Focusing on freedwomen's "idleness" and their fraternization with army troops, the government fretted over their "misplacement." In their steadfast blindness toward the complex structures of black households, military commanders saw black women as literally loose, unfettered by the discipline and order of hierarchy. The inability to conceive of women outside of the marriage relation led to abuse. Not belonging to another person, black women were denied even the most basic right to ownership and control of their bodies. Soldiers and officers sexually abused them, allowed them to starve, threw them out of camp, and denied them access to freedmen's wages or rations. A committee of chaplains protested: "The wives of some have been molested by soldiers to gratify their licentious lust, and their husbands murdered in endeavering to defend them, and yet the guilty parties ... were not arrested.... For the sake of humanity, for the sake of christianity, for the good name of our army, for the honor of our country, cannot something be done to prevent this oppression & to stop its demoralizing influences upon the soldiers themselves?"[74]

To force women away from the camps, the army issued strict orders aimed at crushing freedpeople's independent economic networks. The Union command in Memphis enacted General Order 75, commanding, "Every free negro ... must within 20 days enter into the employment of some responsible white person." As the editors of the Freedom History Papers argue, this "virtually prohibited black people in Memphis from working for black employers or undertaking any form of self-employment."[75]

At stake was literally the concept of household. Unable to recognize the independent households of black Union soldiers and their wives or the alternative households made up of extended kin networks in the black community, the U.S. government relied on an enforced system of wage labor to control the "unruly negroes." General Order 75—much like the leased plantation system itself—limited southern blacks' access to property, and firmly placed them under the control not of white masters but of white employers.

To control contact between soldiers and civilians in Vicksburg, Colonel Samuel Thomas ordered that only soldiers with legal marriages be granted passes out of camp. In response, many soldiers married. "At the time," Ellen Ben recollected, "the chaplains were not marrying the men and women [that] went together during slavery times." She continued, "But when the chaplains began to give licenses and marry the soldiers, they went by the hundreds to him." They married, quite literally, "under the flag." As Hester Speed testified, "That means they stood under a flag and agreed to be husband and wife." There was no ceremony, according to Speed, "they just stood under a Union flag." Marriage became a symbolic act of citizenship—the first step in securing rights.[76]

Yet what those rights included was a matter of some dispute. Cognizant of what the obligations of marriage traditionally entailed, some freedmen expected to support and protect their families. As Jarrit Ware remembered, "Pretty much all of us were married again [by a chaplain] so that should they die the wife and children could come in for their money."[77] Of course, while the soldier was alive, his pay did not cover the costs of supporting a family. Black soldiers in the Delta earned only ten dollars a month—and had to pay for their uniforms, while whites had their uniforms supplied to them. A black soldier, then, was not paid a family wage. Marriage offered some security. The valuable contacts between family, friends, and neighbors could be maintained. In the meantime, wives went to work.

Yet marriage, and the limited rights it guaranteed, could not encompass the wide range of freedpeople's households. In fact, as historian Noralee Frankel argues, many freedpeople who had married under slavery saw no need to marry again. They felt that slave marriages needed no formal legal validation. Other soldiers tried to bend the narrow definition of marriage to fit their conception of flexible household structures. They simply stretched the truth. One soldier, Jake Morton, recalled that they claimed their sweethearts were their legal wives "because no one but a wife or other relative was allowed to come into the lines and see the soldier." If one had to marry to maintain contact with sweethearts and friends, so be it. As Colonel Lister complained, "enlisted men change their so called wives as often as the regiment changes stations."[78]

Rights, freedpeople discovered, were a double-edged sword. On the one hand, rights involved regulation. By marrying under the flag, freedpeople learned that the state had the right to define what constituted a household. Rights narrowed the household to marriage, and marriage alone. Any other sexual relationship fell outside the law. Moreover, many Union officials felt that freedmen abused the marriage relationship by defining it too broadly. In an act repeated across the Delta, Colonel John G. Hudson ordered that "the habit of marrying Common place women of the town" be halted. "Marriages," he declared firmly, "are disapproved of."[79]

On the other hand, rights also provided a legal foundation for defending one's family. When soldiers in Memphis felt that their families were threatened, they took up arms. Wives, they declared, belonged beside their husbands and not on faraway plantations. Caught in a bind, the Union army relented and upheld married men's rights. Yet while soldiers could successfully fight to defend their marriages, the more flexible households were left vulnerable. The marriage right limited household to a patriarchal unit, ignoring other relationships spanning kin, neighborhood, and sweethearts.

Military service, therefore, played a significant role in forcing freedmen to recognize the political advantages of marriage. By and large, women could evade army regulations by remaining as mobile as possible and by maintaining a broad network of relationships. As soldiers, however, men had fewer choices. They either followed the rules or faced a court-martial. So while freedwomen continued to defend freedom through extended, flexible household structures in camps, in cities, and on plantations, freedmen faced restricted options. One could either marry (and maintain a relationship with some family members) or one could remain single (and have little contact at all). A rights-based freedom, they discovered, began with the individual.

In the military, freedmen chafed at the narrow construction of self based on individual rights. Just as the household could not be easily reduced to marriage, the self could not be easily alienated from the wide web of relationships including family, neighbors, and friends. Yet rights did exactly that. Rights stripped freedom down to possessive individualism, ignoring the self that was constitutive of others. Not willing to trade liberty for rights, some freedmen pushed at the military's narrow construction of individual freedom.

Many soldiers believed that "rights" defined freedom too narrowly, ignoring issues of community, dignity, and respect. In 1865, Private John Higgins of the Fifth U.S. Colored (Heavy) Artillery stood up to his commanding officer and demanded respect. The incident began when his officer commanded him to get water for the troops. Higgins protested, "The colored soldiers are imposed upon, and kept cooped up like dogs. . . . White soldiers are not kept under guard, but allowed to do as they please." At this point, the lieutenant ordered Higgins to be strung up by his wrists for two hours. Higgins later reflected, "I was very severely punished by the Commanding Officer of my company for a very light offense." When he was cut down, Higgins refused to move. Thereupon his commanding officer threatened to shoot him. Calling to his comrades for help, Private Higgins cried, "It is time we took our own part; we have been run over by our officers long enough; if we don't take our own part, nobody will take it for us." He cursed, "God damn any nigger that will stand by and see another tied up for nothing. . . . The niggers are all a set of damned cowards, or they would not be imposed upon so." Higgins, tired of abuse, tried to rally his comrades to act on their sense of justice, not the military's. He was unsuccessful. A military tribunal sentenced Higgins to two years' hard labor for "inciting mutiny and sedition."[80] The power of the state showed its full force. Higgins could not stand up against the tyranny of his officer without breaking the law.

Like Higgins, African-American soldiers faced repeated indignities and hardship. Having won the right to bear arms, most black soldiers discovered that they would rarely be asked to use them. After the fall of Vicksburg on July 4, 1863, officers assigned many black soldiers the dirtiest labor and the most dangerous assignments. Captain O. J. Wright complained to Adjutant General Lorenzo Thomas that, of 842 privates, 718 were on duty. He continued, "With this proportion of the Command on guard and fatigue, day after day, is it to be wondered at when they . . . present an unsoldierly appearance?" Building fortifications, digging canals, and setting up camps, these men probably did not feel like soldiers. As one officer remarked, the service performed by freedmen was usually reserved for "prisoners; undergoing punishment."[81]

Disgusted, Private John Mitchell of the Fifty-third U.S. Colored Infantry deserted. When asked why he ran away, Mitchell responded, "I told the captain previous to going away that I should leave his Company and go to some other if he continued to kick and cuff me about as he had been doing." The judge, General John Hawkins, sentenced Mitchell to "be shot to death with musketry" because his statement proved that "his desertion was premeditated."[82] Unwittingly, many freedmen faced death when rights did not correspond with their vision of freedom.

Under such conditions, freedmen learned more formal means of protest. Taking up the pen, freedmen wrote letters to President Lincoln, to Secretary of War Edwin Stanton, to Adjutant General Lorenzo Thomas, the commanding officer of the U.S. Colored Troops, as well as to their own officers. Charged with mutiny in Vicksburg, sixteen men organized a petition in their own defense. They explained that "by stacking arms. & refusing to do duty . . . We were not aware what the consequences of Mutiny would be." Writing to Stanton, they stated that "we did not intend to in any way injure The government but it was for The purpose of resenting the repeated ill treatment of our officers." Yet the frequent punishments for desertion and mutiny in Vicksburg must have made soldiers well aware that they were acting on behalf of or against "The government," not just their officers. They recognized that they were now a part of the body politic.[83]

Military service left a mixed legacy. Service taught freedmen the full meaning of rights. They learned that rights narrowed the household to marriage, and narrowed group visions of justice to individual responsibility. Rights discounted the voices of the neighborhood. Now freedmen traveled alone. Many, like Private Higgins, learned this the hard way. When he called on his company to defend their vision of justice—when he yelled, "if we don't take our own part, nobody will take it for us"—he was sentenced to two years' hard labor. The neighborhood no longer served as the seat of justice.

Freedwomen, unlike soldiers, could evade the issue of rights. Living on plantations and in freedmen's towns, they continued to rely on a network of family, friends, and neighbors to press for autonomy on their terms. Neighborhoods may have been dismantled, but, outside the military, freedpeople continued to act on the logic of neighborhood to achieve some degree of freedom. Households, not marriage per se, became the foundation of their freedom to define themselves beyond the confines of wage labor.

As freedmen and freedwomen reunited at the close of the war, they carried these two lessons with them: Marriage was the foundation of their rights, but households were the foundation of their freedom. The gendered experience of war, that is, created gendered understandings of rights and the household. Before the war, gender conventions shaped men's and women's roles—what tasks they performed both for the master and for their own households—but gender relations did not make a household. Slave households consisted of a wide variety of relationships and centered on single-sex relationships as well as heterosexual ones. What set African-American households apart was the extent of their reach into the neighborhood.

The war shattered these neighborhoods. The government ignored family ties. In order to produce as much cotton as possible, the U.S. government needed to keep every worker, regardless of age or sex, in the field. It fitted black men, women, and children into the model of competitive individualism and defined each freedperson as an autonomous individual worker. By separating parents from their children and dividing old neighbors, friends, and relatives, these practices disrupted fragile communities already frayed by the upheavals of war.[84]

On the plantations, freedwomen fought to expand their freedom by building fluid and flexible household structures. They discovered that wage work, under the leased plantation system, fell drastically short of even northern perceptions of freedom. The army contracted out their labor for them, they were offered no choice as to where and under what conditions they would work, and the government provided no legal structure for them to uphold their limited rights. By working together, not as individuals but as families, neighbors, and friends, they distanced themselves from wage labor and created a base for economic autonomy. Freedom, from their experience, came from building and sustaining as many connections as possible, enabling them to avoid the power of both employers and the government to regulate their actions. This lesson stayed with them long after the war.

In the military, freedmen found themselves steeped in a formal body politic that promised them a limited set of rights. In return, they had no choice but to compromise. The government required them to give up households for the rights of marriage, community for the rights of individualism, and what freedmen termed "respect and dignity" for the right to wear the uniform of the United States. Political rights, therefore, came at a cost.

By the time the Confederacy surrendered, freedmen and freedwomen had confronted the harsh reality of freedom as defined by the state. On leased plantations, in contraband camps, in freedmen's villages, and in military encampments, they discovered that the government's definition of rights fell short of full freedom. Turning to the most powerful institution they knew, they began to uphold their own perception of rights. Doing so, they began to construct a new politics of household.

2

⁂

Locating Authority

Planter Women and the Shattering of the Plantation Household

𝒜S AFRICAN-AMERICANS freed themselves, many planter women felt exposed—unmasked—as if a vital portion of themselves left with their former slaves. Like Mrs. William Wallace, on the Basin plantation, they found themselves unable to act without the comforting presence of the plantation household. On October 21, 1862, Ann Matthews sat down at her writing desk and nervously penned a letter to Mississippi governor J. J. Pettus. "I am here alone with my two daughters surrounded by several large plantations, without a white man on any of them," she wrote. "It will be impossible for me to remain here and think it *hard, very hard,* that in my old age I will be *compelled* to leave my home. I *can not do* it." Ironically, Mathews had lived "alone" with her daughters in relative peace and comfort since her husband's death several years earlier and probably had been surrounded by "several large plantations" most of her life.[1] Yet, suddenly, both home and neighborhood frightened her.

Why did plantation mistresses feel so vulnerable, so defenseless during the war? Most white women in the Delta understood how to run a plantation. Isolated with their husbands on large estates, many women developed an interest in the crop, knowing when to plant, cultivate, and harvest, where to order supplies, and when to best market the cotton. Widows, like Ann Mathews, ran plantations themselves with the assistance of overseers. They managed their own books, distributed supplies in the slave communities, and kept track of the work cycle. Many plantation mistresses, therefore, had the necessary knowledge and experience to maintain the plantation household during the war. What they lacked was the authority to do so.

Historians attribute the dissolution of slavery, in large part, to planter women's inability to command the plantation household during the war.[2] As slaveholders left for the battlefront, slaves refused to respect the authority of

Fig. 6. Planter-class households changed as white men left for the battlefront. Left largely by themselves, planter-class women attempted to reconstruct a familiar position of dependency within any household they could find. ("The Shannon Family: Lavinia Shannon Mount, Mr. Martin, Grace Shannon, and Alice Shannon, ca. 1862." Courtesy of The Old Court House Museum, Vicksburg, Mississippi.)

white women and overseers. Without the constant application of psychological and physical force, African-Americans rejected the hierarchies of household.

Certainly the actions of black southerners challenged white women's authority. Yet like Mathews, many mistresses crumbled even before a single slave rebelled or questioned their influence. As the plantation household dissolved, planter-class women struggled with a loss of identity. In a world without masters and slaves, they no longer knew who they were. More profoundly, without a sense of identity, planter-class women discovered that they had no foundation from which to act. Defining themselves as dependents, they remained steadfastly committed to the hierarchies of the plantation household even as their households slowly dissolved around them.

The conditions of war revealed that planter women's relationship to the slave society was, in many ways, fundamentally different from their husbands' and was based, in large part, on a gendered understanding of household. As wives, mothers, and slave mistresses, women perceived household relationships differently than men. As heads of households, planter men merged domestic and public responsibilities through the language of command. Paternalism rested on each individual planter's authority over his family—white and black. The planter woman grounded her identity in her positions as wife, mother, and mistress as completely as the man did in his roles as husband, father, and master. Yet each role—wife, mother, mistress—rested on a position of subordination to a husband, father, master. Her authority derived from her relationship with others. Unlike black southerners, elite women in the Delta rarely questioned the hierarchies of the plantation household. Most accepted their position as the dependents of husbands and fathers because those very dependencies secured the privileges of their class.

Planter-class women absorbed and accepted the basic tenets of the pro-slavery argument—that slavery rested on the natural hierarchies between men and women, black and white, represented in the plantation household. Planter-class women's standard of living, their reputation, and, equally important, the demonstration of their natural superiority over others depended on men's mastery of the household.[3] Planter-class men, therefore, grounded their authority in their ability to command, while planter-class women's authority rested on their ability to maintain relationships. Without such relationships, planter-class women felt adrift. Planter men and women shared the same belief in household, but they experienced the household differently. War placed these differences in full view, unsettling and confusing planter women who had fixed their identity to the practices and ideologies of their class. In their roles as mothers, wives, and mistresses, planter-class women faced a constant tension between their authority and their dependency.

This chapter explores planter women's struggle to reconstruct an identity in the wake of war and emancipation. Each stage of the war confronted these women with a distinct set of challenges to their self-perception, as their sons, then their husbands, and finally their enslaved African-Americans left the home front for the battlefield.

First, as their sons left for war, southern women found themselves at the center of a national propaganda campaign. Not permitting women to grieve in private, newspaper editorials across the South fixated on motherhood. In their positions as mothers, women represented a challenge to Confederate national-ism. The nation asked mothers, as citizens, to place political obligation above personal self-interest—to deny themselves the rights of motherhood in order to sacrifice their sons for the Confederacy.

Second, as Union forces entered the Delta in 1862, men of all ages left the plantations to defend the region. Mothers without sons now faced becoming wives without husbands. As important, they became mistresses without mas-ters. Planter-class women found themselves unable (perhaps unwilling) to master a slave labor force. To command slaves, they would be forced to sacrifice the essence of white womanhood as they understood it. Confronting this di-lemma, many women froze. In order to better understand why planter women became immobilized, the chapter will turn to one individual, Emma Shannon Crutcher. In letters to her husband, Crutcher examined the sources of her grow-ing paralysis, granting insight into the social basis of planter-class women's identity.

Agency—the ability to act—is usually associated with independence. Planter women, however, provide an opportunity to study action in relation to dependency, and a self constituted only in relation to others. While these women did not consciously frame a political position of dissent, they chal-lenged the Confederacy as living examples of the contradictions of household. White (but without the authority of their race) and elite (but without the pow-er of their class), planter women were some of the first southerners, during emancipation, to actively confront the unraveling of whiteness and mastery.[4]

Mothers of Sons: White Women and the Problem of Political Obligation

As Drew Faust has argued, slavery depended in large part on "tens of thousands of individual acts of personal domination exercised by particular planters over particular slaves."[5] From the outset of the Civil War, white communities feared disruption and even chaos, as sons and husbands left home for the battlefront. In letters to the governor, white men and women described their vulnerability, predicting slave rebellions, abolitionist conspiracies, and the abuse of power at home by irresponsible men. Suddenly, familiar places and people appeared threatening.

The process of nation building tempered this climate of uncertainty and forced Confederates to define exactly who they were. Ironically, the Confed-eracy was built just as slavery was being dismantled. No doubt these two historical moments assumed paramount—although opposed—significance in the minds of black and white southerners. To build the Confederacy, white southerners had to take a set of assumed practices and beliefs and, in the face of military defeat and gradual emancipation, provide them with enough coherence to maintain and unify a nation.[6] Each white southerner's relationship to the nation and to the institution of slavery had to be reiterated or in some cases defined for the first time.

Men and women of the planter class faced the war from their relative positions within the plantation household. In the Delta, most men and adolescents embraced the war as a grand adventure that confirmed their sense of self. War was romantic and gave purpose to their lives. In typical prose, Bettie Morton exclaimed, "My dear brother you don't know how proud and happy I am to have one so near to me fighting for our Country, our rights." The young men responded in kind. "I had a delightful trip up," wrote Edward Worthington to his cousin Amanda. "We had a lively and jovial time. . . . The Bolivar Troop . . . is composed of a great many gentlemen though has some of the rough class in, though that makes it easier for the upper class for they can be made to do anything that is wanted."[7] For young men and women, war provided both an escape from the ordinary and an opportunity to try out adult personas. Released from the household, young men embraced the chance to assume mastery, dominating men they perceived to be inferior to themselves. Young women, on the other hand, practiced the art of sacrifice and support. They, too, got out of the house—in their case to sew, entertain, and raise money for the cause.

For older men, war was an extension of mastery. They fought to maintain slavery and to defend their right to head their households without government interference. Leaving home, they assumed that women and overseers could carry the mantle of mastery. They feared abolitionist conspiracies and the abuse of power at home, but by and large they believed that their authority could be maintained even in their absence.[8]

Yet within each role, fissures broke open, disrupting the commonplace. Speaking for other women of her class, Kate Sperry recognized that if wartime conditions were carried to their logical conclusion, the day would come when the "masculines will cook, wash, and iron and the ladies attend to business— whew! Won't we have fine times—voting, attending to patients—electioneering etc."[9] As Sperry realized, the war opened up a public sphere for white women. The language of sacrifice was a language of political obligation. Women were asked, as citizens, to set aside family interests for the interests of the Confederacy. White women became recognized political actors, and, as Sperry antici-pated, they claimed rights—not the right to vote, but the rights of wives and mothers.

As mothers, Confederate women confronted the war with opposing inter-ests. On the one hand, they recognized that their families' interests stood with the Confederacy. Their children's future, financially and socially, depended on the survival of slavery. On the other hand, in order to secure this future, they had to sacrifice their sons. Unable to reconcile competing interests, many women tumbled into depression. Writing from the Arkansas Delta, Rebecca Downs told her sister: "I feel like I wanted to talk to you about some of my troubles knowing that you have troubles too. . . . it is a hard thing for me to think and know that my son is gone to face all the horrors of war and liable at anytime to be mangled in the field of battle . . . but other Mothers have to give up their sons as sacrifices and mine is no dearer to me than theirs is to them."[10]

Downs did not suffer a mother's fears in silence; she informed her son James how she felt. Fighting this encroachment on his manly independence, James responded: "I know dear mother that [I owe] some immense debt of gratitude to you[,] a debt which three lifetimes as long as the one I shall live could not compensate should all my days be spent in your service." But, he emphasized, "You *can* Ma & you *must* give up such selfish feelings which are natural in mothers towards their children & consecrate me and Bobby to your country."[11] According to James, his mother lost her rights of motherhood as he reached his majority. Her claim to him might be natural, but in his mind she clearly no longer held any authority over him.

While James Downs labeled his mother's feeling "natural," Confederate nationalists quickly moved to classify mothers' feelings as unnatural. In many ways, mothers represented the sticky problem of political obligation in a society centered on household. According to the ideologies of the household, political rights began at home. A man's right to vote and gain access to full legal privileges rested on his heading a household. Without a household, he lost many civil rights. To wage war, however, the Confederacy called on men to leave home. In leaving, they endangered their household—the very seat of their citizenship. Their slaves might leave, and their families might starve or become dependent upon others. Moreover, homes could be lost and property damaged. White men risked everything. In order to mobilize the population for war, Confederate leaders had to temper these fears. To do so, they turned to mothers.

During the first year of the war, mothers became the butt of many jokes in newspaper editorials. On the western edge of the Delta, M. S. Ward, editor of the *Weekly Panola Star,* swiftly picked up the theme. Mothers, according to Ward, abused their maternal relationships, distorting time-honored truths. In typical prose, he claimed that mothers gave sons "the moral courage to withhold [service] from their country in its hour of need." They confused cowardice with honor, he argued, granting sons an easy excuse to avoid military service. "Some of our youth," he sarcastically remarked, "animated by the first noble, but ill-timed emotion, prefer duty to desire . . . [and] consent to remain at home, rather than give pain to the feelings of a tender parent who has nursed their infancy, watched their boyhood, and imbued their ripening years with the noble principles upon which they now act." Mothers, Ward implied, twisted the teachings of childhood to keep boys from becoming independent men.[12]

Mothers were easier targets than wives, who had legitimate reason to demand that their husbands stay at home to provide for and protect them. As historian Drew Faust argues, when women married, they entered into a social contract with their husbands. Wives willingly submitted to their husbands' authority as long as the men could provide for them. Wives, in other words, were the real threat to the Confederacy. Writing desperate letters to their husbands, they encouraged mass desertion toward the end of the war. Indeed, Faust has gone so far as to argue that the Confederate war effort failed in large part because women demanded that their husbands place the duties of household before the duty to their nation.[13] Anticipating these claims, men like M. S. Ward attempted to define all women as mothers rather than wives. A mother's claim to a grown son could be framed as mere sentimental attachment, not a valid social right.

By placing the focus on mothers, editors asserted the perversity of white women's claims to their men. Mothers, they implied, represented a gender inversion—women with power and authority over men. According to Ward, mothers who placed claims on their sons infantilized them by refusing to accept their maturity and independence. Ward cast the love between mother and child as a comic inversion of courtship. Young men, he argued, were more eager to please their mothers by staying home than to impress young women by going off to war. They wrongly directed the fine sentiments of chivalry and honor at old ladies rather than at sweethearts.[14]

Speaking for themselves, mothers defined their public position in letters to the government, articulating a complex relationship between dependency and authority in their dealings with their sons.[15] Some mothers refused to acknowledge their sons' independence or the state's right to assume "a mother's authority" over their sons. Mrs. C. A. V. Deason wrote, "My Son . . . is young and [in]experienced being under eighteen years of age and though I am willing for him to go and defend our rights, I desire to choose his associates."[16] Other parents were more direct: "What will be their moral condition after being in contact with the Army at that impressible age[?] . . . I should fear Vice and ignorance would predominate over Virtue and intelligence." Echoing the refrains of republican motherhood, these letters imply that without a family influence, boys will be ruined and grow to be irresponsible men.[17]

Most mothers, however, reinforced old boundaries by speaking from a position of dependency. Rather than assuming authority over their sons, many mothers emphasized a physical dependency on their sons for economic support and protection from slaves. "As I am a widow," wrote A. L. Coverly, "with a large family of small children and a number of unruly negroes, mostly men, . . . I take it upon myself the liberty of addressing you for the purpose of having my son C. T. Coverly released."[18] Speaking as women in need of men's assistance, mothers like Coverly articulated the importance of a masculine presence in maintaining social and economic stability. Only a few mothers focused on their emotional distress as a justification for exemption, and those that did made it clear that they were asking the governor for a personal favor.[19] Apparently most mothers felt that their public authority extended only as far as a woman's need for protection. They did not reject the hierarchies of the plantation household. Instead, elite women continued to act from a position of dependency.

War, however, exposed hidden truths about the nature of planter-class women's dependency. Crippled by their dependency upon their children, mothers began to question the value of dependency in society at large. Ann Hardeman, for example, saw her entire family split up during the war. A single woman, Hardeman mothered her five nieces and nephews after her sister died in childbirth. For the most part, Hardeman brought up the children alone on her family's plantation near Jackson, receiving limited assistance from her brother William, who had a family of his own, and only occasional support from the children's erratic father, Oscar J. E. Stuart. During the war, Ann's three nephews enlisted in the Confederate army, and only one survived. Eventually both her nieces left home to help support themselves and their family. Adelaide Stuart went to Richmond to work in the Treasury Department, while Annie E.

Stuart taught school in Mississippi. When all five of her children left home, Hardeman felt her usefulness leave with them. Alone, she could find no meaning to life.

Tortured by depression, Hardeman felt "wholly unprepared" for a life without her children. Day after day, she recorded that she could not get out of bed in the morning. Her sewing was left undone, food became a bother, and she wept constantly. Chastising herself unmercifully, she cursed her dependency upon her children, calling it unnatural and the work of Satan. Depression, Hardeman believed, was God's "scathing justice" for her having assumed the rights of motherhood.[20]

God, according to Hardeman, did not direct his vengeance toward her alone, but toward all southern people. "O that we could have some compromise— some treaty," she wrote, "by which we could *safely* be recognized as free & *Independent People*." Southerners, she continued, "have made ourselves so dependent upon [the North] by our inertness as a people—that we needed a little chastisement & we have had it with a *witness* [God].... To Thee do we look Almighty Father for the guidance ... of this unholy War." As a mother, Hardeman could justify her support for the war only by defining it as an act of God, not men.[21] The South, according to Hardeman, proved to be as weak and dependent as a woman. As a woman, she reasoned, she could scarcely place her fate in the hands of men who acted as women.

Hardeman's oblique criticism of the war embodies planter women's complex negotiation of southern ideology. A southerner to the core, Hardeman never rejected her place within the southern social hierarchy; she never expressed her unhappiness with the war publicly and, in a very real sense, never accepted or admitted her feelings of rebellion even to herself. Recreating a position of subordination in a household mastered by God, Hardeman labored to accept and support the war without question.[22]

Mistresses without Masters: The Contradictions of Dependency

By 1862 war arrived in the Delta, heightening planter-class women's political obligation to the Confederacy. Men's enlistment dropped dramatically as Union troops massed to the north in Memphis and to the west in Helena, Arkansas. In the Delta, white men stayed at home to protect their wives, children, slaves, and property from the invading Union army. Confronted with declining enlistment rates, the Confederate Congress passed the First Conscription Act in April 1862, requiring all able-bodied white men between the ages of eighteen and forty-five to leave their plantations and serve the Confederacy.[23] Both men and women of the planter-class immediately wrote the governor to protest the draft.

White women's response to the Conscription Acts reflects their gendered understanding of the household. When the first act passed in April, thirty-five women organized themselves and petitioned Governor Pettus. They requested that one man, George Mayfield, be released from service, arguing that "men are very scarce now, and if they are taken from 35 to 50 years of age many a family will be left destitute of anyone to see to thier business they cant attend to themselves." Surely George Mayfield could not manage the affairs of thirty-five families. Yet white women demanded that a white man remain in their neighborhood. Two issues were at stake. First, women did not want to negotiate business transactions themselves. Second, women feared the slave communities. Another petition stated that "the said neighborhood comprises in its population a very large proportion of slaves and the whites are only women and children helpless and defenseless their husbands and fathers being absent in the army."[24] Without white men, planter women felt cut adrift.

In response to such an outcry, the Confederate Congress passed the Second Conscription Act, exempting from military service one white man from each plantation with twenty or more slaves. The Second Conscription Act is traditionally interpreted as class legislation intended to secure the planting interests of the Confederacy. Yet Ann Eliza Hurst "alone" on her Yazoo River plantation echoed a common belief among planter women in the Delta when she provided a gendered interpretation of the law: she referred to it as the law "promising that every woman owning slaves . . . shall have a man detailed" to protect her.[25] Without the traditionally masculine forces of mastery, planter women felt exposed.

Why would capable, often forceful women feel unqualified to act? Living on the frontier, Delta women frequently helped their husbands and managed quite large home industries that fed and clothed their families and slaves. The answer lies in planter women's definition of household space in the years before the war. A plantation mistress's status rested upon her confinement to certain places.[26] Planter women crossed these borders with reluctance.

Planter women's definition of public and private followed a particular logic that differed from men's. They feared stepping outside the borders of the household. For planter men, the private domain of household encompassed the entire plantation—home, fields, woods, and swamps, not to mention their wives, children, slaves, and hired help. For planter women in the antebellum Delta, the boundaries of household were drawn closer to home. Planter women did not feel safe outside the secure confines of home and garden. At issue was not a refusal to leave home, but a perceived inability to function outside the family. Moving out to the fields or into the world of business represented a severe, unmanageable disruption of their identity as elite white women.

For planter women, the first boundary of household was the border between the home and the fields. Recall Ann Matthews's plea to the governor: "I am . . . surrounded by several large plantations without a white man on any of them." Not once does she mention that each of those "several large plantations" had a very large African-American community. Yet that was exactly her message, and the message of countless other planter women.

Before the war, planter women seldom interacted with slaves working in the fields. Minerva Cook, living just south of Vicksburg, recorded almost daily news of Jane, Ida, Jessy, Mary, and Hester, who worked for her in the house and garden. She trusted the bondsman Jessy to market the voluminous goods her household produced—eggs, chickens, milk, butter, pigeons—and she praised her tireless seamstress Jane for sewing "faster [and] neater . . . than any one I ever saw white or black." Visiting the quarters, however, Minerva changed her tune, exclaiming, "I do not think it is a good plan for anyone who is civilized to ever have a word to say to Negroes. Their language is so horrible and vulgar."[27] While planter ideology extended the rhetoric of family out to the fields to include all slaves, few planter women looked outside the narrow domestic sphere defined by the needs of their white family.

Vulnerable outside the home, most white women in the antebellum Delta were hard-working and capable managers within the garden gate.[28] The Delta's harsh environment gave women's work heightened urgency and importance. Isolated in the swamps, Delta families could not count on friends and neighbors to help them cope with hard times. Towns were far apart, and getting to them was difficult. Mud, often knee deep, made roads impassable much of the year. Louisa Burrus in Bolivar County complained, "I have seen little if any of my neighbors for some time as the road is too bad even for riding on horseback." She continued, "We have had no fruit, a poor garden, & little or no poultry, added to this we can scarcely get any supplies. . . . We do not like to go on steamboats or receive goods by them."[29]

To get by, planter women worked. As Ellen Hyland explained to her father, "There is a great deal to be done in the way of improvement which is rather fortunate as it will give us something to do until we get accustomed to the lonely situation." Hyland managed a garden, twenty dairy cows, and "between twenty and thirty young turkeys"—all dedicated to feeding her family.[30] In her 1858 journal, Minerva Cook described a typical day. She rose at five, woke the children and read them a chapter of the Bible, checked the kitchen, ate breakfast, made sure the slaves were at their posts, skimmed and churned milk, cut out three skirts, and supervised two slave women's sewing—all before noon.[31]

Despite their abilities, planter women rarely conceived of themselves as partners with their husbands. Even when their skills surpassed their husbands', they defined themselves as dependents. The troubled relationship between Minerva and Jared Cook demonstrates this point.[32] Minerva Cook expected everyone to be as capable and efficient as she was. Only two enslaved African-Americans, Jessy and Jane, lived up to her standards. Her husband Jared failed completely. Sharply dividing the household into men's and women's spheres, Minerva pushed Jared to live up to his obligations. The house itself became the Cooks' principal point of contention. She maintained tight order within, while he let the exterior fall into disrepair. For ten years she asked him to make repairs, and for ten years he told her to "hush and quit complaining." Avoiding their home altogether, Jared spent most of his time in Vicksburg, drinking with friends. When he did come home, Minerva was quick to give him a piece of her mind and then run to the children's room for protection. At night she often found herself hiding "in the small bed with the children," her eyes wide open "until the clock struck two."[33]

Jared accused Minerva of stepping outside a woman's place. She protested, writing, "Men have it in their heads that the very moment their wives find some fault and tell them of it that they wish to rule." She continued, "It is not so with me. I love him, respect him and fear him to this extent that I do not wish to wound his feelings."[34]

Women were wise to fear their husbands. Southern law provided women little protection. As dependents in their masters' households, women had few legal rights or privileges except those granted by their husbands. All women, therefore, were extremely vulnerable in public. One had to be poor, black, or desperate to venture into a world that offered no protection whatsoever.[35] Household represented security even for a woman facing a drunken husband. Minerva needed Jared to act for her.

The second boundary of the planter women's household was the border between the plantation and the neighborhood. Antebellum planter women did not cross this border without the protection of men, white or black. Consider

Minerva Cook: she never went to market herself to sell her goods but counted on Jessy, an enslaved African-American man, to act for her. Likewise, planter women rarely rode off their plantations alone. To protect their honor, they usually asked a black man to accompany them. In both cases, black men acted as representatives of the master's household. By traveling with white women or by venturing into public for them, they protected plantation mistresses from breaching the borders of household.

As the property of their husbands, married women could not legally transact business for themselves under the laws of *feme covert*. Widowed women could represent their own interests in public, but few chose to. Planter women did not venture into the world of men. Mary Bateman's journal provides insight into how widowed women perceived the boundaries between public and private on the plantation and in the world at large. Her aunt Re managed a large household of relatives—nine women and one small boy, more than a hundred slaves, a warehouse, a riverboat landing, and a steam gin. Bateman's diary makes clear that Aunt Re made all the important decisions regarding the management of the plantation. She chose whom to hire and fire. She decided to expand their boat landing and construct a new warehouse, and she carefully managed her taxes so as not to lose land. Aunt Re made these decisions at home on the plantation. She left the implementation of each of these decisions, however, to a trusted white man—in Aunt Re's case either a relative, Richard Campbell, or her neighbor Mr. Bell.[36]

The plantation also had public and private boundaries. Every Sunday, Aunt Re "gave out allowance," distributing food to the enslaved African-Americans. She reserved this duty for herself and kept the keys on her person. Her niece Mary managed the home, but Aunt Re "provided for" the slaves. This was the only breach of the boundary between home and field. Aunt Re never appears to have checked on the fields or visited the slave quarters. She did fire and hire overseers, but only with the assistance of Richard Campbell. She interviewed each man, but Campbell or Bell extended the offer of employment and paid the overseers. Under such a system, life could get complicated. When a man stopped by to be hired, Aunt Re would speak with him, but then someone had to send "Frank over to Richards to get him to come over." Richard would perform the actual hiring.[37]

Single women, managing large plantations, rarely crossed these domestic boundaries of household before the war. Why then did many Confederates believe that planter-class women could take up the reins of mastery once their husbands left home? Two possible explanations account for their faith in the women. On the one hand, as the actions of Hyland, Cook, Aunt Re, and scores of other Delta women attest, women were capable managers. On the other hand, planter men must have assumed that the women's class position and their whiteness—with its authority firmly grounded in hierarchies of household— could carry the weight of mastery even in the men's absence.

African-Americans quickly challenged these planter-class conceits. Many refused to accept plantation mistresses' authority in the absence of white men. Writing Governor Pettus in March 1863, Mary B. Carter complained that her "servants" were "under very little control and not doing half work . . . and the neighborhood is greatly disturbed by soldiers trading with the negroes." She continued: "on good authority I say 'pantaloons should help petticoats' or in more modern phraseology coats should help crinolines."[38] Simply walking away from slavery, many African-Americans across the Delta slowly made their way to the Union lines.[39]

Planter women's fears of "unruly negroes" were never fully realized in the Delta. Only three rumors of black violence upon white women were reported to the governor.[40] This is even more remarkable considering the presence of several black Union regiments in the Delta. In Yazoo County, a black Union soldier was accused of whipping a white woman, but unfortunately little evidence survives to indicate the circumstances behind these incidents or to verify whether they existed at all beyond people's imaginations. The majority of planter women's complaints centered on blacks leaving the plantation or refusing to work. The ability of African-Americans to demonstrate their freedom and their own free will terrified planter women. Mistresses felt personally threatened and violated as blacks slowly claimed the abandoned plantations around them, selling cotton, scrap lumber, or anything remaining in the big house.[41] No personal violence needed to occur for white women to feel that terrible forces were unleashed.

Not only were white women's familiar duties disrupted by war, but uncertainty forced planter women to expand their vision to the plantation at large and to assume a limited authority over field work and field hands. The press remained curiously silent on the issue of planter women's new responsibility as plantation managers. The virtual absence of any public discussion of plantation mistresses in a time when thousands of women suddenly found themselves forced to act alone as both master and mistress attests to white southerners' inability to reconcile what to them appeared to be the oxymoron of female leadership. Not only did this fly in the face of proslavery ideology, which emphasized women's dependency, but, as some planter women's experiences suggest, it tore apart women's sense of self.

Uneasy, white women turned to the institutions of the state and tried to establish a personal relationship with the governor, hoping to receive his favor. Alone, and without connections, women hesitantly requested that the governor hear their pleas. The letters begin "Please accept my apology for the liberty I take in addressing you"; "Pardon me for thus annoying or troubling you"; "I would not again intrude on you but"; "I appeal to your generosity"; "It is not my wish to be obtrusive but ..." Uncertain of the obligations of the state, planter women tentatively crossed the boundaries into the public sphere to press their case.[42]

Planter women specifically requested that masters, not just any white man, be assigned to them. Women placed great confidence in each individual master's ability to control *his* slaves. The head of the household, they believed, could best manage his "family." Echoing this belief, District Judge Robert Hudson went so far as to suggest that the governor require that all absentee owners reside on their plantations for the duration of the war.[43] Even in the case of absentee ownership, where any relationship between master and slave was abstract at best, Hudson believed that the master was best suited to govern. A man's ability to acquire wealth, Hudson implied, reflected his natural leadership.

Ironically, slaves probably did respect planters more if they were widely recognized in the community—not because slaves recognized their master's superiority over other white men but because social reputation gave these men control over community resources necessary to maintain the coercive structure of slavery.[44] As the planter wife Lucie Armstrong aptly noted, ruling and regulation went together in Delta communities. "Darling, it requires some ruling spirit like yourself to regulate everything in our neighborhood ... and if the neighborhood misses you as much, you can see how perfectly helpless and dependent I am without you."[45] Community leaders like Armstrong had the power to organize slave patrols and local militias, and they had the ear of their neighbors. By 1862, however, social power was not sufficient to maintain slavery.

As Union troops began working their way down the Mississippi River from Memphis to Vicksburg, slaves dropped what they were doing and left the plantations. By June, many white women had lost their faith in mastery. Men's power, they realized, relied on physical strength. And not all masters had the strength to command. These women requested that the governor send them any strong, young, active, white male who could force African-Americans to work or just to stay. They discounted the abilities of older men, the crippled, or the infirm. Mastery was age-specific; white men had to be young and fit enough "to keep the negroes in proper subjection, to make them work and prevent them from thieving &c."[46]

As the household crumbled around them, some women reconstructed their own households out of whatever they could find. They did not use this moment to press for independence; instead they struggled to ground themselves within a new hierarchy. Take the case of Sarah Garrett. In 1864 Sarah Garrett found herself alone and destitute at her home near Canton, Mississippi. According to court records, Garrett asked three African-American men—a barber and two draymen—to share their wages with her. The men, former slaves of hers, were by this time in business for themselves. The unnamed men decided to help Garrett by supporting her financially and helping her transact business.

At this point, the state stepped in to prevent what was perceived as a dangerous and subversive act. Declaring that the three men were still enslaved and, therefore, the responsibility of Garrett (rather than the other way around), the district court punished Garrett for letting three "slaves ... go at large & trade as freedmen." She was fined five hundred dollars and sentenced to sixty days in prison.[47]

Garrett's actions clearly threatened the court. Her sentence was unusually harsh, suggesting that much more was at stake than the simple act of (in the court's terms) a widow hiring out her slaves. Garrett's request exposed the contradictions of race and gender embedded in planter women's identities. Like most plantation mistresses, Garrett demanded that she be protected and provided for as a weaker subject. Though some women in the absence of white men fled in terror from ex-slaves, Garrett turned to freedmen as a comforting masculine presence. Like white men, freedpeople provided food and shelter and, unlike the plantation mistresses, were familiar with business and trade negotiations. Moreover, freedpeople had ready access to Union forces and the active trade in goods and cotton. According to white gender relations, freedpeople shared the characteristics of protector and provider associated with white masculinity. While Sarah Garrett needed the security of household hierarchies, most African-Americans completely rejected any concept of voluntary submission. The self-conceptions of Garrett and these freedmen resulted in a disturbing upset of what white southerners believed to be "natural" inequalities.

Unable to assume mastery, a few white women like Garrett consciously rec-ognized their dependency upon African-Americans.[48] As the plantation house-hold crumbled around them, white women attempted to reconstruct a familiar role for themselves in any household they could find. Planter women did not question hierarchy; instead they searched to locate a place of dependency in a world where the traditional boundaries of race, class, and gender were being redrawn.

Emma and Will: Exploring the Limits of Selflessness

In the towns and cities, many white women crossed the border between private and public space by volunteering to nurse, raise money, sew uniforms and flags, and by engaging in charity. The movement from domestic to public space was less risky in urban areas. Elite women were less isolated from one another, and slaves were less likely to outnumber whites. In cities, elite women could rely on the institutions of government—the police and the courts—to secure physical safety outside the home. Moreover, in cities, mistresses personally knew the African-Americans residing in their homes.

Yet urban elites also struggled with the tension between women's selflessness and independent action. The correspondence between Emma and William Crutcher reveals how this transferral of women from the private to the public sphere rocked the foundation of southern marriage relations and planter-class women's sense of self and shows that a woman need not be alone on a plan-tation or even managing a household herself to have her identity threatened by war. Emma and Will's letters clearly demonstrate that the household was as much an ideology as a lived reality. One did not have to administer a slave-holding household to adopt its principal tenets. As Emma's letters indicate, planter-class women, regardless of where they lived, defined themselves as subordinate to men while still perceiving themselves as active and able mem-bers of an elite, with duties and authority over others. Yet in Vicksburg, as on the plantation, the conditions of war exposed irreconcilable contradictions between dependency and command and eventually undermined planter-class women's ability to act on their own authority. As a newlywed living in town, Emma did not lose sons to the war, nor did she face daily challenges by slaves. What Emma did confront was an inability to reconstruct a self capable of inde-pendent action.

Marrying William Crutcher in 1861, Emma Shannon declared that her marriage would be "a democracy, not a monarchy."[49] Emma, the extremely well educated daughter of Marmaduke Shannon, the editor of the *Vicksburg Whig*, was self-confident and opinionated. Encouraged by her father to read widely and take an active interest in current political affairs, Emma balked at assuming a position of dependency. Marriage, she felt, could be a partnership. Within a year, however, the experience of war reversed Emma's thinking.

At the outset of the war, Emma tackled her new responsibilities from a well-grounded understanding of her authority as a member of the planter class. While Will marched off to war as a captain in the King Cotton Guards, Emma busied herself on the home front by joining the Ladies' Aid Society, nursing at the City Hospital, and helping to organize the Free Market to distribute food and clothing to the deserving poor.

Emma was not alone in entering a more public sphere; the circumstances of war feminized the southern home front. With a growing number of men volunteering and later being conscripted into the army, the white population on the home front became predominately female.[50] The government encouraged women to take an active role in supporting the Confederacy both materially and emotionally. Planter women responded to the call, "knowing that we could not bear arms, and being unwilling to sit idle." They aided their "Country's struggle for her rights" by supplying local troops with uniforms, blankets, and bandages.[51] Expanding on the traditional household duties of caring for the sick and distributing food and clothing, mistresses acted on their belief in the natural superiority of southern social institutions. They assumed that if each person played a part, the South and southern institutions would emerge victorious.

Planter women, however, soon demonstrated the limits of Confederate nationalism. By acting on the principles of states' rights and the sanctity of the household, they defined the Confederacy in very narrow terms. As the members of the Ladies Soldiers' Aid Society of Palmetto remarked, "We are few in number but willing to do according to our ability for the Miss . . . troops generally apart from furnishing the members of our household." The focus on local troops, on providing for "our regiment or any other from our County," echoed throughout the correspondence from ladies aid societies. While willing to supply their kin, "their brothers and friends," planter women were less interested in helping other, more needy regiments. The *Panola Star* repeatedly raised the specter of class conflict if the women of Panola County continued to provide only for "their men," letting poorer men go without.[52] Obligation apparently stopped short of helping those outside one's acquaintance or, as the editor of the *Star* pointed out, one's class.

With her mother-in-law, Emma helped elite women and planters create the Free Market. The Free Market originated with an advertisement placed in a local paper by Emma's mother-in-law, Emma C. Crutcher, and Mrs. Howe, a commodity merchant's wife. To help feed the families of soldiers gone off to war, they requested donations of meat, vegetables, and grains from local planters. They established a structure whereby a different woman each month organized the distribution of food to approximately eighty families. Initially the Crutcher's slaves Ella and Fred performed the actual labor of delivering food to each house, until the senior Crutcher offered the use of part of his carriage room so the ladies could "come and distribute themselves."[53]

Emma interpreted her work at the Free Market as an opportunity to help her husband. She made it her duty to assist every family who had a soldier fighting under Will's command. As the creation of the Free Market indicates, the war placed working-class women in a precarious position.[54] The Confederate Army was slow to issue pay, and when it was issued, women had no assurance that their husbands would forward enough of it home for them to subsist. By the second year of the war, many working women were finding it difficult to make rent payments.

Tensions at home could undermine a southern soldier's patriotism. Therefore, by assisting these soldiers' families, Emma helped secure their continued loyalty both to her husband and to the Confederate army. Whenever a pressing concern arose, such as a sick child, a missed paycheck, or an absence of letters, Emma intervened, passing personal messages through Will to the soldier involved. "[T]ell Mr. McCarthy, private in the King Cotton Guards," she wrote, "that his wife is in a situation to need all the help he can give her. . . . even two or three dollars from his pay, would assist in paying her rent. . . . she and her four babies are in a state of utmost destitution." Emma covered rent payments when they could not be met, interceded with her husband when pay was late, and even offered to take families of the King Cotton Guards with her when she planned to flee the city.[55]

Emma sympathized with these women as women, but dismissed any serious comparison between her feelings and theirs.[56] Womanhood was an uncertain bond. In her mind, working-class women were another race, like Yankees and African-Americans. Emma always preceded any reference to soldiers' wives with "Irish," "German," or "Dutch."[57] She described Mrs. McCarthy as "about the most modest, Irish woman I ever saw" and mused that "they feel (in some degree, at least) what I would." Emma realized that as a woman without a husband, her situation was in some ways similar to theirs, but she was reluctant to transpose her own feelings onto working-class women. A great believer in heredity as an explanation for emotions, intelligence, and physical strength, Emma designated people outside her class and race as fundamentally different.[58] Sisterhood, according to Emma, was an illusion only skin deep.

Emma's duties seem to have provided her a great deal of satisfaction, in large part because they enabled her to get involved, to a limited extent, in military affairs. Throughout the war she took an interest in military campaigns. In her letters she often expressed her frustration "at the idiocy of generals." Yet she always took care to apologize for these opinions and acknowledge that she had no expertise from which to speak about such matters.[59] With the soldiers' families, on the other hand, she could bridge this gap by making military matters a domestic concern. Emma felt free to comment on recruitment, pay, the fears and hardships of the home front, and the character of the army as it related to the people under her wing.

As Will's wife, she worked at the Free Market to fulfill her duty to him. She stepped into the familiar role of mistress, distributing provisions in order to meet her obligations to her husband and to those under his command. As Emma said, "It tends to make you popular with your men, which is worth a great deal of trouble."[60] Planter-class women understood the authority of their position within the household and attempted to expand this position by defining more and more people as their "sons," their "children," their "people."

Yet there was a question as to where Emma's duty should end. Emma, in replicating the personal, face-to-face interaction of household in her relationships with soldiers' families, extended the Crutchers' circle of obligation. But as a mistress and a wife, she acted on her husband's authority. Will repeatedly warned Emma about assuming a responsibility for others that *he* did not want to assume. Emma's actions made soldiers and their families too familiar. Acting out her perception of household relations, Emma got to know each soldier's wife. She personalized the command.

Will was uncomfortable with Emma's construction of this rapidly growing household. He teased, "The whole company has the highest appreciation of the Capt. lady, much higher indeed than they have of the Capt. himself." He was troubled by the demands made upon Emma. He insisted that she bore no responsibility for the soldiers' families, and he wanted her to end her relationship with the "Irish community who think they have a point blank right to infringe upon your time and patience because they have a husband in the King Cotton Guards."[61] In Will's opinion, Emma's concept of household threatened the hierarchy of his command by opening the door to reciprocal duties and obligations.[62] He frequently reminded her that her first obligation was to him, and that as a mistress and wife she acted on *his* authority, not her own.

The pressure to reinscribe her activities within the boundaries of marriage came not only from Will but from within Emma as well. In their correspondence, the Crutchers played with the word *property,* not to refer to houses, furniture, or horses, but to Emma herself. As a new bride, Emma was the only member of Will's household; they joked that damage to her beauty or health would erode his only asset—namely, Emma. Increasingly, Emma found herself caught between being a person (with duties and responsibilities as an individual) and a physical object (her husband's most prized possession).

To better understand her role, Emma began to analyze the two women she knew best, her mother and her mother-in-law. For Emma, they represented the central virtue of white womanhood—selflessness.

Emma's mother, Lavinia Shannon, was the mistress of a very large and noisy household. The mother of eleven, Lavinia showered attention on her children to ensure that none got lost in the crowd. As one would expect, chaos often ensued; in Emma's words, her mother got "into a good deal of trouble sometimes." Emma blamed her father for her mother's disorganization. Marmaduke Shannon, according to Emma, never added "his authority to hers . . . and thus things tangle up."[63] In Lavinia Shannon's case, selflessness needed to be augmented by her husband's authority to be effective.

Emma's mother-in-law, Emma C. Crutcher, could not have been more different. Organized and efficient, Mrs. Crutcher managed her small household and served as the leader of several benevolent organizations. Before the war, she was active in the church and, once the war broke out, she founded the Free Market and organized nursing services. Emma contrasted her mother's "self-sacrificing" duty to her family with her mother-in-law's selfless involvement in benevolent organizations. "I never knew before how selfish I was, until I saw your mother's daily life, for, though my mother is . . . self-sacrificing she is in a measure compelled to be, by her large family of young children." Emma C. Crutcher, on the other hand, practiced selflessness outside the home.

Emma's choice of words to describe the two women is suggestive. Emma associated action with a sublimation of self. For Emma, the choice lay between selfishness and selflessness.[64] Too much self, according to Emma, did not produce power and action in women, but rather laziness and narcissism. Caught in a paradox, she needed a self to act, but she had to abdicate that self, in her mind, to act effectively.

Emma could act with conviction only in relation to her husband and not as an individual herself. Determined to find significant work, Emma asserted herself in February 1862 by declaring that she was either going to Nashville to become a professional nurse under Felicia Grundy Porter or joining her husband on the battlefront. Reversing her position in the next sentence, she added: "You ought to use your *authority* when you don't like anything. I'll mind when you put your foot down."[65] Emma tried, but had difficulty, conceiving of a space outside her relationship with her husband. She understood herself through her relations with others—through the social relations of the antebellum South. Although Emma's class position granted her authority, that authority was contingent upon her husband's approval.

By the second year of the war, this realization left Emma feeling disembodied and detached from the war, her husband, and even herself. "I am just tired of sitting in this room by myself . . . writing dull letters . . . in a commonplace way about commonplace people and commonplace things." She sat reading history and poetry, which she found "terribly aggravating, when *history* is being acted by my own countrymen just around me everyday; and I *know* that we two contain in our souls the essence of all the poetry that was ever written."[66] Despite her active involvement in the war effort, Emma felt removed—as if she were just reading, not acting.

When they married, Emma had perceived marriage as a democracy, a partnership between two equals.[67] War, however, forced her to reevaluate her position. "When we were married," she explained, "I had by no means made up my mind that you were henceforth to be the *head* and governor, the *monarch* of our little kingdom. . . . I felt very rebellious. . . . So you ought to be thankful for this absence—we ought to, I mean, for placing us in our proper, relative positions. . . . I can give up the reins to you."[68] Emma resigned her position as an equal partner in the household, warning that "your only subject is of a very unruly, willful character, so you will have to be very patient. Besides she married you without recognizing the *right* you had to claim obedience, and she has just begun to see it clearly."[69] Emma had no reason to resign herself to a position of dependency, but the fact that she did indicates her confusion and her inability to find any significance in her actions outside of marriage. Unable to locate a sense of purpose outside the home, Emma turned to her marriage and defined herself in relation to her husband.

Like hundreds of women on plantations across the South, Emma confronted the boundaries of her authority and discovered the limits of women's independent action. Ironically, Emma's confusion was contained, having little impact on the community despite her active involvement in public service. Notwithstanding the Confederacy's emphasis on white women's activities outside the home—in hospitals, markets, sewing circles, and government agencies—their work at home, on the plantations, held the key to victory. In Vicksburg, far from the site of domestic struggle, Emma faced these challenges unnoticed. For Emma, the crumbling of the boundaries of female authority remained a personal crisis.

Emma's letters mark the path taken by many planter women faced with the upheavals of war. Planter women found themselves in the paradoxical position of representing authority while being limited themselves by another's authority. As members of their class they felt compelled to act, while as women they were unsure of how they could legitimately assume this authority.

Emma Crutcher's confusion, her flight from independence into the protective arms of her husband, provides a rare insight into the collapse of the Confederacy. Ignoring the larger topics of slavery, government, and military tactics, the Crutcher correspondence reveals the fracturing of planter-class identity under the strains of war. Caught in the contradictions of her class, race, and gender, Emma was unable to locate a source for the authority she thought she needed to exercise. Displaced, Emma searched uneasily for a familiar position within the boundaries of southern social relations by inscribing herself more and more completely within the bounds of hierarchial marriage relations.

White southerners' personal identities were chipped away as each border was crossed, challenging their sense of authority. Just as slavery had been maintained by thousands of individual acts by particular planters over particular slaves, the "peculiar institution" crumbled as white southerners lost their sense of self and their sense of mastery. Individually, women's confusion may have gone unnoticed, just as Emma's withdrawal from community activities drew little protest from those around her. On the borders of their class and race, planter women were sitting on the fence of southern social relations when it collapsed. Planter women located their authority in the construction of a self dependent upon others.

On the plantation, the shattering of planter women's identity carried grave implications for the survival of slavery and the Confederacy. Unable to master, they watched their sons, husbands, and former slaves walk away, carrying off the only world these women knew. As they tried to assume mastery over slaves, they discovered that they carried neither the authority of their race nor the resources of their class. Scrambling as each boundary of identity was challenged and crossed, planter women sought shelter in the one institution that had once guaranteed them strength and authority: the household. Planter women never created a separate political consciousness that would replace the structures of domestic hierarchy; instead they searched to relocate their sense of self and their sense of authority in the familiar institution of household.

Planter women did not question social hierarchies. Deeply invested in slavery for their livelihood and their sense of self, planter women struggled to maintain their vision of the plantation household. Yet, without the cornerstone of slavery, they faced an impossible task.

3

♣

The Perversion of Defeat

The Crisis of White Manhood

"*I* AM HERE in the Swamp ... trying to start a crop with a few freedmen—who do not at all times jump when I speak to them," complained George Torrey in 1866. "I have come to the [same] conclusion that the girl did, the first night that she was married—She said she was mighty scared when she went to bed. She would lie first on one side, and then on tother. But at last concluded she would lie on her back, and take the chances—So you see, I have come to the conclusion, not to fret, about things I cannot control."[1]

Like Torrey, many planter men personalized the cost of emancipation through bizarre narratives of defeat. Tales cropped up of men becoming women, whites becoming black, ladies hired out by poor whites, and "Yankee schoolmarms" taking up with "black bucks."[2] The unspeakable had come to pass—black men rose and took up arms against them, and black women asserted claims to their families, the land, and the crop. With emancipation, white men faced a topsy-turvy world where everyone assumed a new position. Weakened by the loss of mastery, planter men feared that their whiteness and their manhood would slip away. In the Delta, white men protested African-American freedom by characterizing it as an absurdity. Emancipation, they declared, was as unnatural as attempting to transform independent men into dependents—or, in Torrey's words, of trying to reconstruct grown men into vulnerable virgins. White men's attempts at humor revealed new truths. Mastery, whiteness, and manhood lost their moorings as the plantation household dissolved. Lashing out, planters labeled emancipation a gross perversion of natural law.

Planter men's response to defeat demonstrates that political consciousness was not separate from personal identity. For planter men, emancipation was replete with gender and racial inversions, threatening their understanding of themselves, and upsetting familiar power relations. Any challenge to their

THE LAST DITCH OF THE CHIVALRY, OR A PRESIDENT IN PETTICOATS.

Fig. 7. Stripped of their slaves and subjected to defeat, planter-class men feared the loss of masculine authority. The national press fed on these fears by portraying Jefferson Davis in petticoats, fleeing from Union soldiers. ("The Last Ditch of the Chivalry, or a President in Petticoats," by Currier and Ives. Courtesy of the Division of Prints and Photographs, Library of Congress.)

political power was interpreted as a challenge to their most intimate sense of themselves.

In response, they acted on antebellum constructions of power and privilege. In the antebellum Delta, whiteness, manhood, and mastery were inseparable. To be assured of full civil and political rights, a man needed all three. Each was represented in the social relations of household. Before the war, mastery of one's household guaranteed a white man his most basic rights—the right to vote, the right to legal protection, the right to conduct business, and the right to travel freely across the landscape. Most important, the household provided a man with an independent living. He was not, at least in theory, beholden to any man. This independence, this freedom from corruption and influence, marked white men and set them apart from dependent people—namely, women, children, slaves, free blacks, and hired hands.

Of course, antebellum mastery alone did not give one full political privileges. One had to be white and male. Black men headed free households, and so did women of both races, but their race or gender denied them basic legal rights. Southerners, like most Americans, defined blackness and womanhood as biological markers of a dependent nature. Conversely, neither whiteness nor manhood alone guaranteed a white man full rights. A white man without a household was dependent upon another man for his livelihood, and so he was denied full rights of privacy. His employer could regulate his domestic and personal affairs. In short, one had to possess whiteness, manhood, and a household to be fully independent.[3]

Emancipation threatened this understanding of political rights. What was white manhood without mastery? Emancipation, Union occupation, and defeat exposed the fiction of white men's independence. Planter men found themselves "dependent" on free labor, "dependent" on their women for financial support, and, in the case of some six thousand lamed men, literally "dependent" on others for mobility.[4] More profoundly, without the plantation household, domestic authority no longer translated into public authority. Emancipation and Reconstruction extended state regulation into what had always been defined as a man's private domain. Stepping into the household, the Federal government freed men's slaves. Not stopping there, new labor laws regulated a man's relations with his work force. Moving into the household, the state began to regulate marriage, legalizing interracial relationships and making divorce more attainable.[5] One by one, these laws forced open the gates of the plantation, undercutting landowners' control of labor and of their families.

Planter men responded to emancipation by turning to the household, their traditional seat of power. There was only one problem—the antebellum household no longer existed. Planter men continued to assert their power in the time-honored fashion, only to discover that emancipation had fundamentally altered the political terrain. Honor became dishonor as emancipation transformed the politics of household.

This chapter explores the connections between planter-class men's identity and the reconstruction of their political consciousness by examining three different responses to emancipation. White men's responses varied from the personal to the political to the ideological. On the most personal level, some men collapsed into hopeless depression and alcoholism. They discovered that they no longer had a foundation from which to act. As young men they had assumed they would inherit their fathers' mastery, and when that dream died, they collapsed from grief. Others lashed out in vicious acts of violence. In order to reclaim their antebellum political privileges, they refused to relinquish past rights. Denying that the loss of the household stripped them of the right to dominate the political sphere, they continued to police their homes, their neighborhoods, and the state through traditional rituals of violence and mastery. Still others worked to advance white supremacy. Weaving fantastic narratives of racial and gender inversions, racial ideologues attempted to classify people by race and gender rather than social position. They argued that white male authority was grounded in white men's biological nature. A white man's race and his gender guaranteed him, and him alone, full political privileges.

Each response—depression, vengeance, and mythmaking—built upon antebellum traditions of household hierarchies. Even as their individual households dramatically changed shape, white men did not reject the politics of household. Like white women, they did not, and in many ways they could not, reject their commitment to the hierarchies of the household. Yet each planter faced the same question: How could one express dissent when the very foundations of one's identity suddenly held little meaning?

The unraveling of planter men's identity began during the war. In 1862, white male mastery took direct hits in the Delta—in April, the Confederate government instituted the draft; in June, Union troops freely patrolled the Mississippi River; and all through the spring and summer, African-Americans began to run for freedom. In 1863, when the Emancipation Proclamation went into effect, former slaves donned Union uniforms, and on July 4, 1863, Vicksburg fell and was occupied by Union troops. Under these conditions, mastery proved elusive at best. Exposed, planter men found their authority questioned at all levels—by their wives, their children, their former slaves, and the yeomanry.

Several incidents during the war reveal the sudden reversals of power. In the summer of 1863 a white man, Charles Brick, discovered several black women celebrating their independence by going from home to home and taking choice pieces of clothing and furniture. Brick ordered them to stop. They responded by telling him that now that they were free, they had the right to slaveholders' property. Brick shot one woman in the leg, claiming he had the right to shoot "runaways." Suddenly Brick found himself surrounded by a crowd of black men, who proceeded to whip Brick and, placing a gun to his head, demanded that he call them "master."[6] Without sole access to the use of violence, white men discovered that mastery was easily transferred from one race to another.

Unable to comprehend black men's mastery, Confederate captain William E. Montgomery reported to Governor Clark that a "band of 300 armed negroes" burned down Judge Shall Yerger's plantation in the Delta. These men, he continued, "must have been Curry's gang of Thieves blacked." Montgomery made the quick assumption that these men must be white in blackface. Yet they could just have easily been African-Americans, as he had at first suggested. The Delta sheltered numerous African-American guerrilla troops during the war who operated both legally, under the command of Union forces, and extralegally.[7] Perhaps Montgomery and other planter-class men could not fathom former slaves taking up arms against them. To recognize blacks as fighting men fundamentally undermined their understanding of race.

Portraying black soldiers as unwitting dupes of the Yankees, local newspapers tried to explain away black southerners' actions. "[N]egroes have quitted the Yankee lines in disgust," proclaimed the *Memphis Daily Appeal*, "and returned to their masters, horrified at the bestiality, wickedness and degradation of their would-be liberators."[8] Only beasts, not men, they reasoned, could perform these acts of violence. Only white men masked in black, or black men dressed as Yankees, or Yankees exposed as beasts could explain the inversion of plantation hierarchies, and the essential perversion underlying these acts.[9]

Beyond racial inversions, planter men confronted class conflict during the war. On May 24, 1864, Judge Robert S. Hudson warned local authorities that the yeomanry were taking over planter property in the Delta with impunity. Spewing forth one insult after another, Hudson wrote that "the counties of Leake, Attala, Neshoba, Winston and other [hill] counties are now ... emptying their filthy, base, disloyal, deserting, stealing, murdering population into Yazoo. ... They pretend to go there to get corn to live on, but their real object is to avoid our army, steal, plunder and be with the Yankees. ... the whole crew male and female are unfit to live any where." The outraged Hudson continued, "Joel Williams & his son Jo. and his sons in law Mask and Peterson are at one of Maj. Vaughn's or Boylans places [and] ... gave parties to deserters and danced over the downfall of Vicksburg & all our defeats." He concluded: "The Yankees will reward them with the places they have located upon."[10]

As the unity among white men dissolved, planter men responded by stripping poorer men of their claims to mastery. Lacing their discussions of the yeomanry with references to gender transgression, planters accused poor farmers of rejecting the most fundamental tenet of household—a man's authority over his wife. Yeomen women, from Hudson's perspective, were running amuck, loosed from the fetters of manly control. "The women," he emphasized, "are far worse than the men and are responsible for most of it. ... The state is now under the tacit rule of deserters, thieves, and disloyal men and women. . . . nearly all the women are openly at work to weaken our army."[11]

Planter men rarely faced women's dissent within their own households.[12] For the most part, planter women expressed their disappointment by constructing a mythic past rooted in a safe and harmonious plantation household. Sarah Buckner, however, confronted her father directly. On June 27, 1865, Buckner publically disowned her father. Declaring her longstanding loyalty to the Union, Buckner proclaimed that her father no longer represented her interests. She defiantly stated, "My Father's opinions *often very often* disagreed with his familys." Writing to Mississippi's new governor, she swore that "your opinion on the subject of the preservation of the Union I adopted & never waned the open expression of opinion,—& a determination to influence all I could to feel Ceession was wrong & would be our ruin." As the plantation household collapsed, she broke free from her father. She sought refuge with the Yankees since he no longer had the power to protect her. After all, if manhood was grounded in mastery, how could women respect men who were not masters?[13]

Each incident openly revealed that planter men could no longer assume that they had mastery over African-American men and women, yeoman farmers, or, in Buckner's case, his own daughter. Stripped of the traditional vestiges of authority, planter men were unmasked. Startled, they made the rude discovery that their identity—their standing in society and their knowledge of themselves—was not fixed but fluid, susceptible to the ignominy of defeat. Without the plantation household, all the familiar definitions of master and slave, black and white, male and female no longer seemed to function. Suddenly it became unclear exactly who was dependent upon whom.

Isolated incidents, like the ones described above, gave planter men fair warning of what they would witness after the war. Yet no one could have prepared them for the initial shock of finding their households destroyed, both literally and figuratively. After the war, some men collapsed, unable to find meaning in an unfamiliar environment. Others set to work. Building on the law, extralegal violence, and the power of the pen, they attempted to reconstruct a position of mastery. Both forms of dissent provide insight into how planter-class men struggled to regain a coherent sense of self as their society—and their identity—fractured and fell apart.

Union officer J. A. Hawley observed, "It is quite noticeable that the women and *young* men as classes, are more bitter & vehement while the older men—

more versed in business & more polite[—]are found to regard more shrewdly their interests."[14] As Hawley remarked, older and more established men in the planter class quickly proclaimed loyalty to the Union in order to maintain their business interests. Voting themselves back into office, they took control of the state and its laws and quickly passed what became known as the Black Codes.

The Black Codes restricted the rights of freedpeople. First, the laws made it illegal for blacks to rent land in the countryside. Second, they required all freedpeople to carry proof of employment. Third, black southerners could not own firearms. And fourth, (black) children could be apprenticed to (white) guardians should their parents fail to provide for them. The laws systematically placed freedpeople back under the control of white male heads of household, but this time as wage workers, not as slaves.[15] Planters, relying on the force of the state, secured their economic dominance and their mastery by once again laying claim to their family "white and black."

The state legislatures, however, paid a considerable price to pass the Black Codes. Demonstrating their defiance, they outraged Northerners who felt that former Confederates were attempting to reinstate a version of unfree labor. Even worse, according to Yankees, southerners were accomplishing all of this legally, using the very same government they had openly rebelled against one year before.[16]

Southern men also faced a blank stare of incomprehension at home. White women and young men perceived the former Confederates' willingness to compromise as the ultimate form of submission. By rejoining the nation, white men appeared to have turned their backs on the southern cause. "Country, my country," wrote Amanda Worthington, "my spirit chafes at thy forced submission to our foe & in my soul the fire still smoulders & waits for a chance to burst forth once more with renewed vigor, and do battle for *VENGEANCE, VENGEANCE, for our wrongs!*" Women like Worthington feared that white men were betraying the Confederacy. "I did not want Father and Willie to vote," Worthington confessed, "but they thought it best to do so. . . . I feel that I have no country, and the affairs of the United States Government will never have the power to interest me." Unlike Sarah Buckner, who openly rejected her father, women like Worthington could not blame their loved ones. Instead, they expressed their anger through a fierce patriotism. "I wish I could have voted," Worthington exclaimed. "My vote would have been *for the soldiers forever.*"[17] Women and children fiercely clung to the past, refusing to accept the terms of surrender and questioning the valor and judgment of white southern men.[18]

In March 1867, Presidential Reconstruction came to an abrupt halt. White southern men had overstepped. Congress responded by passing the Reconstruction Acts and dividing the South into five military districts. The U.S. government required each southern state to pass the Fourteenth Amendment, granting African-Americans citizenship, before it could be reinstated in the Union. Under the new legislation, each southern state's representation in Congress was reduced in proportion to its disenfranchised black voters. This act placed planter men in open competition with the Delta's black majority.[19] The bottom rail moved to the top.

White men responded to the loss on a number of different levels. Those with the least power—the young men—suffered the most extreme reactions. They, like their mothers and sisters, saw defeat as betrayal. The older generation had failed them, leaving them without their true inheritance. In many ways, they could not mature because they could never assume mastery over slaves.

The young men's experiences can be loosely grouped into two categories. Some were paralyzed with grief and literally became feminized as they turned to parents, daughters, or wives for support. Others initiated the extreme wave of violence that shook the South after the war. Refusing to submit, they stepped into the alternative political space created during the war and used extralegal activities to wield power in its rawest and most violent form. Both responses required planters to reposition themselves—in the household in the first instance, and in the community in the second. Young planter-class men acted on principles learned during slavery, most notably those of force and submission, but found themselves transferred outside the accepted power structures.[20]

Alcoholism and depression gripped the South after the war, crushing the younger generation. Boys during slavery and adolescents during the war, many young men had never been able to prove their manhood on the battlefield. They grew up only to discover that they could never follow in their fathers' footsteps as heads of plantation households. In their minds, they could never mature into grown men because emancipation stripped them of mastery, the one vocation that truly marked manhood and independence. Many young men balked at leaving the plantation for work in business, law, medicine, or engineering. Like most southerners, white and black, they believed that working for another man signaled dependency. Stymied, some men sank into hopeless despair.[21]

In 1865 Edward Stuart, Ann Hardeman's only surviving nephew, returned home to find that the family plantation had been sold, his aunt who had raised him had left, and his sisters had been sent off to find work. Cut adrift, Stuart took a job as a mechanic in another part of the state. Raised as a member of the elite, Stuart suddenly found himself working for wages and snubbed by the very people he viewed as his social peers. He complained that "there are few of the purseproud ... aristocracy, or would be aristocrats, that care to fraternize with a mechanic how-so ever deserving.... such fellows have more to lose than I by the non-association; but a denial of those advantages that were expected for me diminishes the pleasures of social intercourse."[22]

In Stuart's case, his distress was sharpened by his sisters' apparent strength. Forced to leave their home and find work, Adelaide and Bettie Stuart served as a constant reminder that Edward had failed to provide for his family. "I would rather submit to any drudgery," he declared, "than my Aunt Ann or Sisters should be reduced to work."[23] Yet both came to pass. His sisters went to work, and he submitted himself to drudgery. As a consequence, Edward simply disappeared. Unable to face family or friends, he severed all ties with those who had raised him. They never heard from him again.

Edward Stuart was only one of many who found paid employment—engineering, medicine, business, or artisanal labor—demeaning. Facing an uncertain future, many young men found it impossible to act. The *Weekly Panola Star* warned, "Shall an unpardonable indifference relieve you of the weighty demands that self and the world have upon you? Can not these considerations induce you to ... doff that indolence ... ?"[24] Parents, struggling themselves to make the transition to free labor, pushed their sons to find a profession. Caroline Kiger constantly reminded her son William that "it would not do for you to quit the University now. I am exceedingly anxious that you should have a profession to fall back on." She had reason to question his fortitude. William Kiger valiantly went off to the University of Virginia every fall, and every winter, just before exams, he returned home. First he tried a course in engineering, then medicine, but homesickness crippled him each time. Yet as his letters make clear, he longed not just for his family but for the past. "[I have] no one to cheer me in my lone solitude or to make my pulses bound with ecstacy by the simple sweet words *'Christmas Gift.'* In my imagination I saw each loved face and heard each treasured voice.... Again & again did I wish that I could be a child once more to pass through those happy scenes.... I feel and know that the happiest portion of my life has been spent and I look forward to the future with an uneasy troubled mind." He was acutely aware that with emancipation he had no household to become master of, and for William this meant no future. Sinking deeper and deeper, he despaired of "trying to do so much, and breaking down just as you are nearly through, and failing in everything, is too much time lost to gain nothing."[25]

By and large, older men fared better than the young. Because they had matured before the war, they possessed a well-developed sense of their own power and authority and, as Chaplain Hawley remarked, "more shrewdly regard their interests."[26] Yet exceptions did exist. Some older men slowly faded away rather than face a new South. Jean Smith wrote long, despairing letters to her sisters describing their father's inability to take command and act after the war. Awkwardly she set about trying to manage the plantation on her own. In January, as it was time to settle up with her father's sharecroppers, she discovered that they had been marketing the cotton on their own and "they refused to tell where they had sold it and were very impertenent, so much so that I thought it best to return to the house . . . to urge Pa to try and find out where it was. . . . I was sure Pa could attach the cotton. . . . he thought he knew where the cotton had been sold but he [said] he really did not know how to act in the matter. . . . Every day I am convinced how foolish it is for us to look for Pa to provide for us." Smith continued to try to consult her father, "knowing what respect was due him," but repeatedly his only response was to continue reading his "novel" while remarking, "I do not know what to do, this thing living off of other people I do not fancy myself."

Jean Smith felt frustrated as her father forced her to assume the masculine role of protecting and providing for him. Writing to her sisters, she confessed that "such an unableness on Pa's part to make my life easier . . . unnerves me [and] I cannot stand longer and I feel at times my reason is tottering and another great sorrow will make me a lunatic." As the farm failed, she and her younger sister were "shut out from society" because they had no proper clothes to wear and no free time to "improve" themselves. She believed that their father, by assuming the dependent position, threatened to strip them of their womanhood and leave them genderless as neither men nor women. Torn between her loyalty to her father and a desperate need to rescue herself, Smith reasoned that "it would never do for us to leave him but already our sacrifice has been great on his account."[27]

While some men lapsed into a helpless dependency with the loss of mastery, others clung to the remaining vestiges of southern manhood—namely, force, intimidation, and honor. Mastery, at its most basic level, relied on the use of brute force. A white community's safety depended upon white men's ability to maintain order at home. To this end, the head of a household had the right to use force in punishing any member of his household, white or black, man or woman. The law restrained him just short of murder. Violence was not seen as disruptive so long as it was authorized by the head of a household. A master's words and actions were informally recognized as law.

Many white men, therefore, perceived violence as a cornerstone of civil order—as state-sanctioned behavior. Before the war, violence was the legitimate right of all white men, regardless of status. A white man, whether master or hireling, could legally use force against any black southerner by serving on a slave patrol or local militia. In whippings, beatings, and sexual assaults, white men expressed their right to rule. Moreover, the proper use of violence represented a noble virtue. Any questioning of a man's honor called for a duel or a beating. Ritualized violence thus served as the foundation of chivalry and honor.[28] The display of force secured white men's control over all others—both black and white.

After the war, many southern men ritualized violence once again, but this time outside the legitimate structures of authority. Under Republican rule, elite white men discovered that much of their former lives, and their former selves, now stood outside the law. The foundations of law and order constructed in a slave society—whippings, slave patrols, and other physical means of controlling black bodies—were now illegal. White men had a choice. They could either accept their position in a free-labor society or assert the customary rights to dominate black southerners. Asserting old privileges, however, required them to transgress the law and move into an extralegal world of violence.

Not only were the old forms of violence illegal, but Mississippi's 1868 constitution severely limited white men's access to citizenship, the franchise, and jury service.[29] Forced from the legitimate political sphere by the Reconstruction Acts, white men became outsiders. They made this movement so easily, so unthinkingly, because—at least in their minds—it was only the reconstruction of social space in the postwar years that made white men's violence transgressive.

Laying claim to public space, William Davis, a former Union soldier with the Third Colored Cavalry, walked up the street in Yazoo City with his wife and another black woman. Former Confederate colonel J. J. B. White took offense at this and suddenly stopped and stared. Davis "asked him what he stopped for.... he replied I stopped to let that god damned bitch pass meaning my wife ... he called me a god damned black son of a bitch and also told my wife he would kill her." According to R. S. Donaldson, Acting Assistant Commissioner for the Freedmen's Bureau in northern Mississippi, such actions were common. "It is surprising how little concern is Manifested on the part of the Citizens for the killing of a negro. But let a negro brush against one of the 'Chivalry' on the side walk, or fail to give him wide berth on the street, and they act at once call on both civil and military authorities to punish the 'insolent intolerant Nigger.'"[30]

Freedmen's Bureau agents throughout the Delta numbingly reported countless incidents of murder, arson, and robbery. Donaldson reported that "outrages are being daily committed by white men, and by white *women* too, upon freedmen, by shooting, stabbing, whipping, and otherwise cruelly misusing them." In Vicksburg, Calvin Holly concurred: "I think the colored people are in a great many ways being outraged beyound humanity, houses have been tourn down over the heades of women and Children.... The Rebbles are going about in many places through the State and robbing the colored people of arms money and all they have and in many places killing." In Yazoo City, Agent T. Sargent Free decided: "The Southerner is worse now than before the war. He is a played out chivalry. . . . During the war, he occupied himself mainly in massacreing and starving Union prisoners. Now he pleasantly passes his time shooting niggers or cutting off their ears or hunting them out of his neighborhood with bloodhounds."[31]

The killing and robbing was not random. Disputes centered over African-Americans' claims to the crop, personal property, and, by 1867, the right to vote. Any sign of independence on the part of freedpeople, no matter how small, unleashed ruthless acts of violence.[32] Near Greenville "a black man was sent to jail for raising a few hundred pounds of cotton for the support of his family."[33] In Yazoo County the mere presence of freedpeople living in town rather than on a plantation infuriated white men. Aiming to "break up the free niggers," these men destroyed every single article owned by nine black families. "[T]he colored people were having a . . . quilting then a dancing party. . . . a company of white men, supposed to number about twenty (20) came up suddenly, set fire to the buildings, then surrounding them, began, and for some time continued to discharge fire-arms. . . . The white men drove the colored people away and went around picking up bundles and other articles of property and throwing them into the fire." No object was too small to be stolen or destroyed. "The poor people were thus, at this unseasonable hour, scattered adrift without shelter, without clothing or other property."[34]

The men responsible for most of these crimes, it was rumored, came from good families. As children of violence, the war had shaped their adult identity.[35] They scoured the countryside and refused to disband guerrilla troops formed during the war. In 1865, Bureau officer Donaldson remarked that "many outrages have been perpetrated against the Freedmen by whipping them and in some instances killing them....it is hoped that the 'gallant young men' who have come home from the army will settle down to follow some lawful occupation."[36] His hopes proved futile. These troops were slow to disband. Long after the Confederate surrender, the Delta was the site of prolonged guerrilla warfare. Testifying before a Senate committee in 1868, attorney G. Gordon Adams recalled that "in the counties of Warren, Hinds, Washington, Issaquena, and Bolivar . . . there was a great deal of violence of the very worst character."[37] Freedmen's Bureau reports read like a litany of guerrilla warfare. From 1865 to 1867, Carroll County experienced a reign of terror culminating in a complete breakdown of law and order when black citizens registered to vote.[38] In 1867 Freedmen's Bureau agent J. B. Webster declared, "This . . . district is one of the most lawless in the state. It was infested by a gang of desperados known as Morrells Gang. . . . During the war this district was infested by a gang of Guerrillas and . . . upwards of three hundred stragglers from the [Union] army were murdered."[39] Although the Senate investigations into the Knights of the Ku Klux Klan uncovered little activity in the Delta, Freedmen's Bureau agents suspected their involvement in these gangs.[40]

White southerners attempted to legitimize their illegal behavior by cloaking themselves in tradition. Calling themselves "guerrillas" or "militias," they sanctioned their behavior as a police or military action. Joining secret societies such as the Knights of the Ku Klux Klan, they likened themselves to a fraternal order. As historian Stephen Kantrowitz argues, elite men believed that only they had the right to "pass judgment on state policies and veto those they disapproved."[41] Yet they suddenly found themselves outnumbered by black voters. Violence, they claimed, was their only recourse. Robing themselves in ritual, they carefully planned their assault on Republican Party rule.

Of course, the use of violence to overthrow a government is undemocratic. Planter men faced a disturbing contradiction, which they consciously or unconsciously addressed in their use of disguises. In the Delta, white men engaged in organized violence wore white hoods, blackened their faces, or donned robes. These masks functioned on both a practical and a symbolic level. In many ways, they served simply as costumes worn to conceal a person's identity. But as disguises they were particularly ineffective. Everybody knew who wore the masks. Four men in Carroll County donned blackface to attack Richard Harris, a black lessee. The men were immediately identified as "the sons of the best men in the county" because they rode their own horses. Charles Coe, of DeSoto County, reported "that parties of white persons are in the habit of riding about the county... in the night & visit the negro cabins.... [They] disguise themselves with masks &c," but he recognized their clothes. In the small Delta communities everyone knew everyone else, including, apparently, their clothes and horses. Masks hardly disguised a thing. Because masks were such poor disguises, most white men rarely bothered to wear them, committing depredations in broad daylight.[42]

So why did white southerners feel the need to disguise themselves? The white hoods and gowns might be attributed to fraternal orders or perhaps even to the robes of priests. Perhaps these white southerners meant to lend themselves the moral authority of the sacred by wearing these garments and performing ritual acts. If so, their move into a sacred realm is suggestive. The political structure no longer sanctioned the rights of all white men to police the actions of blacks. Conceivably, white southerners responded by wrapping the violence of slavery in rituals with sacred overtones.[43] Their actions mirrored those of white women who, by 1866, were erecting monuments and organizing services to honor the Lost Cause. Both white men and women actively set out to mythologize the past and, as historian Charles Wilson argues, baptize it in blood.[44]

Yet the use of blackface reveals a tension—an inherent discomfort—with this shift to extralegal activity. Moving outside the law, white southerners literally found themselves taking on the role of the dispossessed or disenfranchised. Emancipation undercut white men's mastery. Both the Republican Party government and free labor served to underscore white men's dependence on others for political representation and economic livelihood. Like George Torrey, many white men feared that they had become "dependents" resembling women, blacks, or poor whites. Perhaps acting on what they perceived as a bizarre racial inversion, they blackened their faces and, in fury and distress, recognized themselves as the "other."

Their rhetoric helps illuminate their actions. As white men circumvented the structures of law and government to subvert an imposed system of order to which they fundamentally objected, they felt subjugated. During the war, the image of the enslaved white man shackled by the imperialist Union army dominated Confederate war propaganda: "robbed of our property and humiliated in the dust at the feet of our Yankee masters ... we shall have passed through the pupilage of dependence and submission, degenerated and degraded; then forsooth, we will be worthy to re-enter the glorious Union. . . . In short, before we can again become freemen, we must first become slaves."[45]

In yet another twist of logic, however, blackface symbolized power as well as powerlessness. By stepping outside the legal system, white men took on the power of the mob. Seeing themselves as politically powerless, they rioted to protest the injustice of the current political order. By blackening their faces, they initiated "insurrections" reminiscent of slave rebellions. They used the power of the uncontrolled and uncontrollable to protest and to terrorize. They were a carnival run amuck—white dressed as black, men as dependent as women, the scions of society upholding disorder.[46] They were conscious of their transgressions. As outlaws, they masked themselves as blacks, or preachers, or a curious amalgam of both, and questioned the legitimacy of the new social order. Emancipation effectively perverted the master.

Emancipation upset the antebellum's neat correlations between social hierarchies of class, gender, and race. Not surprisingly, white southerners became obsessed with defining what was "natural" in order to police the changing political boundaries. Everywhere they turned, white southerners saw gross perversions of racial order. "The great distinctive elements of our population have been thrown into unnatural, and, as it were, antagonistic relations. . . . That blacks and whites are each a distinct, peculiar people, no man in his sense will pretend to deny."[47] The problem was that, without slavery, many did indeed deny just that. Emancipation, destroying the plantation household, unraveled the skein that tightly integrated and related race to gender to class.

Before the war, white southerners understood race, class, and gender not only as biological distinctions but, more important, as social distinctions, not so much located on the body as defined through relations of dominance. They understood race and gender identity more in relation to the institutions of slavery and the family than as discrete biological units.[48] From white southerners' experience, race and class and gender could be understood only in relation to one another. Yet after the war, each suddenly stood alone. The destruction of slavery exposed the inherent contradictions in white southerners' most basic understanding of themselves and each other. The "natural" order was perverted.

During this period, white southerners became more and more wedded to explanations of natural law to define distinctions between manhood and womanhood, and between black and white. They attempted to locate racial and gender identities firmly on the body. The social system might change—black men could become free—but their bodies remained unchanged. Biological explanations of difference promised to cement clear racial boundaries which were threatened by emancipation. Obsessed with the disruption of what they saw as "natural inequalities," white men complained that "fanatics, ultras and mischief-makers must have no apology for their foolish schemes, for resisting the natural-laws, the unconquerable repugnance to social equality . . . which opposes and denounces the proposition of investing the colored freedmen with equal social and political rights with the white freemen"[49] (see figure 8).

Moreover, white southern commentators employed natural law to shame their enemies. Yankees, they declared, twisted reality. Only beasts, they argued, could fail to see "natural" biological distinctions. Yankees, no better than animals themselves, threatened to destroy civilization. In 1863 the *Mem-*

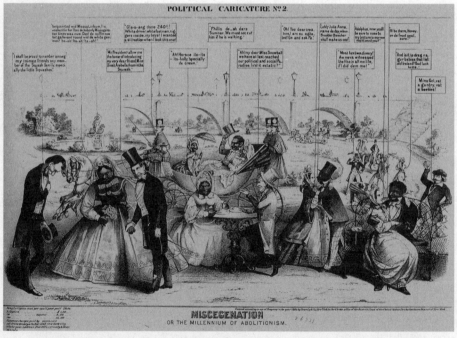

Fig. 8. Reconstructing race, many cartoonists, journalists, and intellectuals portrayed whiteness and blackness as biological markers of social difference. ("Miscegenation, or the Millennium of Abolitionism." Courtesy of the Division of Prints and Photographs, Library of Congress.)

phis Daily Appeal opined: "The promiscuous mixing of races contemplated by negro philanthropists will not be effaced until white laborers in this country-side are degraded far below their present level. The Gorilla has sufficient common senses to understand this." By implication, Northerners and African-Americans did not have the common sense of gorillas. Moreover, the editors charged that Northerners and freedmen were beasts masquerading as men. Allowing them to rule would be like placing animals in power over men. "It would be about as wise to turn a score or two of monkeys into a large china establishment . . . and then beg them not to break the elegant vases. . . . His monkeyship would be apt to 'grin horribly a ghastly smile' . . . and then turn around to prosecute his work of destruction." Editor W. G. Brownlow inquired, "Do you ask me to make a pointer out of a poodle? . . . a peach out of a crab apple? Can you change a carrot into a melon? . . . You can not undo what God has intended. . . . It is, therefore, simply impossible for you to change an African into an Anglo-Saxon."[50] The quantity and scope of these stories grew exponentially as freedmen were granted suffrage. The status of slavery could no longer be used as a justification of difference. Distinction, therefore, was transferred onto the body.

White southerners repeatedly described black equality in sexual terms. The mixing of the races was literally "promiscuous" in their eyes. An article titled "MISCEGENATION" reported that a white auctioneer was observed sitting "down to the table and ate dinner with a big buck negro. They appeared to enjoy each other's society amazingly."[51] The writer ignored the fact that the two eating dinner together were men and that no sexual attraction appeared to be evident. Social equality with freedpeople was perceived as a crime against nature, a sexual trespass. By linking social distinctions with biological differences, white southerners saw emancipation as an act of sexual perversion.

On one level, the sexualizing of racial equality revealed white men's horror that former slaves were now recognized as men, with all the accompanying rights and privileges of manhood. As heads of their households, black men now held power over dependents. For white men, African-American political rights were threatening enough, but freedmen's private privileges were even more disturbing. As masters of households, African-American men could suddenly claim dominion over any woman—black or white.[52] Not surprisingly, rumors of black men carrying off white southern women grew rampant. The *Memphis Daily Appeal* reported, "A young lady of the highest respectability . . . was over-taken by a negro man and forcibly drawn from the high road into the woods"

for "vile purpose." This story was printed as an "apt illustration of the consequences of converting a mass of concentrated ignorance into freedmen with
an unlimited conception of the liberty and power they acquired at the same
time."[53]

Yet the obsession with rape also reveals the confusion and outrage that white
southerners faced without the familiar boundaries of slavery. No one and nothing could be taken at face value. This confusion is evident from the first moment
of emancipation. In 1863 a white women reported that she was raped by a
"yankee but . . . probably a negro."[54] Apparently, white men and black were not
easily distinguished.

Likewise, the identity of white womanhood fell into question. The *Coahomian* of Friars Point featured a story in 1866 in which a bridegroom discovered
that his wife's hairpiece "was made out of wool (which wasn't a sheep's either,
for it was too black, and we thought, kinky). . . . oh horrors! those beautiful
curls. . . ."[55] White women, apparently, could not be trusted. After all, if black
southerners could throw off the mask of a slave, could not white women throw
off the mask of whiteness? The boundary between nature and artifice had been
ruptured.

The rhetoric and practice of inversion, therefore, grew out of the legacy of
war and defeat. The war gave white southerners women who refused to be
conquered, blacks who acted "white" by assuming mastery over themselves, a
yeomanry that laid claim to the land, and Yankees who moved in and out of
received racial, social, and sexual etiquette without any apparent knowledge of
the boundaries they transgressed. As the power relations of slavery were disrupted, the most basic definitions of what it meant to be black or white, male
or female, yeoman or planter collapsed. If planters had not considered it before,
emancipation taught them that race and gender were tied not to the body but
to the body politic.

In moments of crisis and social change, people use the tools and skills that
are familiar to them to establish their place and to ground their sense of authority. As southern society began to tear apart at the seams, planter men did not
discard what they knew. They stuck to the familiar, acting on the principles of
the household. They claimed that to do otherwise was a perversion of natural
law.

Yet in refusing to change, planters confronted a perverted vision of themselves—their sons refused to mature, their violence became illegal, and whiteness shifted on its foundation. Moreover, planter men could not recognize

themselves in Mississippi's laws or government. The state no longer represented them or reflected their understanding of the social foundation for power and authority.

Clinging to what they knew was theirs, planter men tightened their grip on their land. No one, they claimed, could pervert their Constitutional right to property. Yet African-Americans did exactly that. Measuring freedom in their autonomous control over their households, African-American men and women challenged planters' command over the land. Freedpeople acted to secure liberty for themselves and their kin by working together to lay claim to their labor and to the valuable products their labor produced. On the plantations, the question was not whether the past was past, but who and what would reconstruct its legacy.

II

Forced Intimacies

Reconstructing Households in the Postwar Delta

$\mathcal{W}$AR SHATTERED the Delta. Returning home in 1865, Delta southerners found their homes and households in pieces. Despite this,
they continued to return. Freedwomen came from the cities, their men
from the military, planters from the battlefront, and planters' wives, such
as Emma Crutcher, from homes in Texas and Alabama where they had
sought refuge from the war. On the plantations they greeted those who
had stayed behind, and faced each other as a community for the first
time in almost four years. No longer separate and apart, they set to work
recreating a society based, according to theory, on the principles of free
labor.

Part II, "Forced Intimacies: Reconstructing Households in the Post-
war Delta," turns from an examination of the impact of emancipation on
southern identities to a consideration of how the older structures of
household reasserted themselves and challenged the reconstruction of
rights. During the war, black men, white women, white men, and black
women relocated a sense of their individual and group authority in the
plantation household's relative absence. Yet as black and white, men and
women, came together again, they faced a multitude of complex ironies
in the construction of new households. They may have grounded their

sense of authority in their various perceptions of household, but the households themselves crushed as many freedoms as they created. Could a person ground individual rights in an institution that, at its heart, was hierarchical?

In essence, households were relational. One person's independence was based on the dependencies of others. What remained unclear was who exactly headed the households—in other words, who was independent? And, on what terms was this independence accorded? What obligations did the heads of the households have to their dependents, and could dependents also claim individual rights in the new post-war society?

Interestingly, few southerners abandoned the household. Instead they still grounded domestic, economic, and political life in the structures and ideologies of the household. Yet each person carried his or her own separate vision as to what constituted a household and which rights rested in these constructions. Seeing themselves in relation to one another, they never thought to separate themselves from the body politic. Each and every person knew that no boundary lay between the personal and the political. Indeed, the permeable boundary between self and society produced a vicious irony. It laid the foundation for political, economic, and domestic rights while, in the same instance, it worked to strip away those very rights.

Part II begins in the home and moves out to the plantation, the courts, and the legislature. Chapter 4 examines the roots of political consciousness embedded in African-Americans' negotiation of gender relations at home. Chapter 5 explores how these hotly contested domestic relationships grounded the complex renegotiation of labor in cities and plantations. Chapter 6 turns directly to the question of citizenship as expressed in competing terms by white men, white women, black men, and black women in Mississippi courthouses. The final chapter offers an examination of Reconstruction politics. Each chapter asks how the household framed dissent and how it acted as the very seat of those oppositions by combining public and private, and intimately intertwining individual rights (or independence) with domestic hierarchies (or dependence).

4

⚜

Husbands, Wives, and Sweethearts

Gender Relations within African-American Households

*I*N 1866 SILAS CLEAR mustered out of the Forty-seventh United States Colored Infantry. His first action as a civilian was to walk into Vicksburg and claim Mary Jane Kelley as his wife. Mary Jane was "cooking and working for some white people," Silas recalled, and "they told me I could not have" her. Silas bided his time. He returned to his home in Washington County, saved his money, and the next spring brought "Mary Jane up here." From that moment forward, Silas Clear declared, "Mary Jane has been owned by me as a wife... and has always been called by my name."[1]

Silas Clear used the language of the plantation household to describe his marriage to Mary Jane. Marriage, from his perspective, involved ownership. Mary Jane was transferred from a white master to an African-American husband without skipping a beat—at least that was Silas's story. Mary Jane remembered it differently. According to Mary Jane, she was indeed working for a Mrs. Fisher in Vicksburg when the soldiers mustered out. But her work for the Fishers was just one job out of many she had taken during the war. During the war, and indeed after her marriage, Mary Jane moved frequently, demonstrating a personal freedom within a web of obligations to others. Her story was not just the movement from a white man's household to her husband's. Rather than emphasizing the household as a patriarchal hierarchy, Mary Jane placed interdependency and obligation at the center of her narrative.[2]

Silas Clear was Mary Jane's third husband. Mary Jane met and married her first, Jim Garrett, on the Everhope plantation during slavery times. They never had a wedding ceremony, but she took his name and lived with him, and they considered themselves husband and wife. She and Garrett had one child, but they split up after a few months. As Mary Jane recalled, "We separated because he wanted a women named Angeline and right away I took up with Ed Kelley." Mary Jane and Ed lived with his father, Isaac, during slavery, until Ed and Mary Jane ran away together on a Union gunboat. Adam Metcalfe, who traveled with

Fig. 9. With emancipation, freedwomen and freedmen debated the meaning of "family" and the nature of men's and women's authority within various family types. ("Negro Family, Hewn Log Cabin." J. Mack Moore Collection. Courtesy of The Old Court House Museum, Vicksburg, Mississippi.)

them, recalled that Mary Jane and all the other women were "put off the boat at Hawes Harris' landing." Metcalfe's choice of the words "put off" implies that he felt others were acting for them, providing women no role in shaping their freedom.[3]

Mary Jane, however, took matters into her own hands. She went to work for Joe Miller on a plantation across the river from Vicksburg, where she could visit Ed. After Ed was shot and killed in Yazoo City, she left the plantation and went to work for the Fishers until the soldiers mustered out. Here, her story and Silas's diverge. She testified that she went down to Davis Bend after working for the Fishers and then returned to Vicksburg. "I had been living at Davis Bend for awhile & Fannie Cox—Ed's mother sent for me to come to Vicksburg & when she was sick I waited on her until she died." Only then did Mary Jane join Silas Clear in Washington County. The Union army and the Fishers tried to limit Mary Jane's mobility, but she managed to make her own way, maintaining contact with kin and community.[4] Silas interpreted these actions as a demonstration of Mary Jane's dependency. She, however, did not interpret dependency as a limitation, but rather as a cornerstone for expanding her personal freedoms.

The stories of Silas and Mary Jane Clear demonstrate the structures and languages of the household that informed freedpeople's definitions of freedom. Both Mary Jane and Silas rejected planters' definitions of the plantation household. Neither accepted a white man's mastery in the intimate relations of household. Yet they did not discard what they knew. Instead they framed their dissent to white authority through often competing definitions of household.

This chapter explores how African-American men and women negotiated the meaning of household authority after the war. Mary Jane and Silas Clear's stories demonstrate that African-Americans debated the meaning of household, and often on gendered terms. Both men and women claimed the household as the foundation of their rights. But they disputed exactly who held these rights and on what terms.

On a practical level, African-American men's and women's differences stemmed from the fact that they experienced the war very differently. From Silas Clear's vantage point in the military, Mary Jane did not appear free—she still worked for white people who, in his mind, refused to permit her the mobility that "free labor" implies. So from his perspective, she simply moved from the white household into his own. White men no longer mastered Mary Jane; he did. As a wife, Mary Jane served as a symbol of his manhood and his freedom. In essence, the marriage covenant was the foundation of Silas's rights, leaving him poised to claim social and, perhaps, political equality with white men.[5]

Yet Mary Jane was not tied to a white household for the duration of the war. She claimed her liberty by moving at least five times between 1863 and 1867. Certainly, the Union army and various white employers circumscribed Mary Jane's actions. Yet, in her account, Mary Jane emphasized her freedom. Emancipation did not free Mary Jane from her household. Instead, freedom granted her the liberty of acting on family ties. Mary Jane ascribed each move to the desire to be with, or give assistance to, kin. Household informed her every move.

Several rich archival collections grant insight into the Delta's black communities after the war. These communities' gendered discussions of freedom appear in census records, pension applications, labor contracts, and formal complaints filed with the Freedmen's Bureau. Census records and labor contracts provide the bare backbone of African-American household structures in the city and countryside in 1865, 1866, and 1870. These records are fleshed out by the pension applications filed by widows of black Union soldiers following the war. To qualify for a pension, a woman had to prove she was married to the soldier. Since antebellum southern law forbade slave marriages, pension examiners had to interview entire communities to confirm the widow's claim. These records, as historian Noralee Frankel wonderfully illustrates in her book *Freedom's Women*, reveal how black Mississippians defined marriage in contrast to other types of male and female relationships.[6] The Freedmen's Bureau complaint files build on these records by highlighting issues of dissent. The complaints provide insight into how men and women contested authority within their households, and how they defended their relationships against intrusions by employers, government agents, and white southern terrorists.

Read together, these records clearly demonstrate that neither the household nor individuals' understandings of the household were static or fixed.[7] No single pattern of an African-American household emerges. Not all men claimed patriarchal authority in the same ways and not all women rejected dependency. Like most people, African-American men and women held, and expressed, contradictory points of view simultaneously.[8] Yet most agreed on one point: Freedom was intimately connected with the domestic relations of the household.

Redefining Dependency: Alternative Households during the War

The conditions of war significantly altered the foundations of patriarchal authority. War undermined male mastery, white and black, by separating men and women, the weak and the strong, young and old. The meaning of household was open to question as families scattered across the Delta. After their unique war experiences, it was by no means clear that men "owned" their families or that families were willing to be owned again.

On the most basic level, the war destroyed the plantation household. With emancipation, white men no longer held any legal right to claim African-Americans as members of their household. Suddenly, white men's patriarchal rights extended to their white families alone.

Yet, despite Silas Clear's claim to the contrary, a simple transfer of patriarchal authority from white to black men did not occur during the war. Heavy Union enlistments of all able-bodied black men between the ages of eighteen and forty-five guaranteed that many African-American men simply were not present to take their places at the head of their families. To bridge the distance between themselves and their families, many African-American soldiers married. Some, like Silas Clear, defined marriage as the first step in claiming equality with white men. They became masters of their own households. Others defined marriage more liberally. Frequently, they married in order to be granted access to sweethearts and kin who lived outside the Union camps. These men expanded the definition of marriage to include the flexible relationships established during slavery. Regardless of how soldiers defined their relationships, military experience taught them that marriage accorded them rights.[9] Some defined this right as the simple ability to leave camp to visit lovers, while others defined this right as their ability to assume the privileges and obligations of the head of household. Marriage was the foundation for rights.

Or was it? On the plantations, in the cities, and in makeshift camps, a wide variety of household relationships, not marriage alone, served as the foundation for freedom. Moreover, black women, children, the old, and the disabled subtly, and perhaps unthinkingly, altered the nature of authority within their households during the war.

Without many men on the plantations or living in town, patriarchy was a theory at best. Power did not flow through the head of the household. Instead women, children, and older men relied on a dense web of relationships to carve out a modicum of personal freedom. During slavery, the neighborhood helped serve this function. The war, however, shattered many neighborhoods. To compensate, African-Americans turned inward, counting on their household relationships to help them make ends meet.[10]

Flexible households helped freedpeople create a private space away from employers and military commanders. The House-in-the-Woods plantation provides a glimpse into these household networks. In 1865, seven African-American families contracted to work for E. P. Brickell. Of the seven families, none was nuclear. Three were headed by men, four by women. Lilsy Henderson, Hannah Napier, and John Johnson lived alone. The other four households listed at least one worker. George Washington worked with his daughter Katie. Jenny Williams and Hannah Dicey lived together and raised a child, Priscilla. Sophy Fall, a mother of three, had Edward, age twelve, to help work the cotton. And Charles Cohen, who was blind, lived with his mother, Ellen, age sixty-five, and his eight-year-old daughter. Ellen went to the fields each day while Charles worked at home. Also listed were six orphans ranging in age from seven to fourteen, who counted on the various families to take them in and sustain them.

For the African-Americans on the House-in-the-Woods plantation, forming a household proved necessary to keep body and soul together. Sharing a home, they depended on each others' contributions.[11]

These families did not use the moment of emancipation to reject household hierarchies. Instead they built upon relationships of independence and dependence and subverted their meaning. All members of the household, with the exception of very young children, signed a labor contract with E. P. Brickell to work on the cash crop. Signing the contract insured that they could remain in their homes, be paid cash wages, and be issued "provisions, clothing, and medical attention." Yet the law limited their legal right to privacy. As historian Laura Edwards argues, by 1866 southern labor laws placed agricultural workers under the master-servant laws. As "servants," workers were considered by law to be domestic employees. As a consequence, employers had the right to dictate their actions around the clock. As former slaves, however, black men and women were well aware that no dependent was as powerless as the law might suggest.[12]

All seven households made it abundantly clear that Brickell had little power over their work lives, much less their private lives. Each family designated some labor for the crop, but put equal, if not more, effort into maintaining personal gardens and raising livestock. This practice was widespread. In an official report on leasing in the Delta, T. P. Anderson estimated that fewer than one-third of those residing on plantations worked the crop, while the majority worked for themselves raising corn and other vegetables. The households might be dependent on wages—and, perhaps more important, dependent on Brickell for the right to stay in their homes—but their actions argued that dependency on Brickell did not strip them of all personal autonomy. By devoting so much effort to their own crops and animals, they marked off the territory of their independence. They could choose what to do with their bodies and when to do it, within the limits imposed upon them.[13] They were dependent on each other and on wages, but this dependency enabled them to maintain their privacy. Perhaps paradoxically, they gained a degree of independence through relationships of dependency.

This level of privacy was seldom possible during slavery. In the antebellum plantation household, white southerners defined independence and dependence as polar opposites. Only the white male head of household was independent. He was subservient to no one. This independence gave him legal rights and privileges and guaranteed him perhaps the most precious gift—privacy. No one had the right to interfere in his domestic affairs except in the most extreme cases. His independence stood in sharp contrast to the dependency of his wife, children, slaves, and hired hands. These members of his household fell under his dominion. Since they were his responsibility, he had the right to interfere in any aspect of their lives. Nothing was private. He could dictate what they ate, what they wore, whom they married, where they traveled, or what church they attended. The law upheld the distinctions between independent and dependent people by granting African-Americans, women, and domestic servants few, if any, legal rights. According to theory, dependents only had those "rights" that masters decided to grant them.[14]

Moreover, many whites, North and South, considered the African-Americans who stayed on the plantations and farms during the war—black women, children, the old, and the disabled—to be the most dependent members of society. Two related definitions classified them as dependent. First, they were dependent because of their position in the plantation household; they fell under the control of the head of the household and, therefore, held no rights over their own person.[15] Second, African-Americans were considered dependent "by nature." Blackness, womanhood, age, and lack of physical strength disqualified a person from being able to control his or her own actions. According to proslavery thought, each of these factors made a person susceptible to the undue influence of others. Whites believed African-Americans could be manipulated and thus did not deserve independence. Indeed, many white Americans believed independence to be physically impossible for African-Americans because they were, by nature, weak in either mind, spirit, or body.[16]

Yet for the families on the House-in-the-Woods plantation, the choice between independence and dependence was not an either/or proposition. Black women, children, the old, and the disabled were dependent on each other and dependent on wage work. But they raised the barrier of privacy. They carved out a niche for independent action and secured as much autonomy as possible for themselves and their households. In doing so, they redefined the nature of plantation household authority. Dependency, in their eyes, did not mean acquiescence or loss of personal freedom. Instead, they reinterpreted the conservative hierarchies of the plantation household to expand their rights and privileges.

Flexible households, therefore, framed African-American dissent to wage labor, the leased plantation system, and freedpeople's subordinate position to white employers. Of course, African-Americans' reliance on flexible family forms was not unique. Throughout the United States, working-class families—North and South, white and black—turned to fluid household structures to help make ends meet. In the North, white workers married and divorced without legal sanction, and in the South, poor white families adopted many of the same elastic household structures as African-Americans.[17] Yet in the post-emancipation Delta, flexible family forms held added significance. For many, they symbolized freedom. They upended the plantation household and, with it, many of white southerners' expressions of power and authority. By claiming rights from a position of dependency, freedpeople rechannelled the flow of power within households. They questioned who had rights and on what terms.

Coming Back Together: Postwar African-American Household Structures

When the young black men mustered out of the Union army, they did not challenge or upset the alternative household structures established by freedpeople during the war. Together, African-Americans emphasized personal autonomy by working to construct an alternative economy where neither they nor their families would be beholden to just one white man as an employer. While many men and women formalized their relationships by marrying during and after the war, almost as many built on slave traditions of household, emphasizing a wide range of relationships.

Not limiting "family" and "household" to formal marriage vows, African-Americans recognized the validity of at least three household structures connecting men and women—"taking up," "sweethearting," and marriage.[18] Each involved sharing a house, work, skills, and, in most cases, love. Yet the mix of these ingredients distinguished one type of relationship from another.

According to freedpeople's testimony, "taking up" referred to a long-term relationship between mature adults. Men and women took up for primarily financial reasons, although varying levels of attraction and commitment ran through these relationships. By and large, it was difficult to sustain a household alone. Consequently men, dependent on women's skills, exchanged room and board for cooking and washing, while women counted on men for additional income. Lewis Williams recalled that Anna Hayden "was not my wife and didn't pass as such. My first wife was dead and I needed a housekeeper and Anna was poor so I let her make a home here."[19]

Freedpeople consistently identified the question of support as a critical distinction between taking up and marriage. When freedpeople took up, they kept separate accounts and often, but not always, separate beds. In her application for Jefferson Boose's military pension, Jane Boose claimed that she had lived with Cap Wilson but never married him. To prove this, she pointed out that she always bought her own rations, paid her own bills, and never shared his bed.[20] According to Boose, they shared a house but maintained their personal autonomy.

Since "taking up" did not necessarily imply sexual relations, some black churches recognized it as a legitimate relationship. Soon after the war, Anna Hayden's church accused her of fornication for sharing a home with Lewis Williams. Because their arrangement had lasted for three to four years, church members became suspicious that Hayden and Williams shared more than just a house. Upon investigation, however, the church demonstrated that Hayden "paid her own way" by cooking and washing for Williams in exchange for room and board. In fact, her neighbors testified that Hayden's wages "helped build" the house. In addition, Hayden emphasized that, while they shared a house for four years, it was "a two room house and he [stayed] in one end and I in the other end." Proof of financial autonomy and the lack of evidence that she and Williams ever shared a bed cleared Hayden of the charge of fornication. Like other members of the black communities, Hayden's church recognized the legitimate difference between "taking up" and "sweethearting."[21]

"Sweethearting" did involve sexual relations. Many women sweethearted with a man for a year or more, without considering the relationship a common-law marriage. Isabella Harris testified that Levi Anderson "had been visiting me as a sweetheart. . . . But we never married." She continued, "I don't know how long we were sweethearting, but I had one miscarriage by him. I never had any children for him." Having children, however, did not transform sweethearts into marriage partners. As Dock Townsend testified, Anna Hayden "had one child by me and stayed with me two or three years. We had no license and were not married."[22]

Freedpeople's testimony in pension applications reveals that they defined the distinction between sweethearting and marriage based on a woman's financial and sexual independence.[23] Daniel and Maria Bell briefly lived together on the Vicksburg waterfront. Maria did laundry and cooking while Daniel picked up jobs on the docks. They extended this financial relationship to a social one, going out together, visiting and drinking. Yet their friend Taylor Young remembered Daniel saying "she was no wife of hisn" because Maria Bell "was most everybody's wife."[24] Robert Hudson also complained about his "sweetheart," outlining a long list of grievances explaining why Emily was never his wife. First of all, he said, she did not treat him right. Seeing other men, Emily asserted her sexual independence. Second, Hudson pointed out that he did not provide for her, but paid her for cooking for him. Third, they never worked on a crop together. Working a crop involved a year-long commitment and a level of trust unusual outside of marriage. Finally, Hudson declared, "none of the folks on the plantation called her by my name." Not just Hudson but the entire community agreed that Emily and Robert never formed a marriage of any kind.[25]

In the pension records, therefore, freedpeople defined sweethearting and taking up as the obverse of marriage. By sweethearting or taking up, men and women could maintain personal boundaries. They shared much and were dependent on one another, but maintained a degree of personal autonomy and control over resources.

In contrast, marriage represented a blending of resources and identity. Charles Byas succinctly defined marriage in his description of John and Julia Anderson's relationship. Byas made four points. First, he stated that the Andersons were married because John "spoke of [Julia] and her children as his wife and children." Second, he explained that John provided for his family. John Anderson, according to Byas, always "bought and carried home provisions." These first two statements indicate that men played a dominant role in constructing a marriage. *John* called Julia his wife, and *John* provided for his family. In other words, John played the patriarch by claiming Julia and providing for her. Byas's next point, however, complicates this simple assertion of male authority. The Andersons, he stated, "treat[ed] each other as husband and wife." Julia was not simply owned by John, she played an active role in constructing the marriage relation. She had to act married, and no doubt had a right to expect John to act married as well. Finally, Byas declared, the Andersons were married because they "have been so recognized and considered." For a marriage to be finalized, the community had to confirm and recognize the partnership. Certain group standards had to be met. Marriages had to be performed daily, on a public stage, to be valid.[26]

The emphasis on performing marriage left some room for individual interpretation. For many marriages, there was no wedding day. People came together and, over time, created a common-law marriage. There was no precise moment of signing a contract and agreeing to a specific set of rights and obligations. Men and women could negotiate the terms of marriage within certain parameters. According to freedpeople's testimony, those community standards included long-term commitment, the sharing of income and re-sources, sexual fidelity, and the woman taking the man's name. A violation could end a marriage.

Freedpeople "quit" their marriages when the relationship failed. If a spouse ceased acting married, then the aggrieved husband or wife left. Charles Mitchell recalled the night that his friend John Hunter divorced. John "went home one night," Mitchell remembered, "and found some other man occupying his place in the Bed that he thought should be his solely. He quit her." Not waiting for lawyers or bothering to go to court, Cornelius Washington's wife divorced him by physically taking "the license back." Nealy Graham discovered that his fourth wife was divorcing him when she "got her wagon and husled her things off." Many freedpeople took the rights and obligations of marriage quite seriously. If a spouse failed to perform his or her duties, the other partner could, and often did, act on his or her perceived right to end the marriage.[27]

African-Americans thus significantly redefined legal marriage, fitting it into the spectrum of flexible household structures. By taking up, sweethearting, forming common-law marriages, and quitting, African-Americans skirted the law—at least from the government's perspective.

Cracking down on what he defined as promiscuous behavior, Mississippi's Commissioner of Freedmen Alvan Gillem called for state regulation of African-American households. "The courts alone," he declared, "can establish a radical cure." In one year, from 1867 to 1868, Gillem established procedures to rapidly enforce marriage and divorce laws. "I have caused the proper steps to be taken to bring this matter before the Civil Courts," he stated, "and shall urge that offenders be brought to trial and punished."[28] Yet a Bureau agent in Tupelo reported, "I feel confident these acts are not done through ignorance of the law . . . [b]ut from a want of a will to comply with the law."[29] Rejecting the legal enforcement of marriage, many African-Americans emphasized that marriage was a changing relationship and not a fixed legal contract. They upheld marriage while simultaneously reinterpreting its meaning.

Contradictions abounded. On one level, freedpeople recognized that marriage was an important step in declaring citizenship rights. After all, one of the first rights granted to freedpeople was the right to marry. In 1864 the United States Congress proclaimed that former slaves were legally married if "the parties had habitually recognized each other as man and wife, and lived together as such for . . . not less than two years." In 1865 the conservative Mississippi legislature concurred, stating that "all freedmen free negroes and mulattos who do now and have heretofore lived and cohabitated together as husband and wife shall be taken and held in law as legally married."[30]

Yet, on another level, freedpeople contested the state's narrow definition of marriage rights and continued to define marriage on their own terms. Privileging flexibility, many freedpeople fit marriage into a broader understanding of household. They could dissolve marriages because marriage was only one of many options. The presence and acceptance of a wide variety of other household structures—taking up, sweethearting, living with friends and kin—made marriage more flexible. These alternative households provided a safety net, permitting married men and women a certain freedom to define who owed what to whom. If wives took sweethearts or if husbands wandered, their spouses could dissolve the marriages. Counting on friends and family, men and women could make ends meet. They could take up, sweetheart, or share a house with kin. For many, marriage was not an unbreachable contract. Instead, freedpeople placed marriage within a broad spectrum of fluid and flexible households.

Negotiating Marriage

What did freedmen and freedwomen expect from the marriage relationship? They recognized that marriage was a foundation for civil rights, yet they debated what those rights entailed. For some, like Silas Clear, marriage involved ownership. Marriage gave a man legal control over his household. For others, marriage involved mutual obligation. A man and a woman needed to act married in order to legitimately be married in the eyes of their community. Neither definition dominated. The practical fact that African-American men and women depended upon one another subverted any claim to patriarchal authority. Yet the law undermined any claim to mutual dependency by upholding a husband's legal control of the family's resources. Contradicting themselves and each other, freedpeople debated the nature of rights.

Marriage tentatively conferred on a husband patriarchal authority over his wife and children. Remember Charles Byas's statement that John Anderson *named* Julia as his wife. Likewise, Silas Clear claimed he *owned* Mary Jane, and that Mary Jane was called by his name. Freedwomen, like white women, lost their legal identities to their husbands upon marriage.

Yet most freedwomen described marriage in positive terms. Abuse, many claimed, signaled the end of a marriage or provided a clear indication that no marriage had ever occurred. For Anna Hayden, marriage granted a woman rights, protecting her from men's exploitation. Anna Hayden met Lewis Williams soon after the war. Her husband, Samuel Hayden, had been killed in combat, and she had lost three children to disease. According to a neighbor, Dock Townsend, Anna "went crazy about Lewis Williams and tried to marry him, but he wouldn't have her." Yet Anna and her surviving son, Henry, stayed with Williams. Anna cooked and cleaned for white people, managed a truck garden, and chopped cotton, while Henry helped Lewis by working as a drayman. Many in the community commented on the relationship. Townsend recalled that Lewis "didn't treat [Henry] right for [Henry] was sickly and they killed him by making him drive a wagon in bad weather." Iverson Granderson agreed that the relationship was abusive, commenting that "Williams held himself higher than Anna and wouldn't take her out with him." Most declared that such a relationship did not constitute a marriage.[31]

For her part, Anna stated flatly, "Folks who say I acted like his wife don't know what they are talking about. Me and my boy Henry were his slaves more than anything else and he took our wages."[32] Anna felt owned by Lewis Williams. And, unlike Silas Clear, Anna Hayden felt that ownership was no foundation for marriage. Idealizing marriage, she argued that a husband would never treat her the way Lewis Williams did. A husband would recognize her rights. But which rights? Hayden implied that no husband would take a woman's wages. So what exactly would a marriage consist of, according to Anna Hayden? Did she expect to be able to control her own wages in a marriage (emphasizing her rights) or did she expect to be provided for by her husband with those same wages (emphasizing his obligations)? Or did she believe that marriage, at its core, emphasized mutual respect—a relationship where such abuse was inconceivable? What did a marriage signify?

Some women (and some men) defined marriage as the right to be supported. The law, after all, gave a wife the right to her husband's financial support and, conversely, granted a husband control over his wife's wages. These rights, however, did not play out as neatly as the law implied. For women, marriage could be preferable to sweethearting or taking up because as a wife a woman could sue her husband for support. Many women did exactly that. Employing the power of the Freedmen's Bureau, married women demanded that men meet their obligations. Recognizing the power of legal marriage, women like Harriet Bordan carried their marriage certificates with them to force the Bureau and their husbands into action. Marriage license in hand, Bordan complained that "her husband left her and does not support her or his child." Caroline Denby had no marriage certificate. She stated that "her husband had left her and lives with another woman. He has sold the house over her head and taken away her marriage papers." Yet even without marriage papers, the Bureau acted in her favor. Rose McClellan, confident that her common-law marriage was legal and legitimate, expected the Bureau to recognize her rights as a wife. On January 28, 1868, she hiked through miles of Delta swamp to Rosedale. Once there, she asked the Bureau officer "to find her husband." Randolph had disappeared into Sunflower County, and she was destitute. Rose demanded support as his legal wife. The Bureau agreed that she was owed that much.[33]

If support made a marriage, Susan Griffin reasoned, then her refusal of support constituted a divorce. By not acting married, Susan quit her husband. First, Susan moved out of their home. Second, she resisted his efforts to provide for her. For two years her husband brought her "meat provisions." Each time he appeared, Susan rejected him, throwing the meat out. The marriage, from her perspective, was over. Each time she threw the meat out her front door, she let the entire neighborhood know that she had quit her marriage.[34]

The question of support, however, was not as clear-cut as the marriage covenant implied. An equal number of men and women petitioned the Bureau for their spouses' support. Glen Edwards, for example, requested an order from the Bureau agent in Yazoo City to force his wife, Liza, to permit him to live with her. She refused on the grounds that he beat her, and that she had a job as a cook and did not want to support him. Likewise, Willis Maddox asked the Bureau "to compel his wife to follow him away from the plantation." She refused. Maddox responded by demanding her wages.[35]

In fact, the bourgeois definition of the marriage contract—where the wives depended on their husbands for financial support—was almost impossible for African-Americans in the Delta. Few black husbands could "support" their wives. Each family member had to find work as soon as she or he was able. Men and women were physically dependent on each other for survival. Husbands, therefore, often demanded that their wives support them. By law, a married man owned his wife's wages.[36] And by necessity, many men needed their wives' support to get by.

Not surprisingly, some men and women chafed at this mutual dependency. Marriage encroached on personal autonomy. No longer owned by another, both men and women jealously guarded the most precious gift, the right to privacy. They acted on the principle that they had the right to control their own bodies—to work when they wanted, to see whomever they desired, and to simply say "no."

Like women, some men rejected the "ownership" of marriage. Marriage simply involved too much obligation, and chipped away at personal freedom. Henry and Frances Bush's relationship is a case in point. Henry Bush was just one of many men who would not tolerate plantation life after the war. Every year, Bush signed a contract to work on shares and then drifted off to fish for a living. Leaving his family on a plantation near the banks of the Mississippi, Bush traveled up and down the river, coming home only when he felt like it. Many men in the Delta "worked the River," passing back and forth between Arkansas, Louisiana, and Mississippi to find work during the farming season. The rivers running throughout the Delta created an easy highway, linking communities scattered by war. Men used the river both to maintain their autonomy and to keep in contact with relatives and comrades. Using his engineering skills to travel with a "gin-ring," William Asberry cleaned cotton from September through January, then repaired gins during the winter. After that, he returned home to Vicksburg. Some men, like Henry Bush, avoided wage labor altogether. Often working in a community of men, freedmen gathered driftwood for sale and fished together, returning to their families when they had money in their pockets. Some men never returned. Jane Graham's husband simply vanished. "He was out of a job," she recalled, "and going to hunt work and went off and did not come back to me."[37]

Women, by and large, understood the impulse to avoid wage labor. Yet few women "took to the river" with their husbands. River work was a masculine culture, often violent and physically grueling, and required constant mobility. Jobs for women were scarce, especially if a woman bore the responsibility of children. In Frances Bush's case, she had to care for thirteen children. So for thirteen years, while Henry lived as a river man, Frances stayed with her children on seven different plantations. Then, having had enough of plantation work, she packed up her children and went to Arkansas City and moved in with Henry.[38]

Henry, apparently accustomed to independence, ordered Frances and their children out. Frances remembered, "He did the separating. He said he couldn't live with us any longer. He used to fight me and the children didn't allow it." The fighting centered on support. Henry "was not a drinking man. He just had a mean heart. He worked very little. He never gave either me or his children a penny of his pension." Their son David recalled that "he did not support her. She supported him."[39]

After her marriage dissolved, Frances Bush did not return to sharecropping. Instead she moved back to Washington County and settled in Greenville, entering the urban labor market. Like Henry, Frances avoided working for any single employer at this stage in her life. Her options, however, were more limited than Henry's. So while Frances searched for work, she, like many other women, moved in with a friend to share a home and expenses.

The wage labor market provided limited alternatives for African-American women in small Delta towns like Greenville. Women could work as cooks, domestic workers, nurses, teachers, or field laborers for daily, weekly, or monthly wages, or they could work by the job as seamstresses, laundresses, prostitutes, or bakers. Independent businesses required licenses, but the municipal governments granted few, if any, to freedwomen.[40] Women, however, could skirt the law and open restaurants or after-hours clubs, or peddle pies and cakes. Given these reduced options, Frances chose to take in laundry and work as a prostitute. Neither choice provided easy money. As a laundress, a woman spent her days bending over cauldrons of boiling water. She pounded clothes and scrubbed them, bleached them and wrung them out, hung them up to dry, and then heated irons on coals to press them. The soap, bleach, and starch left hands chapped and bleeding; the wringing, pounding, and lifting tested every muscle in the body, and the heat through the long Mississippi summers must have tried every ounce of patience and endurance. The money was not good, either. Yet as historian Tera Hunter argues, laundresses carved out a degree of independence—they worked at home, often with friends, and saw their employers only once a week.[41]

Prostitution also allowed Frances independence. She could work only when she needed money and regulate her own hours and pay. She testified to the pension examiner, "I was paid fifty cents to a dollar every time I had sexual intercourse with a man. I never did it except for money and never had any particular man." Frances saw nothing wrong with prostitution. She did not hide her work from the pension examiner. She argued that prostitution, being work, should have no bearing on whether or not she should receive a widow's pension for her husband's service to the Union. She repeatedly stated, "I cannot name any one with whom I have maintained sexual relations since the death of Henry

Bush." From Frances's perspective, prostitution was work, not intimacy. Since she did not ever marry or sweetheart with another man, she saw no reason to be disqualified from a United States pension.[42] Prostitution, like washing, had its concomitant dangers. No doubt Frances faced violence, humiliation, and a loss of personal control at various times during these years. However, she never returned to field work; she never lived with another man; and, as her open statement to the pension examiner suggests, she never felt that she did anything morally or legally wrong.[43]

Frances Bush, and many other members of the Delta's African-American communities, adopted a more flexible definition of what constituted a household than did the pension examiners. Between marriage, sweethearting, and taking up, freedpeople experienced a wide variety of households. Each relationship suggested a distinct pattern of authority and obligation between men and women. The border between independence and dependence in these relationships was never fixed. The gender relations sketched out by the marriage contract appear to be paradoxically contested, reversed, and upheld at the same time.

The connection between freedom and households, therefore, contained numerous contradictions. Flexible households enabled men and women to carve out a measure of autonomy—to avoid dependence on a single employer, to resist abusive relationships, and to secure a degree of personal freedom. Freedpeople's acceptance of the porous boundaries between marriage, sweethearting, taking up, and families based on kinship or networks of friends permitted a degree of individual freedom. This freedom, however, was not grounded on individualism or independence per se. Instead, freedom centered on a recognition of interdependency. Freedpeople did not—and could not—choose between independence and dependence. Indeed, this distinction was a false dichotomy. As African-American household structures indicate, freedpeople recognized that freedom rested on their relationships with others.

Combining resources in a wide range of flexible and fluid household structures, African-Americans carved out a niche of autonomy from the law and from wage labor. They provided a potent threat to northerners and white southerners alike. African-American households, therefore, stood at the center of the Reconstruction battles over labor and politics. The ambiguities of household—the way in which domestic relations linked independence to dependence, freedom to inequality, and rights to obligations—provided a middle ground unevenly marking the territory between land and labor, worker and employer, and the white household and black. As black households faced white households on the plantations after the war, a battle over rights began, and it began in the home.

5

❧

Rights and Obligations

Marriage, Alternative Households,
and the Reconstruction of Plantation Labor

O NE SUNDAY in March 1866, Tom Edwards stormed into his home and demanded that his wife fix him something to eat. She refused. Edwards, blinded by rage, began to beat her mercilessly, screaming, "I told [her] to get me something to eat and if she dont get it I'll be damned if I dont make her get it." Edwards's anger and his wife's stubborn refusal to obey his orders provide visceral evidence of the struggle for authority within African-American households after the Civil War.

But there is more to the story. Tom Edwards's fury must be read in a larger context. Minutes before Edwards entered his cabin, he had been confronted by his employer, Nathan Bedford Forrest—a former Confederate general renowned for his ruthlessness. That Sunday, Forrest, angered by a workers' protest organized and led by Edwards earlier in the week, decided to demonstrate his authority. Marching down to the former slave quarters, Forrest demanded that all workers use Sunday, their day of rest, to clean up *his* property. The workers might be free, but they lived on *his* land and in *his* houses. As their landlord, he ordered them to clean the entire area. In response, Tom Edwards entered his home and proceeded to beat his wife. The houses might belong to Forrest, but Edwards's wife belonged to Edwards. He asserted his mastery.

But there is even more to the story. Forrest, hearing Edwards's screams (and no doubt the screams of his wife), entered the cabin and ordered Edwards to stop his assault. Edwards refused. At that point, Forrest picked up a stick and proceeded to beat Edwards to death.[1]

On the surface, Forrest's actions make no sense. In order to protect the health and well-being of one worker, Forrest murdered another. Clearly, Forrest's motive was not to protect life, but to demonstrate his ultimate control over every person on his DeSoto County plantation. With each blow, Forrest

Fig. 10. By 1866, cotton represented the family wage—a wage controlled by men. ("Cotton Ginning Time, Depot Street." J. Mack Moore Collection. Courtesy of The Old Court House Museum, Vicksburg, Mississippi.)

declared that manhood alone did not guarantee mastery. Tom Edwards, as a worker and as a black man, was not the master of his family or even the master of his own fate.

At issue was the question of who had the right to command and control freedpeople. Did the newly free men and women have the right to assume authority over themselves and their dependents—women, children, and the elderly? Or did planters still bear the ultimate authority to command the bodies of their workers, both on the job and at home?

Forrest's actions demonstrate how the black family, especially the male-headed nuclear household, deeply threatened white southerners' sense of order. As planters saw it, black households stood between landholders and their right-ful control of property. Blurring the boundary between property in land and property in people, many planters "in a violent heat" whipped, raped, beat, and shot African-Americans.[2] The inability to separate people from property was, in many ways, the legacy of slavery and the plantation household. For four years, planters had fought to protect their independence—their undisputed mastery over what they often termed their "family, white and black"—only to return home defeated and discover that African-Americans had established independent households in their absence.[3] Moreover, these households—comprised mostly of women, children, the old, and the disabled—had laid the foundation for an alternative economy that threatened the viability of the cotton economy.

Planters' reactions to the black households were inconsistent at best. On the one hand, planters feared the independent economy established by women and dependents. They recognized that flexible households formed a formidable foundation for freedom—a freedom based on communal, not individual, rights. On the other hand, they felt visibly threatened by black men asserting any kind of mastery over the black households. If black men assumed the right to head their households, they should, according to tradition, be granted the right to vote. Caught on both sides by conflicting interests—the first economic and the second political—planters lashed out. They could not accept any of the African-American expressions of household.

But planters had no choice in the matter. Emancipation destroyed the plantation household. A planter no longer had any legal claim to a family consisting of his wife, children, and enslaved African-Americans. One of the first rights the United States government granted freedpeople was the legal institution of marriage. As masters over their households, African-Americans achieved an important measure of independence.[4] The abolition of slavery forced planters to relinquish control over a tremendous portion of their former household.

Black and white southerners' struggle over household resulted in the emergence of a distinctive family type in African-American communities during Reconstruction—the male-headed nuclear family. Despite planters' open and frequently brutal hostility to African-American families, evidence strongly suggests that the nuclear family structure not only survived but flourished on plantations after the Civil War.[5] Many historians argue that these nuclear families attest to the resilience of the black family under slavery. Indeed, families struggled to reunite after being torn apart first by slavery and then again by war.

Yet the nuclear family was an exception to the rule within African-American communities.[6] "Families" may have reunited and survived, but they were not nuclear families. Before, during, and after the war, the nuclear family was by

Table 1. Rural versus Urban Household Types

Region	Nuclear households	Complex households
Urban (N=1,668)[a]	801 (48%)	867 (52%)
Rural (N=1,838)	1,636 (89%)	202 (11%)

Source: 1870 Manuscript Population Census for Bolivar, Sunflower, Tunica, Washington, Yazoo, and Warren Counties, Mississippi, U.S. Bureau of the Census, rolls 186 and 187.

Note: The urban areas tabulated are Greenville (Washington County), Yazoo City (Yazoo County), and Vicksburg (Warren County).

a. N=number of households.

no means the only legitimate relationship in the Delta's black communities. Marriage was only one of many options. Freedmen and women could "take up" with others, "sweetheart," form common-law marriages, live with friends or relatives, or marry. In fact, nonnuclear households dominated the cities and the countryside until 1866. Then, suddenly, they vanished on the plantations. By 1870, nuclear families comprised 89 percent of all African-American households remaining on the land. In contrast, nuclear families comprised only 48 percent of households in the cities. In many ways, the development of the nuclear family could be cast as an aberration. It was only on the plantation that the nuclear family became the predominate household structure (see table 1).

So the question remains, why did marriage become the most viable option for black southerners only on the plantation? What relationship existed between the construction of free labor and the emergence of this one particular household structure—the male-headed nuclear family? Why did the rich legacy of flexible family forms fail to thrive on plantations after the war?

This chapter explores the politics of marriage in the reconstruction of plantation agriculture. In many ways, the African-American nuclear family resulted from the intense negotiation over property rights and the meaning of free labor in the Delta after the war. Both black and white, male and female, recognized "the household" as the foundation for their rights and freedom. Yet each carried a competing understanding of just what constituted a household and exactly which rights and freedoms it secured. As black households contracted with white households, their competing concepts of authority clashed. Just who owned what and on what terms became open to question as contests over labor and over property swept into the domestic realm.

To Limit Their Freedom: Planters Confront African-American Alternative Households

The dominance of the nuclear family was a pointed response to the wartime economies, created largely by women, both in towns and in the countryside. Returning home in 1865, planters found their vast plantation households replaced by small, self-sufficient black communities focusing their energies as much on foodstuffs as on cotton. Former masters suddenly found themselves dependent upon their former slaves. As Inspector General T. Sargent Free reported, "it seems hard to the former master, that he should lose all control of his slaves, and see them possessors of property accumulated in his absence." He explained, "The former master returns [home] only to find himself a poor man while what little there is to subsist on is the hard earned food of the Freedman generally, who claims his produce . . . he has rightfully earned . . . by his industry." With typical bureaucratic understatement Free concluded, "This feeling sometimes engenders . . . a cruel display of malicious & vindictive passion, terminating in violent heat . . . the white man being the aggressor."[7]

In many ways, freedwomen were the unspoken center of this debate. During the war it was primarily women who had developed and nurtured alternative economies both on the plantation and in the city. In the process, many had accumulated a fair amount of property.[8] Defeated at war, soldiers marched home only to find themselves defeated once again by what they must have seen as an odd assortment of women, children, and older men. Furious to discover that people they had always designated as "powerless" were in fact demonstrating a good deal of power, planters lashed out. According to former soldiers, the resulting violence was worse than—or at least as bad as—any war. "I would rather storm the Vicksburg Batteries," wrote one Union man, ". . . than attempt to live [as a freedperson] on a good many plantations far from our lines."[9]

Planters directed much of the violence at perhaps the least physically threatening members of the black community—older men, women, and children. When Harriet Murray had the audacity to request her wages, Dick Porter "took her to the woods . . . with the help of another man, one sat on her head the other . . . striped her of all her clothes naked, her hands were tied up at a limb . . . two candles were burned out in the time occupied whiping her." Harriet Murray may not have possessed the physical strength to fend off her attackers, but she certainly possessed something these white men feared. Simply by being able to control her own labor, she and others like her demonstrated the real power these "dependents" held.[10] That small bit of control—the ability to decide when to work and for whom—could secure a degree of autonomy. Planters feared that women like Murray would choose not to work, or work only when they saw fit. The freedpeople's independence, in large part, came from their ability to direct most of their labor to gardens and livestock and away from the cash crop.

In 1865 freedpeople asserted their power. The labor contracts signed that year demonstrate just how much control the "old and weak" could wield. Freedpeople managed to force planters to permit them time and resources to commit to their personal crops. The 1865 contracts, unlike those signed a year or two later imposed few restrictions upon the production of cotton or garden produce or the raising of livestock. Instead, landlords agreed to furnish freedpeople with the "grounds they have in cultivation" in order to "raise such crops as they choose."[11] William Fulgate in Yazoo County permitted the inevitable, stating that freedpeople could "cultivate as much land on their own account as may desire." On Eveline Purvis's place freedpeople grew rice, potatoes, and watermelons, while on M. B. Lamb's and J. P. Wilson's farms freedpeople grew cotton as well as produce. On the Linvale and Vanderling plantations, freedpeople secured themselves a weekend. Sunday was traditionally a day of rest, but on these plantations Saturday was also set aside for people to work on gardens.[12] By expanding upon traditional rights to cultivate and market crops in individual garden patches, freedpeople secured a degree of independence. Moreover, these contracts represented planters' open recognition of freedpeople's claims to property gained during the war, be it their right to the crops already sown and cultivated or their right to livestock. Granted, these were small concessions, especially considering the low wages paid to plantation workers in 1865. What is significant about these contracts is that freedpeople remained focused on securing and maintaining an independent livelihood. Their efforts demonstrate a stubborn reluctance to accept a position as a wage laborer or to negotiate, whether for wages or shares, within that system.

Both planters and agents of the Freedmen's Bureau recognized that the success of these small household economies threatened plantation agriculture. Well acquainted with the legacy of emancipation in the Caribbean, the U.S. government and planters alike hoped to tie the workers back to the land. "If the negroes in the South are left as they have been in Jamaica ... the same results of desolation, decay and abandonment will follow. ... [N]egroes [will] abandon the plantations and collect in towns or villages [and live] by stealing, begging, or petty jobbing."[13]

Where the Freedmen's Bureau saw disintegration into a peasant economy, planters rightly perceived a real challenge to their property. As southerners, both planters and freedpeople associated household with the control of people and property. As white southerners immediately recognized, freedpeople's constructions of household economies expressed personal freedom. Moreover, the African-American alternative households provided a basis for freedpeople's independent production of goods.

In the eyes of white southerners, a horrible inversion had occurred. African-Americans usurped the power over planters' "households" to lay claim to property. This property, in turn, gave freedpeople a measure of latitude. They were not completely dependent on wage, and they were not completely beholden to former masters.

Planters acted to crush freedpeople's independent production of goods. Targeting African-American alternative households, planters made it clear that the plantation would no longer serve as a haven for the old or the weak. By 1866 labor contracts indicated that dependents were not welcome on plantations. Suddenly alternative household structures became an exception rather than the rule on plantations.[14] Moreover, the contracts dramatically diminished independent ownership of livestock and control over garden plots, which formed the backbone of the alternative economy. Instead, plantation work became a stage in the life cycle—an option for only those freedpeople who married and settled.

Plantation labor became so associated with the nuclear family in the Delta's black communities that working a crop together often signaled marriage. As Robert Hudson put it, "I just considered [Emily] my woman, not my wife. ... She did not help me work the crop." Couples moved to plantations after they had formalized marriages, and women often returned to town after losing a spouse. Contracting for a crop meant sharing debts and profits, and for women it meant trusting a man enough to feel confident he would not leave with the majority of the proceeds.[15]

By 1866 fewer and fewer planters contracted directly with women. More than half of the freedwomen worked the land under the supervision of squad leaders or husbands.[16] In less than a year, nuclear families dominated the plantation workforce, reversing the pattern established during the war and in its immediate aftermath. This one form of the household had become essential to the production of cotton across the South.

Emancipated Workers: Property, Family, and African-American Households

So why would planters make this concession to black manhood in 1866, and why would they encourage one family type over another? In many ways, freedpeople forced planters to accept the autonomy of the black household. Freedpeople simply refused to work on plantations where former slaveholders still claimed the rights of mastery. Yet even while planters apparently agreed to contract with families, their response to this restructuring of authority was contradictory at best. They were not about to grant black households all the rights and privileges accorded to plantation households before the war.[17]

In 1866 planters launched a charge at the specter of free labor by boldly heading in several directions at once. Eventually sharecropping would dominate the Delta landscape, but from 1865 through 1880 labor arrangements twisted and turned, advancing in one direction, then retreating into another. Gang labor, squads, renting, and sharecropping existed side by side as landlords juggled their books between cash wages, share wages, and sharecrops.[18] No single pattern of contracting emerged in the 1860s, but planters established specific terms that fundamentally shaped the course of events.

The contracts registered with the Freedmen's Bureau in 1866 set two precedents that would never waver, regardless of labor arrangement. The first was the establishment of the nuclear family as a work unit. In 1865 the majority of freedpeople contracted as individuals. In some cases, households were listed together, but only one-quarter of the contracts were written explicitly for fami-

Table 2. Labor Contracts Signed by Family/Individual, 1865 and 1866

Year	Contracting as nuclear family	Contracting as individual
1865 (N=51)[a]	13 (25%)	38 (75%)
1866 (N=98)	52 (53%)	46 (47%)

Source: Labor contracts for Washington, Issaquena, Tunica, Yazoo, Sunflower, and DeSoto Counties, AC, RG 105, M826.

a. N=number of contracts.

lies. By 1866 the percentage of freedpeople contracting in family units more than doubled (see table 2). The second precedent established the landlord's concentrated effort to limit freedpeople's direct access to the marketplace. Planters greatly reduced access to garden plots and truck farms and would not tolerate the cultivation of commodity crops on those plots. In essence, the 1866 contracts stipulated that cotton production was to be the principal focus of freedpeople's attention.

Planters were willing to loosen their grasp on individual workers in order to tighten their control over the market in land and cotton. Planters attempted to use the nuclear family structure to crush freedpeople's independent production of goods. If planters could undermine the alternative economies established during the war, they could achieve two goals at once—produce more cotton and limit freedpeople's economic independence.[19] Planters worked to assure that their ownership of every acre, animal, and plant would never again be brought into question by the claims of a moral economy.

Ironically, the family proved critical to planters' control. First, employers shifted the burden of caring for dependents from themselves to the male head of each household. Marriage, they reasoned, brought obligations and few rights. Jerry Lightwood explicitly defined James Rowe's manly obligations, writing, "he will keep good and orderlee conduct among his family that he will see that his children are ordely and in case of roodness on ther part that he will chastize them for the same."[20] By contract, Lightwood bound Rowe to maintain discipline in his family—and not just any form of discipline. Rowe agreed to teach his children not to overstep the boundaries of prewar racial etiquette by any acts of "roodness." Rowe's job now depended on disciplining his family.

Equally important, planters refused to contract with individual members of black households. Instead they contracted only with the heads of the households. After signing a contract, African-American men (or women) became responsible for providing for their own families. Planters used marriage to put an economic squeeze on black families. With their meager pay, workers discovered that they now had to provide for dependent family members. Virtually all employers stated that they would issue food, clothing, and medicines only for family members working the cash crop. Using typical language, Marietta Heard stipulated that she would provide food for only those "Employees going to the fields." Further, she required that her "Employees" agree to "clothe themselves and pay their own Doctor's bills."[21] Reversing the trend established by the 1865 contracts, planters en masse refused to care for the needs of anyone not working the cash crops.[22]

These restrictive clauses threatened extended families and the alternative economy simultaneously. Those not working for the employer placed an economic burden on their families. This forced all able-bodied people into the field, and must have discouraged families from taking in the very old, the young, or the disabled. Single women with children simply could no longer afford to work the crop. In November 1865, agent Thomas Smith warned that "a large surplus class of persons must inevitably be thrown off many plantations.... The class which I refer is composed of the aged and infirm, of orphaned and abandoned children, of unmarried women with large numbers of little children too young to work." Agent Smith continued, "Everywhere that I went I was met with the question, what are you yankees going to do with the women and children?"[23]

Moreover, families had to think twice about withdrawing men's or women's labor from the field. If a woman chose to "stay at home," her family would have to pay for her food, medicine, and clothing. She had to be able to guarantee that her work marketing produce, raising livestock, fishing, or laundering would cover her expenses. Anyone not working the crop became a potential liability, rather than a source of independent income, for the family.

Docking family members for not working the crop was not leverage enough. Planters knew that women could make a sizeable income from truck gardening and raising chickens. Isaac Harris's wife, for example, earned $46.50 raising chickens, nearly matching his yearly wages of $64.75.[24] So plantation owners used their status as landlords to assert authority. In 1866 they stipulated that workers could not raise livestock or maintain gardens on the employer's property. The number of gardens dropped dramatically. That year, only 11 percent of the sampled contracts permitted gardens, whereas 43 percent had permitted

Table 3. Labor Contracts Permitting Gardens and Livestock, 1865 and 1866

Year	Gardens only	Gardens and livestock
1865 (N=51)[a]	22 (43%)	8 (16%)
1866 (N=98)	11 (11%)	1 (1%)

Source: Labor contracts for Washington, Issaquena, Tunica, Yazoo, Sunflower, and DeSoto Counties, AC, RG 105, M826.

a. N = number of contracts viewed by the author.

them in 1865 (see table 3). Moreover, one-third of those planters allowing gardens specifically stated that the land be used "for food only." Aware that freedwomen gardened for profit, Andrew Shotwell went so far as to specify that women be granted less land for crops than men.[25]

Then there was the chicken factor. Many women, like Isaac Harris's wife, must have raised and sold chickens and eggs. Not surprisingly, in 1866 contracts began to specify that chickens could be raised if, and only if, they were not raised for sale.[26] Planters forbade all other animals. By 1866 only one percent of the labor contracts permitted workers to keep any type of animal.

In 1868 the state legislature, backing planters' property rights, dramatically overturned traditional fencing laws, further reducing freedpeople's ability to raise livestock. The new law made owners of livestock responsible for fencing their animals in. The law permitted the confiscation of any animal responsible for "injury upon the property of others," and subjected the owners of the wayward animals to an initial fine of two dollars, plus seventy-five cents for each day the animal was held in custody.[27] Workers earning ten dollars a month could hardly afford these fines and no doubt lost the animals to landowners.

For many planters, these laws did not go far enough. Mississippi's legal code protected each individual's right of property. Whites could not contain their fury that black southerners had established a legal claim to property that had been taken from plantations as the spoils of war. Throughout Reconstruction, freedpeople lodged hundreds of complaints against white southerners for shooting their cows, stealing their horses, taking livestock to cover debts, and even threatening their lives.[28] On April 28, 1868, Frank Moore walked to the Freedmen's Bureau office in Rosedale and lodged a complaint against James Upshaw. He claimed Upshaw took two sows, eight pigs, one cow, and one calf. Benton Bowen reported that his employer refused to pay him, and when he demanded his wages, the landlord threatened to "shoot him and take his cow." John G. Shuth took a horse; N. G. Coulter took a freedwoman's hog and all of her corn; Z. T. Nichols took James Bobo's mule.[29] Livestock had helped freedpeople secure a degree of independence. A horse, a mule, or an ox kept freedpeople from having to rent landlords' mules to plow. The hogs brought in a sizeable profit and served as a good food supply. Without the animals, the alternative economy was crippled.

Female-headed households, especially those with small children, were especially hard hit by the new conditions of labor. During the war, freedwomen maintained a degree of economic and social distance from commodity production by pooling the resources of the family. Women, children, and elderly freedpeople managed not only to maintain themselves but to legally acquire property during these years. The conditions of the new contracts undermined the ability of the black family to expand its resources outside the production of cotton. Without access to land, freedpeople could not produce for themselves or maintain the livestock they had acquired during the war. The household economy, developed largely by women during the war, became more and more dependent upon a single source of income—wages or shares paid for the production of cotton. Controlling the land, planters exerted a heavy hand in the development of free labor. Shifting the responsibility for dependents onto black families, planters effected an enormous wage cut that drove the less commercially successful households off the land. In doing so, white southerners hoped to guarantee themselves a strong and able-bodied workforce.

White Men Confront Black Manhood

They got that and more. In May 1866, freedmen recently discharged from the U.S. Army returned home to take their places as heads of their households. To accept the black household, white southerners had to welcome back former slaves who not only had rebelled and claimed their own freedom but had physically destroyed slavery, defeated their former masters in battle, and stood in victory over them as members of the occupying army. The independence and defiance of workers was troubling enough, but, at least as workers, freedpeople remained familiar. Soldiers, however, wore the badges of their transformation. Guns, uniforms, and ready cash from paychecks and bounties displayed black soldiers' masculinity and independence. So while planters wished to undermine women's alternative economy on the plantation by tying the black household directly back to the production of cotton, they feared the consequences of their actions. They needed male labor, but they were not willing to accept black men as heads of household.

One has only to remember Forrest's murder of Tom Edwards to recognize planters' outraged denial of black men's rights as the heads of their households. From the southern perspective, claiming mastery over one's household was the first step in establishing political rights. With emancipation, black men became free men, and many, like Tom Edwards, claimed their rights as heads of household. In the Delta, where blacks outnumbered whites by as much as five to one, planters faced a serious challenge to their political domination.[30]

The fear of black male suffrage haunted white southerners from the moment of their defeat. Suffrage, they assumed, would follow race, not class. As early as December 1865, the Friars Point newspaper the *Coahomian* urged the importation of white labor in order to guarantee planters' political domination of the state. "[I]f we supplant the negro with the European, it will give us just that much more power in Congress," an editorial stated. It went on to specify how planters' political power should be used: with a Congressional majority "we will have the force to guard the country . . . and force the negro to honest labor or drive him, by starvation, to seek his proper associates—the radicals of the North."[31] Political rights, according to the *Coahomian,* were synonymous with the right to use physical force and violence.

Therefore, while upholding the nuclear family with one hand, many planters worked systematically to disrupt it with the other. Black families might be accepted, but only on certain terms. As far as planters were concerned, acceptance did not mean a relinquishment of control.

When hundreds of African-American Union soldiers mustered out in May 1866, planters faced what was, to them, an awful dilemma. They needed workers, but they feared and despised Union soldiers. "No soldier," one freedwoman desperately warned, "shall return to the County and live."[32] As symbols of black manhood and the promise of civic equality, soldiers presented a grave challenge to white political authority. These men represented the full significance of Union victory. In incident after incident, white southerners tried to physically destroy any manifestation of black manhood. One man had his blue shirt ripped off him as he walked down the road in Yazoo County. His assailant threatened to "kill him if he ever saw him again with a yankee coat on."[33]

The Black Codes, written in 1865, starkly demonstrated white southerners' refusal to accept African-American households. Conservative legislators reasoned that wage workers were dependents. They worked on another man's land and owned no real property, which meant they were like servants. As servants, they lived and worked as members of their employer's household. The employers, therefore, maintained the right to discipline their workers' behavior both on and off the job. As dependents, moreover, African-Americans deserved no civil or political rights. The Black Codes limited African-American testimony in civil courts, making it impossible for freedpeople to file lawsuits. The Black Codes also outlawed the ownership of "firearms, dirks, or knives"; they required each freedperson to have a lawful home or employment and carry written evidence of such; they taxed each freedman one dollar a year and imprisoned him as a vagrant if he could not pay. According to law, freedpeople were required to obtain a license to preach, sell goods, and live in town and perform "irregular work." No freedperson could rent or lease land except in cities, and only then if the civil authorities agreed. Each act denied freedmen the rights of manhood—the rights of property, the right to defend and protect oneself or one's family, the right to legal protection, and the right to travel freely.[34] Blurring the boundaries between property and self, white southerners outraged the nation. These actions were interpreted as a clumsy attempt to reinstate slavery in a new guise. Yet after four years of war and three years of emancipation, the Black Codes had more to do with southern limitations of freedom than being a desperate effort by whites to redefine slavery.[35]

The 1865 Apprenticeship Act demonstrated white southerners' refusal to relinquish the authority of household. The act placed orphans and any children with indigent parents under the guardianship of others until they came of age.[36] General Oliver O. Howard, director of the Freedmen's Bureau, agreeing with such logic, permitted the enforcement of this law as long as no distinctions were made by race.[37] Hoping to construct a free labor system built upon republican craft traditions, which would maintain white men's place at the head of black household, Howard carefully dismissed charges of racial prejudice by drawing on northern conventions of household economy. Like apprentices in a craft, masters promised black children training, education, and a suit of clothes in exchange for unpaid labor.

Enforcing this law, both northern and southern whites ignored black household and community structures. The government authorized the legal apprenticeship of children cared for by aunts, grandparents, siblings, and informal guardians. Frequently, white southerners took children away from working mothers and apprenticed them, using the argument that a woman's wages could not sustain a family; more often than not, however, children's wages provided the glue in the household economy. Apprenticing these children, planters controlled their labor for free, leaving their relatives without emotional or financial support. Reasserting themselves as heads of the plantation households, planters demonstrated their unthinking belief that the black household, whether independent or not, existed as an extension of the plantation itself and therefore was subject to the owner's best interests.

Across the Delta, planters built on the logic of the Black Codes to disrupt black households. By 1866 it had become common practice for planters to sign labor contracts with the male head of household and not individual family members. Using this leverage, they then proceeded to "discharge" the male head of household at harvest time. Planters believed that women could pick cotton as fast as men, or faster. By throwing men off the land during the cotton harvest, planters used the family contract to obtain the same crop with cheaper labor.

Following this common practice, H. F. McWilliams threw Albert Wadlington off his plantation in September 1866, exactly when the cotton bolls began to burst open. In this case, McWilliams accused Wadlington of beating his wife, Anna. So when Albert left, Anna and five children stayed to finish the year. When it came time to settle up, Anna and the children received payment for their labor only, and not Albert's. Despite the amount of cotton they had produced as a family, they received only the low wages paid women and children. For Anna, contracting as a wife left her with nothing. Without her husband, she lost a man's share of the crop over which her woman's labor had worked long and hard. For his part, McWilliams got a crop at bargain prices. But the case did not end there. A full year after the final settlement, the Bureau ordered McWilliams to settle with Wadlington. Ruling in Wadlington's favor, the Bureau forced McWilliams to pay him his wages and the wages of his wife and children.[38] Anna, at this point, lost any right to her own wage.

The lessons of this free black family speak more to the subject of hierarchy than independence. Contracting as a family, they were bound to each other for the year—which, if the allegations of abuse were true, left Anna and her children balancing economic needs against their physical well-being. They had few choices, but McWilliams made their choices even narrower. Intruding upon their family, he assumed the right to break it apart.

Every fall, planters drove black men like Wadlington off their plantations. And each year, freedmen walked many miles to lodge formal complaints with the Freedmen's Bureau agents, protesting their loss of wages. Planters claimed that these men had broken their contract by leaving the plantation. Freedmen protested that planters had forced them off the land while keeping a tight hold on their women and children.[39]

So while white southerners, in order to tie workers back to the crop, forced freedpeople to work in family units, they refused to accept the implications of personal and political freedom implied by the black male-headed household. Instead they fiercely reinforced their undisputed dominance, not only over the work, but over the body of each black southerner as well.

The charges of physical abuse most graphically highlighted the grotesque battle over household. Blacks protested when whites beat them, women protested when their husbands beat them, and black men and women protested when whites beat them for beating each other. People beat each other with whips, sticks, boards, guns, and fists, planting an imprint of their mastery over others.[40] The complex web of abuse reflected the struggle on the part of blacks and whites to assert independence and control by commanding others by force.

In 1867, John Evans beat Mary Johnson for beating her daughter, and Captain Gentry and William Brown beat Willis Maddox for beating his wife.[41] These beatings clearly did not reflect the planters' desires to protect Maddox's wife or Johnson's child. Instead these planters assaulted and murdered freedpeople for usurping white male authority. The planters identified violence—the right to punish and command another through force—as a demonstration of power and authority that only they had the right to control. The black household undermined this authority by investing husbands and parents with the same bloody presentation of mastery.

In case after case, whether through murder (*Edwards v. Forrest*) or the control of property (*Wadlington v. McWilliams*), white southerners refused to recognize either freedpeople or the black household as separate from themselves. Ignoring family ties, white southerners brushed aside freedpeople's right to self-determination. Black men could be murdered and beaten for asserting selfhood, black children taken from their homes and bound as servants, and black women beaten or employed as sexual slaves. In crushing waves of violence, white southerners exploded with calculated rage, physically branding the land and the people.

Emancipation forced a reconstruction of power, but planters did not relinquish control. They retained similar power, but on new terms. A. T. Morgan, a northerner who settled in the Delta after the war, witnessed the demise of the plantation household and planters' struggle to understand the source of their power after emancipation. He commented on the fierce struggle over property and free labor, writing, "I believe that the question is not altogether one of race or color, but, that, back of the race question and stronger and more merciless & cruel than it is the question of capital and labor." The battle, according to Morgan, centered on the control of labor, land, and cotton. Yet the struggle over property involved large concessions by planters. They risked much by partially recognizing African-American men as the heads of their households.

Could planters insure that partial relinquishment of control would not develop into a complete loss of authority? Morgan believed that planters counted on older intimacies of the household to tide them over. Planters granted themselves the right to police African-American households. "The attitude or relation," according to Morgan, appeared to be "that of 'keeper' & 'sweetheart' or 'mistress' and not of employer & laborer and of 'white' man & 'black' man." His choice of words is telling. Each of the relationships he mentioned—"keeper" and "sweetheart" and "mistress"—is a sexualized and highly gendered term implying a dependent relationship. Taking their position as the "keepers" of "sweethearts" and "mistresses," white southerners described freedpeople in a dependent—if illicit—relationship with white men. Moreover, they counted on what Morgan described as "the closest relations known to the two sexes of the human family."[42] The foundations for political, economic, and personal power were marked by a relentless assertion of intimacy by white men. The plantation, from the planters' perspective, remained their private domain.

To control land and labor, the Delta's planter class worked to crush alternative African-American households from 1865 to 1867. Working alongside the conservative state legislature, planters exercised their mastery as landlords to force workers into a position of dependency. Yet, in doing so, they opened the door to African-American manhood rights. As the number of male-headed African-American nuclear households increased exponentially on the plantations, planters encountered men claiming patriarchal privileges regardless of race. Freedmen disputed the basis of white male privilege by laying claim to black families and, as important, to the fruits of their families' labor. Claiming citizenship, African-American men pushed the state and federal governments to intervene on the plantations and bring public power to bear on what white men claimed was a private domain. Yet not just black men claimed the privileges of citizenship—freedwomen also went to court and sued their employers for an infringement of their rights. They too claimed household privileges, but on different terms than many freedmen. In suits and countersuits, the people of the Delta, black and white, male and female, contested the meaning of citizenship. Together, both black and white households forced changes on themselves and on each other.

6

⚜

Going to Court and Claiming Citizenship

Property, Patriarchy, and Alternative Households

AFRICAN-AMERICAN men and women forced the issue of citizenship
from the first moment of emancipation. Moving beyond resistance, men
and women took public political action, filing suit and pressing charges against
anyone infringing upon their rights. Long before the first African-American
man served in the Mississippi state legislature, freedpeople demanded that the
government—state and federal—represent their interests. Just what those interests were, however, was a matter of dispute. From 1865 to 1870, freedpeople
debated the nature of rights within their homes and neighborhoods. In turn,
the planter class, faced with emancipation and African-Americans' constant
legal claims, weighed their options. Planter men and planter women, themselves, began to redefine the basis of citizenship.

Remember Tom Edwards. In the spring of 1866, Edwards beat his wife. He
paid for that act with his life when his employer, Nathan Bedford Forrest, picked
up a stick and pounded him to death. The struggle between man and wife was
also a struggle between white man and black for the mastery of the African-
American family. Yet the story unfolds further, revealing another layer in the
politics of household.

When Forrest killed Edwards, he murdered the plantation's undisputed
leader of the African-American community. Edwards had confronted Forrest
that spring, demanding that Forrest abide by the terms of the labor contract
signed in January. Earlier in 1866, Forrest had had trouble finding workers. His
reputation preceded him. So, in a rare moment, workers had forced Forrest to
compromise. "Some of the best hands," Forrest recalled, "told me they would
not have a superintendent to direct them as they knew how to work as well as
any white man."[1] The point was clear—no white overseers. Forrest capitulated
and signed the contract.

Fig. 11. Who's missing from this picture? Men and *women* used the civil courts and the Freedmen's Bureau to claim rights as citizens. ("The Freedmen's Bureau," *Harper's Weekly,* 1868.)

In less than a month, Forrest violated this agreement. He hired two overseers, former Union officers, to supervise the labor on his plantation. He hoped, no doubt, that the blue uniform would disguise the whiteness of their skin. His plan failed. "For several weeks past there was a spirit of insubordination," reported Freedmen's Bureau agent George Corliss. Freedpeople resented the overseer's "efforts to get them to work a proper number of hours each day . . . and refused to work or obey Mr. Tann." At that point, Tann fell back on a form of punishment common in the military and threatened "to tie one of them up by the thumbs. At this," Corliss reported, "they nearly all quit work and . . . went over to the other place and got their chief (Tom Edwards) and some of his followers, who came back with a Spencer rifle." Rather than use the rifle, Edwards organized the workers into a "procession" and demanded concessions. His concluding act was to send a man downriver to the Friars Point Freedmen's Bureau office in the next county for help.[2]

This was the final lesson of the Forrest incident—the private domain of the plantation was now vulnerable to outside intrusion. Forrest was furious. His plantation, in his mind, was about to be invaded. By calling for a Bureau agent, Edwards demonstrated to Forrest the new laws of freedom. Former masters no longer had complete control over their workforce, nor were their plantations sacrosanct. Workers and government agents now paraded around Forrest's land at will. The boundaries between family, the plantation, and the state slowly folded in upon themselves as freedpeople called on the government to serve their interests.

When Nathan Bedford Forrest reneged on the terms of his labor contract, Tom Edwards called on the Freedmen's Bureau to defend his rights. In the process, he lost his life. Yet hundreds of freedpeople in the Delta took this chance. They demanded equal treatment before the law. As freedman Calvin Holly argued in 1865, "I think the safety of this country depens upon giving the Colered man all the rights of a white man, and especialy the Rebs." Writing to the Freedmen's Bureau, Holly declared, "let [freedpeople] know that their is power enough in the arm of the Government to give Justice, to all her loyal citizens."[3]

The courts stood on the front lines of freedom. In the early years of emancipation—before the United States government granted African-Americans citizenship and before freedmen won the right to vote—black southerners aggressively demanded that the government intervene on the plantations and defend their rights. Of course, as long as former Confederates controlled the Mississippi government, few civilian courts agreed to hear their cases. Yet freedpeople persisted. Their actions spelled out their determination. Planters, taking notice, began to redefine the boundaries of their households to preserve former privileges.

Taking their cases to court, planter men, planter women, freedmen, and freedwomen expressed competing definitions of citizenship. The differences are striking. Planter men and women worked in concert to privilege property over traditional household hierarchies. Expanding the Married Women's Property Act, planter men gradually forfeited bits and pieces of the household to their women. They counted on their wives to support them, gambling that a mutual commitment to maintaining class privilege would override women's desire for independence. Of course, planter women had already demonstrated this faithfulness during the war. To guarantee privilege based on property, both planter men and women willingly sacrificed strict adherence to the ideologies of the household.

In contrast, African-American men and women maintained a commitment to household relations, albeit with a contested vision of what those relationships entailed. In doing so, African-Americans grounded citizenship not on property but on a complex web of social relations, involving rights and obligations to others. In many ways African-Americans articulated a concept of rights based on what sociologist T. H. Marshall termed "social citizenship."[4] Social citizenship, unlike civil or political citizenship, does not privilege property rights. Instead, social citizenship recognizes social relations as a form of capital.[5] An individual alone might not possess resources, but that individual's social ties to community, household, and the state provide value—social capital. Many freedpeople, therefore, challenged any definition of rights based on property ownership alone.

The uncoupling of these two foundations of citizenship—property and social relations—reflect the political unraveling of power based on the antebellum plantation household. Before emancipation, the two were inextricably linked. A white man's independence—his ticket to full political and legal privileges—rested upon his mastery over his land and over all who resided upon it. The abolition of slavery destroyed any easy correlation between property in land and property in people. Determined to control capital, planters emphasized a citizenship defined in terms of property rights. They attempted to defend the borders of their plantation from government or legal intrusion. Freedpeople, however, challenged this assertion. Claiming rights as citizens, they brought the law onto the plantation and demanded that everyone, regardless of property rights, fall subject to legal enforcement. In the courts, planters and freedpeople expressed the underlying bases for their visions of power and authority.

Property as the Foundation for Rights: Planter Men and Women and the Reconstruction of Household

From 1865 to March 1867, white conservatives wrote the new laws of freedom. Empowered by the fact that African-Americans could not vote, planters attacked the rights of workingmen.[6] They took control of the legal system and worked to secure what they now saw as the ultimate foundation of their authority—property.

Three legislative issues—labor laws, lien laws, and the Married Women's Property Acts—were cornerstones for rebuilding planter-class privilege. On the one hand, to maintain control over workers, planters attempted to reassert older forms of the household—to demand that all workers, by law, fall under their employers' jurisdiction. On the other, to maintain control over landhold-ings, planters gradually transferred legal authority to their wives, consequently undermining traditional gender hierarchies of the household. One common thread ran through the two responses—property rights.

First, the conservative legislature's labor laws defined agricultural wage la-bor as a domestic relation. As historian Laura Edwards argues, conservative law-makers used the Black Codes to classify African-American laborers as either "domestic" or "menial" labor. Legislatures across the South determined that agricultural laborers rightfully fell under master-servant laws. From the courts' perspective, farm laborers had no special skills and owned little property. Therefore, they could not be classified as independent people. Farm workers were free, but dependent, laborers. They needed masters. The Black Codes, like laws in the northern states, gave employers special rights as "masters" of un-skilled workers.[7] They could regulate the domestic lives of their workers, in-duce them to labor by using year-long contracts, and use the vagrancy laws to compel "idle" people to work.

Of course, African-American workers were neither idle nor propertyless. Yet planters believed that freedpeople's property rightfully belonged to the land-lord. After all, planters argued, freedpeople's goods had been produced on their employers' plantations or had been acquired while African-Americans were still enslaved. Either way, freedpeople's property fell under the landlord's do-minion.

Second, the legislature enacted lien laws designed to limit the rights of wage laborers. The lien laws were arguably the legislature's clearest expression of disregard for freedpeople's property. A lien is a legal claim to another person's property. At the beginning of the crop year, planters needed to borrow heavily in order to purchase supplies—mules, seeds, plows, and other equipment. During slavery, a planter borrowed from a commission merchant, who held the planter's property (slaves and cotton) as collateral against the loan. Merchants, in other words, held a lien on the planters' property. With emancipation, plant-ers could no longer use slaves as collateral. Instead they had to mortgage their crop or their land. Commission merchants, however, were reluctant to loan money to planters based on their crop alone. Free labor posed a risky invest-ment.

To entice merchants to loan planters money, the Mississippi legislature passed a new lien law granting merchants the first lien on the crop. The lien law stated that once the cotton crop was harvested and sold, planters were obligated to pay off their debts to merchants first.[8] At the end of the year, planters discovered that once they paid off their personal debts, there was nothing left for workers. So from 1865 to 1866, many African-Americans across the Delta received no wages for their work.[9] Free labor literally meant working for free. Thus the lien law reflected planters' belief that crop transactions were private—a business relationship between themselves and their creditors. Laborers, from the legislators' perspective, had little right to interfere in this personal matter.

The lien laws notwithstanding, planters felt vulnerable. Remember George Torrey's comment: "I am here in the Swamp ... trying to start a crop with a few freedmen—who do not at all times jump when I speak to them."[10] Planters felt trapped on all sides. On the plantations, freedpeople challenged the rights of property. Regardless of the conservatives' tight control of the judicial system, freedpeople continued to sue their employers. Also, as the previous chapter indicates, freedpeople built on the alternative household to make claims to property. In the marketplace, merchants forced planters to mortgage their land before lending them money. Moreover, emancipation had stripped them of more than half their capital: their slaves. To secure control, planters called on their wives.

In January 1867 the legislature passed a new Married Women's Property Act. The challenge of free labor forced white, as well as black, households to change. To avoid losing their land, planters reconstructed their relationships with their wives. Building on antebellum precedents, planters expanded the Married Women's Property Act, enabling them to turn over family property to women.

Mississippi had passed the first Married Women's Property Act in the nation in 1839. The act created a wife's separate estate, permitting her to own property in her own name. Before the passage of this act, a woman experienced "civil death" when she married. Her husband subsumed her legal identity. A wife could not own property, conduct business, bring suit, or be sued. She had no legal self. Instead she was termed a *feme covert*—a woman covered by the authority of her husband. Of course, some married women protected themselves by hiring lawyers to draw up contracts for separate estates, but the process was expensive and time-consuming. With no protective contract, a husband could do whatever he saw fit with the family's property, including selling the roof over their heads (which some men did).[11] The Married Women's Property Act granted women the right to hold property in their own name. Yet the law only partially emancipated propertied married women. A woman might own property, but she could not sell or manage it without her husband's consent, and he retained the right to enjoy its profits.

During Reconstruction, the conservative legislature expanded married women's property rights. These reforms, however, focused less on women than on the property they owned. Suzanne Lebsock argues that "there was something in them for men and they had nothing to do with feminism."[12] The acts worked to secure family property from men's debts. Building upon the antebellum laws, the conservative legislature raised legal walls of protection around married women's property. In 1867 lawmakers declared that a wife's property "shall be exempt from [her husband's] debts." A husband could personally fall bankrupt while preserving property in his wife's name. Furthermore, a husband could borrow from his wife. If he failed to pay back her estate, she had first claim to his property. A husband, in other words, was legally bound to pay his wife's estate before paying back loans to merchants, wage workers, or cotton brokers. The 1867 Married Women's Property Act functioned as a safety net. By maintaining some property in a married woman's name, a family could protect that property from creditors.[13] Holding on to land was critical. A poor crop year—and there were many between 1865 and 1877—could drive a planter deeply into debt. By emancipating his wife, a husband could protect property—with her cooperation. Husbands could emancipate wives *and* retain control. Manly authority became dependent, in part, on the partial emancipation of married women.

In most instances, white women cooperated with their husbands. Planter women, after all, believed that their political interests lay within their households. During the war, planter women had attempted to relocate themselves back within the secure confines of household authority. After the war, most planter women continued to accept their husbands' authority. Therefore, few women used these acts to emancipate themselves from their husbands' authority. In fact, of the 145 cases brought before the Mississippi Supreme Court under the Married Women's Property Act during Reconstruction, only four pitted a wife against her husband. In the other 141 cases, married couples used the Married Women's Property Acts to protect family property from their husbands' debts.[14] Such was the case in *Wright v. Walton.*

When Sarah Walton married her husband, Charles, she owned a substantial plantation in Hinds County, just south of the Delta. Soon after the war, Charles Walton borrowed money in his wife's name from his commission merchant,

Hamilton Wright of Vicksburg, ostensibly to buy supplies for Sarah's planta-tion. However, Charles apparently used the money for other purposes and lost it all. When Hamilton Wright sued the Waltons, he claimed that since the money was borrowed to run Sarah's plantation, she should pay off the debt. Judge C. J. Simrall disagreed. "It by no means follows," he declared, "that be-cause a wife has separate property she is liable for household and family sup-plies." Sarah was not responsible for Charles's debt, not because she was inde-pendent, but because, in the judge's words, "The fortune of the wife does not relieve the husband from his duty to maintain his family." As head of his household, Charles was held to be the responsible party. The fact that Sarah held property in her own name only worked to the Waltons' favor. The Married Women's Property Act protected their plantation. Essentially, Charles Walton used the act to shelter the family's interests while he continued to take financial risks.[15] Paradoxically, planters could maintain household authority by emanci-pating their wives. As historian Angela Boswell argues, "husbands used the laws protecting married women's property most often as extensions of their ability to provide for their families and of their authority in the household."[16]

Boswell, however, overlooks the issue of married women's consent. Wives, not just husbands, used the Married Women's Property Acts to secure family property. Sarah Walton and countless other women permitted their husbands to use personal property for sheltering family assets. Yet planter men and women did not always define "family" in the same terms.

Conflicts arose when wives placed their children first, locating the family interests in succeeding generations rather than in the sole authority of their husbands. Placing sons before husbands, propertied women threatened to disrupt white men's undisputed mastery over family resources. In 1866 Harriet Theobold expressed concern over her sons' futures. She pressed her husband to permit her to use her property to secure loans for her sons. Samuel, her husband, protested. "In relation to your going security for your sons or any-one else," Samuel wrote, "it was always most decidedly against my judgement & feelings that you should do so. Of which," he testily continued, "you were fully impressed on all occasions when I was called on to express my opinion on the subject." Harriet's hands were tied. Under the Married Women's Prop-erty Act, she could not act alone. In order to transact business with her own property, a wife needed the consent of her husband. Yet even partial emanci-pation enabled propertied women like Theobold to assert their interests.

Although she could not act without Samuel's consent, Samuel likewise could not use Harriet's property without her consent. Agreement had to be reached. Neither husband nor wife could act alone when it came to a woman's property.

Propertied women, therefore, gained some leverage over family affairs. Samuel Theobold never agreed to permit Harriet to cosign a loan for their sons. He did, however, grudgingly let her sell property in her own name, pronouncing, "[I] hereby notify all whom it may concern that my wife is fully authorized to sell lots or any other species of property she holds."[17]

Unlike Harriet Theobold, few women aggressively pursued their right to conduct business independently.[18] They continued to help manage plantations just as they had before the war, working to preserve family property by standing by their men. Yet the uncertain economy heightened women's concern for their children. Emancipation stripped planter families of half their income. Before the war the planter class relied on the quick sale of a man, woman, or child as a safety net to help finance a child's education or to cover the losses incurred during a bad crop year. The abolition of slavery stripped them of this security. Suddenly, all family property resided in land and the success of free labor.

Mothers feared the irrevocable loss of family status if children could not be provided with the education, training, and clothing necessary to maintain class position. Recall Jean Smith. After the war, Smith realized that her father "had no head for business." As Jean managed tenants and saw to the crops, he read "*novels.*" To many in the planter class, novel reading represented an indulgent pursuit—a commitment to leisure—usually associated with foolish young women. As her father pursued this feminine pastime, Jean's younger sister Fannie tended cows. Jean said in despair: "It is not right to have Fan running after cow's, and for *Ma's sake*, I want to see her child have better opportunities of improving herself." For her part, Fannie became reclusive, "shut out from society" because "she has no time to improve herself acting in the capacity she is in now."[19] With work-roughened hands, no proper clothes, and no time to cultivate manners, Fannie was no longer eligible to take her place as a member of the planter class. Without money, family name meant little. Planter women, like men, realized that class identity resided in wealth and that manners and bloodlines meant little without it.

Therefore, many planter women took an active role in managing free labor.

They needed capital for their children and themselves. Many planter women became well versed in the ever-changing free labor practices, understanding that family fortunes depended on a "successful" crop year. From 1866 through 1870 Caroline Kiger worked hard to keep her son, William, in school. William's status as a gentlemen—and with it the family's future—rested on maintaining wealth through the "control," as Caroline put it, over freedpeople and the land. "This may be the last session your father may have the ability to send you to College," Kiger wrote her son. "I hope we will make a good crop. The hands are working better than they have ever done." The Kigers did manage to keep their son in school, and Caroline's letters detailed how. They tried to squeeze every penny out of their land and workers by first contracting for share wages, then renting, and then switching back to shares. The problem, according to Caroline, was providing workers some incentive without according them too much independence. Caroline managed this delicate balance herself. In 1868 she wrote her son concerning her troubles with a share-cropper named Wes who "now gets paid a hundred lbs. and is so much pleased with the field that he wanted to draw his rations so that he would not have to come to the house at all." She continued, "I would not agree to this as I did not want him to become too independent and think I had no control over him."[20] To protect her children and her family name, Caroline assumed control over Wes. Most men counted on wives like Caroline—planter women who defined their political rights as extensions of family interests and, most specifically, their children's interests.

The Married Women's Property Act, however, recognized married women's independent action, at least in part. As long as the courts and the legislature remained in the hands of conservatives, these rights would be narrowly construed. Planters could loosen household authority without much risk, confident that wives shared their class interest. Yet by extending rights to former dependents and granting them a measure of autonomy, the planter class opened the door to a renegotiation of political privilege.

Planters, therefore, tightened their control over private property on the one hand by imposing new labor and lien laws, while loosening control on the other through the Married Women's Property Acts. Both actions represented planter men's clear understanding that emancipation threatened the borders of their plantations by raising the question of exactly who had a legitimate claim to the land and the crop and on what terms. As freedmen and women challenged them daily—laying claim to families, labor, and the crop—planters sought partial relief in the legal code.

Claiming Citizenship: African-Americans and the Courts

As citizens, African-American men and women pressed the courts to hear— and record—their understandings of political rights. Claiming the courthouse as a public space, freedpeople challenged the conservatives' unilateral imposition of the law.[21] Equally persistent, the magistrates and judges rebuffed them. In 1865, the Issaquena County Freedmen's Bureau agent O. B. Foster reported: "Freedmen have come to me with cheeks pounded, eyes badly injured, teeth knocked out, and other evidences of maltreatment." According to Foster, they filed charges and "several cases [were] . . . tried before the Justices of the Peace." Each case, however, was "thrown aside by the County Court." Further up the Mississippi River in Greenville, agent W. S. Myers investigated why the courts dismissed so many cases. He reported: "The courts inform me that none but attorneys licensed by the Supreme Court or Circuit Court of this State can appear even as 'next friend' of another and assist him in prosecuting his rights— even before magistrates courts." Moreover, anyone practicing without a license was fined two hundred dollars.[22] The situation was dire. Few licensed lawyers would represent a freedperson, so African-American men and women had almost no access to the courts. Myers advised freedpeople not to sign any labor contracts until their rights could be defended.

Despite the civil courts' lack of response, freedpeople continued to file suits before the justices of the peace. One unnamed African-American woman reported a white man for whipping her. No action was taken. Then she filed a deposition and still received no response. Unwilling to take no for an answer, she "went to [the mayor's] office repeatedly to urge her case in person." According to the Bureau officer, no one responded to her case. When the agent investigated, he discovered that the mayor "stated in open court that he *would not take the testimony of a negro against a white man.*"[23]

Unable to find justice in the county courts, freedmen and freedwomen pressed the United States government to give them a full hearing.[24] They went to the closest Freedmen's Bureau office. In 1865, however, this meant traveling to Vicksburg, Memphis, or Skipwith's Landing—journeys that could take several days. In Memphis, Bureau officer T. Sargent Free reported, "They spring from the counties of De Sota, Marshal, Tippha, Tunica, Coahoma, Panola,

Table 4. Freedmen's Bureau Complaints Filed in the Delta, 1867–1868

	Crop	Wages	Assault	Custody	Theft	Total
Filings by men	162	50	25	4	17	258
% filed by men	91.5	57.5	62.5	26.7	85.0	76.1
Filings by women	15	37	15	11	3	81
% filed by women	8.5	42.5	37.5	73.3	15.0	23.9
Number of cases	177	87	40	15	20	339
% of total cases	52.2	25.7	11.8	4.4	5.9	100

Source: Based on Registers of Complaints, SFO–Greenville, SFO–Friars Point, SFO–Rosedale, SFO–Sardis, and SFO–Yazoo City, AC, RG 105.

Lafayette, and Pontotoc, and penetrate even further into the interior of the state. . . . Hence they go to Memphis to lay their complaints before the commanding General."[25]

The United States government responded. On March 26, 1867, Congress stripped the Mississippi legislature of its power and placed the state under the military command of General Edward O. C. Ord.[26] Targeting the laws and the courts, Ord issued a series of military orders. First, he appointed three African-American men, William T. Montgomery, Isaiah Montgomery, and William Lewis Jr., to serve as constable, justice of the peace, and deputy sheriff respectively in Warren County, thereby forcing the Mississippi judicial system to recognize African-American men's rights before the law.[27] Second, Ord used military powers to dismantle the Black Codes, to impose new labor laws, and to open the Freedmen's Bureau to judicial complaints. Third, Ord changed the lien laws, ordering that workers be granted the first lien on the crop. In other words, workers had to be paid before the merchants.[28]

Complaints poured in. Freedpeople pressed cases of divorce, assault and battery, nonpayment of wages, illegal apprenticeship of children, unfair distribution of the crop, and larceny (see table 4), pursuing an equally wide variety of defendants including family—wives, husbands, relatives, and children—neighbors white and black, and employers of both genders. In pleading their cases, freedmen and women argued that rights went hand in hand with obligations. A person could not have one without the other.

African-Americans' Gendered Expressions of Citizenship

African-Americans, both male and female, framed citizenship rights on household authority. Yet marked differences between men's and women's com-

Table 5. Freedmen's Bureau Complaints Filed for Others/Self

	For spouse	For child	For self	Total
Filings by men	17	3	238	258
% filed by men	6.6	1.2	92.2	100
Filings by women	4	18	59	81
% filed by women	4.9	22.2	72.8	99.9

Source: Based on Registers of Complaints, SFO–Greenville, SFO–Friars Point, SFO–Rosedale, SFO–Sardis, and SFO–Yazoo City, AC, RG 105.

plaints reveal a gendered understanding of the household and therefore a gendered reading of rights. In court, men asserted their position as heads of their households. Freedmen, not women, for the most part challenged white men for control over the crop. They claimed the right to the cotton that family labor produced. At face value, freedmen's actions seemed to represent an appropriation of white men's traditional mastery over family and property. Freedwomen, however, disputed any claim that rights were contingent upon property-holding or household hierarchies. Although women generally conceded men authority over the cotton and, by extension, family labor, this admission did not signal dependency in their minds or disqualify them from entering the public forum (see table 5.) Women, whether married or single or sweethearting, represented themselves, their children, and, in a few cases, their husbands in court to protest physical abuse or breach of contract. The concept of *feme covert*—a woman with no legal self—held little meaning for them. African-American women challenged the laws' assumption that a woman with a father or a husband must absent herself from the public sphere. Instead family, in all its forms, motivated freedwomen to press harder to defend their legal rights. Everyone, they asserted, had access to the political sphere as contributing citizens. The complaints they brought laid bare African-American men's and women's political consciousness—their gendered understanding of rights, and the role of government and the law in maintaining those rights.

Men—and perhaps women—associated manhood rights with the cotton crop. Freedmen dominated the record books when it came to the crop, filing 91 percent of all complaints concerning cotton. The crop was the man's domain. Closely examining these cases reveals freedmen's complex understanding of their public role as the heads of their households.

Freedmen's claims to the cotton crop expressed a multilayered understanding of their rights as workers, as family men, and as equal citizens before the law. As workers, freedmen were engaged in a fierce struggle with planters for their share of the crop. By 1867 most workers contracted with planters for pay in cotton. Workers agreed to raise a crop and harvest it and, in recompense, receive a share of that crop—from one-quarter to one-half of what they produced. The cotton crop was the worker's wage. But it was a fluctuating wage. Neither the worker nor the employer knew the value of the crop (how much it would bring at market or how much a worker could raise) until the cotton was picked and baled. Then the battle began. In many cases, both the employer and the worker had lived on borrowed money to make the cotton crop. So each fall and winter, in order to escape debt and maybe make a profit, they scrambled to get as much cotton as possible.[29]

In November and December, freedmen filed numerous complaints "protesting the removal of cotton before settlement."[30] Planters, usually working at night, moved the cotton to a makeshift landing somewhere along the rivers and attempted to sell the cotton before giving the workers their share. Bureau agent D. W. White reported from Yazoo City: "There is a class of people calling themselves planters who are determined to use Every Method to defraud the laborers no Matter how good the crop might be." Even in a good crop year, White recounted, planters "are now hauling [the cotton] to points on the River below the City for Shipment in order to prevent seizure for Claims of laborers. Thir object is to keep the negro in a state of poverty and degradation in order to make him subservient to thir will."[31] Freedmen responded. They filed complaints. When this did not work, they took up arms.

In November 1867, Richard Coleman led a group of armed freedmen up to Henry Yerger's front door. He "threatened to shoot the overseer unless he gave them their portion of the crop."[32] Unable to control mass protests, Bureau agent D. W. White called for troops. "The negroes," he explained, "have been discharged and are killing stock and stealing indiscriminately & in some instances refuse to leave the plantations." More, he warned, "are buying arms of every discription paying the money for them without regard to the price."[33] As White reported, freedpeople were determined to receive their rightful pay. Most, however, used the Bureau to seek compensation. Report after report told the same story. Men like Willis Keyes led his comrades down to the Freedmen's Bureau offices to complain that their employer "surreptitiously conveyed from said plantation a portion of the cotton crop," sold it, and "converted the money for his own use and benefit."[34] Freedmen demanded that their rights as workers be upheld.

Freedmen's status as workers, however, was often indistinguishable from their status as the heads of their households. By pressing for their rights as workingmen, African-American men also demanded recognition of their household authority. Planters signed contracts with married men, holding freedmen legally responsible for fulfilling the terms of the contract. From the planter's perspective, his only legal obligation was to the head of the worker's household. Acting on this assumption, every fall after the cotton had reached maturity, planters drove freedmen off the plantation. By forcing the men to leave, the planters could claim that the men had broken the labor contract and therefore were not entitled to their wages or share of the crop. Since the planters contracted with men as the heads of their households, planters could dramatically cut down on labor costs while still harvesting the crop with the men's families. Remember the case of Albert Wadlington. When H. F. McWilliams threw Wadlington off his plantation in September 1866, McWilliams got a crop at bargain prices. He had to pay only Anna and the children, not Albert.

Freedmen like Albert Wadlington fought back. Taking his case to the Freedmen's Bureau, Albert claimed his patriarchal rights. Until 1873 a married woman's wage belonged to her husband. Albert, therefore, demanded Anna's wages. And he won. He forced McWilliams to face the fact that, as a married man, Albert possessed sole authority within his family just like any white man.[35] Having contracted as the heads of their households, freedmen demanded that this position be upheld. They caught planters in their own contradiction. While planters defined African-American marriages in relation to obligation alone, freedmen pushed for rights. Filing complaints, freedmen asserted that planters could not obligate black men to support African-American households without according them the rights concomitant with that responsibility.[36] Freedmen took their place as equals among men.

Freedmen used their position as the heads of their households to directly challenge planters' definition of property. Demonstrating a sophisticated familiarity with Mississippi law, W. Harper, Isaac Bryant, and Mark Tony demanded protection under the state's Homestead Act. In 1866 the three men had contracted out their labor in exchange for a share of the cotton crop. At the end of the year, their share of the crop fell subject to debt. They lost everything.

Protesting, they claimed equal protection under the law. The Homestead Act, as most planters knew, protected a man's home from sale by creditors should he fall bankrupt. Planters counted on this law (along with the Married Women's Property Act) to protect their homes from bankruptcy sales. Claiming the same right as heads of their households, Harper and Bryant and Tony traveled to the Bureau agent in Friars Point and declared that their cotton was "entitled to exemptions under the Homestead Exemption Act." In other words, cotton, not just land, qualified as property. By defining property more broadly and demanding that the laws of the State of Mississippi extend to workingmen, Harper and Isaac and Tony challenged planters' privileged status. Freedmen took their place as citizens.

Yet these were not universal rights; they were manhood rights, granted only to men, and only to married men at that. Harper, Isaac, and Tony made their claim in the language of household. The three "made oath that they each were men of family." As heads of their households, they could secure property (and consequently a degree of power) in ways unavailable to women or to men without families. Marriage, therefore, granted men rights that alternative African-American households could not enjoy.[37] Before African-American men won the right to vote, the rights they demanded—as workers, as husbands and fathers, and as men—rested on their position as married men, as masters of their households.[38] They appropriated white men's traditional base of power.

As scholars Nancy Fraser and Linda Gordon argue, "in doing so, they were not simply demanding admission to a pre-existing status," in this case, that of propertied white manhood. "Rather," Fraser and Gordon continue, "they were challenging the grounds on which claims to social resources were made a fundamental aspect of the social order."[39] By claiming manhood rights as the heads of their households, African-American men challenged planters' assumptions of workingmen's dependency. They demanded a workingman's right to the cotton his family produced. Class and race, they argued, could not exclude them from the category of independent men.[40] They, too, had access to valuable property.

Freedwomen did not, and could not, claim rights based on a privileged position within the household. For example, freedwomen rarely contested the division of the cotton crop. Women and children might help produce the crop, but, in public, men represented family interests in the cotton. Cotton was the fruit of family labor. And "family," when it came to cotton, fell under a husband's authority. Women were named in only 15 of the 177 cases (see table 4), and most of those women were unmarried.[41] Instead, as the complaint files indicate, women upheld men's position as the public heads of the household.[42]

Freedwomen, however, did not concede all public space to their men, nor did they relinquish all authority over their households. African-American women instead pressed for rights on two fronts—as individuals and as kin. As individuals, freedwomen demanded their right to control their labor and to protect their bodies. These actions centered on the principle that all people possessed certain individual rights, regardless of their ties to others. The household, in their minds, did not strip them of personal independence. Under specific circumstances—when others attacked their right to their wages, their bodies, or their children—women aggressively defended themselves. In such cases, they did not count on fathers, husbands, or lovers to take their cases to court.

While according men the right to dispute the crop, African-American women aggressively defended their right to their wages. Apparently African-Americans in the Delta made a sharp distinction between the crop and cash wages. Technically, the cotton crop was a wage. At the beginning of the year, many workers agreed to work for a share of the crop. When it was sold, they would reap the profit. Cash wages differed from share wages in that the worker got a set price for his or her labor. Workers receiving cash wages did not gamble on the cotton market. Their employer owed them their pay, regardless of his personal profit. By and large, agricultural laborers contracted for share wages, while cooks, housekeepers, gardeners, and mechanics contracted for cash wages.[43]

Almost half of the cases filed by women centered on wages. Freedwomen, married or unmarried, did not rely on men to represent their interests in cash wage disputes. Instead, most assumed sole authority over what they must have defined as independent contracts. Every autumn, like clockwork, planters discharged wage workers from the plantation. Women, going to the Bureau, demanded their pay. In a typical case, May Edwards woke up one morning to find that her employer had skipped town just when her yearly wages were due. Traveling on foot to Friars Point, Edwards located the Bureau agent and reported that Mrs. F. G. Boyd "owed her 75 dollars for last years labor and that Mis Boyd had left the county permanently." Boyd, however, had left substantial personal property behind. The Bureau agent ordered the public sale of Boyd's property and paid May Edwards her wage.[44] Like Edwards, many women—single, married, sweethearts, and those who took up—personally contracted for their own labor. In doing so, these women, regardless of household structure, carved out a niche of personal space within the private domain of household. Moreover, to defend their personal interests, they willingly entered the public sphere of the courts. The crop and family property may have been designated men's responsibility, but women did not assume that this closed the door to public life. Rather than asking men to represent them, many women readily asserted themselves.

African-American women also aggressively defended themselves against assault. Violence often accompanied the request for back wages. One morning Jane Davis asked for her pay from her employer, Mrs. H. H. Camp. Camp refused. Davis proceeded to "insult her," so Camp picked up a fire shovel and proceeded to beat Davis repeatedly. Davis walked off and immediately reported the incident to the Federal authorities.

Chloe Taylor paid a greater price for asking for her wages. Her employer, Jarvis Keith, "struck her three times with a stick and kicked her in the abdomen causing her to lose the child she was carrying." Keith then proceeded to whip "her boy about eight years of age cruelly who is deaf and dumb." Refusing to backdown, Taylor picked herself up, gathered her son in her arms, and walked into Sardis and reported Keith. She was paid fifteen dollars in damages.[45] Many women did not permit anyone to beat them. They reported husbands, daughters, mothers, and neighbors for physical assault.[46] These women aggressively asserted their right to their own bodies, firmly defining their personal space. Marriage and employment might entail legal dependency, but freedwomen did not permit any claims of dependency to transgress their control over the body itself.

By readily filing complaints over wages and assault, freedwomen asserted their rights as individuals. Their actions demonstrate that, from their perspective, neither the marriage contract nor the labor contract placed them in a position of complete dependency. They were not "owned" by another. Instead, women defined both relationships as contracts where the individuals involved —husband and wife or employer and worker—had specific rights as well as obligations. This was a dramatic reversal from slavery. In the antebellum South, enslaved African-Americans had no rights (at least in theory) and no access to public space. With emancipation, many freedwomen quickly righted that wrong by acting as autonomous individuals within a relationship.

The rights within marriage, therefore, appear very clear-cut and sharply defined by gender. Men represented the family in disputes over the crop and personal property, while women represented themselves in disputes over wages and assault. In other words, men acted as heads of household while women retained rights over their individual interests.

Yet shifting the focus from rights to obligations complicates the picture. Freedwomen pressed for an alternative reading of citizenship based on their relationships with others—as a wife, mother, kin, or neighbor. In fact, women were twice as likely as men to act on behalf of a family member (see table 4). When the need arose, women went to court to defend their children, relatives, and, in rare cases, husbands. Men may have headed their households in matters concerning the crop, but women held recognized positions of authority within the family. Men did not assume complete responsibility for the family, even in the public sphere.

In December 1867, Nancy Ann Mead set out for Greenville to defend her family. Walking into the Freedmen's Bureau office, she reported that Joseph Bloodson refused to pay wages to both her husband and her daughter. Bureau agent William Tidball immediately wrote to Bloodson demanding that he pay his workers. Tidball received no response. Unwilling to let matters drop, Nancy Ann Mead once again traveled to Greenville, where she reported that Bloodson still refused to pay wages. Moreover, Mead noted, he was slyly shipping the crop in the dead of night from a landing downriver. Tidball again wrote a letter informing Bloodson that unless this behavior stopped and he paid his workers, he would face charges of fraud and theft.[47] The records report no further action.

In acting for her husband, Mead was unusual. Women, however, were much more aggressive than men in defending their children's interests. Twenty-two percent of the cases filed by women concerned their children. In contrast, only one percent of all cases filed by men were on behalf of their children.[48] Women reported employers for beating their children, for reneging on children's labor contracts, for refusing to pay wages, or for absconding with a child's portion of the crop.[49] So while freedwomen granted men the right to represent them, they did not relinquish all rights to represent themselves or their families.

Violence itself was an expression of dissent. In order to clearly distinguish their households from their former masters' households, some women and men relied on what they knew—violence.[50] In September 1867, Mary Johnson filed a complaint against her employer, John H. Evans. She reported that Evans had beaten her. Evans countered by claiming that he had beaten Johnson because she herself had beaten her son. Moreover, "the woman whipped the child, after he had forbidden her merely to provoke him." In other words, Mary Johnson beat her child to display her parental authority. She made it clear to Evans that he, a white man, no longer had any claims over her children. Emancipation, according to Mary Johnson, gave her rights of mastery.[51]

The complaint files demonstrate that women, more than men, acted on behalf of family members. And women, more then men, refused to be subjected to any form of personal violence. On the one hand, they attempted to carve out a space of personal privacy, refusing to permit anyone to touch them without their consent. Yet on the other hand, some women connected their personal right of self-determination with the entire community's right for its members to control their own labor.

Standing up for her friends and neighbors, Mrs. Tyrell risked her life by going to the Freedmen's Bureau. In 1866 the Tyrell family and their neighbors agreed to leave Vicksburg and return to the plantations, but only if they were permitted to supervise their own labor. Signing a contract, they traveled to the Murdock plantation in Sunflower County. There the landlord, Mr. Cooper, promptly put the freedpeople under the supervision of a white overseer, John Barkley. Since the terms of their contract had been violated, three men left the plantation in protest. One of these men, Elias Tyrell, was Mrs. Tyrell's son. Unable to find Elias and his comrades, Barkley beat Mrs. Tyrell "with a stick ... tied her thumbs & drew her up by them, he then told her to call him master." Undaunted, Mrs. Tyrell traveled to the nearest Bureau Office and "carried her contract with her. . . . [T]he Squire told her the contract was unlawful." Upon hearing this, the landlord sent Barkley to the Tyrrel cabin the next morning with a loaded pistol.[52]

The actions of Mrs. Tyrell—her refusal to submit to extreme intimidation and her active pursuit of her rights of contract—testify to freedwomen's vigorous involvement in plantation labor politics. Planters like Cooper viewed women and children as pawns. They subjected them to violent abuse in an effort to control "head men" and to demonstrate that landlords, not husbands and fathers, determined the fate of African-American families. Yet many women refused to cave in to the pressure. Instead, they demanded that the federal government, in the form of Freedmen's Bureau agents, uphold their rights of self-determination and the right of contract. After all, Mrs. Tyrell did not simply report personal violence. She carried her contract with her. In pursuing her complaint, she acted on behalf of the entire work force.

As historian Elsa Barkley Brown argues, freedwomen did not cede the public forum to men. Instead, Brown insists, women and children took their place as citizens alongside men.[53] The Delta's history, however, suggests that women defined rights on different terms than men. Women contested men's gendered definition of rights based on patriarchal assumptions of household authority.

Nathan Bedford Forrest, for example, murdered Tom Edwards in a dispute over mastery. Meeting in the quarters that Sunday, both Edwards and Forrest acted on their perceived rights of household. Forrest still defined "household" in the language of the plantation. He believed he had the sole authority to command the labor of every person residing on his property. Edwards, however, defined household closer to home. He demanded the right to oversee his own labor and the labor of his family. The one person who remains masked in the public record is Edwards's wife. Both Edwards and Forrest saw Mrs. Edwards as a symbol of their authority, a representation of their household rights. Yet Mrs. Edwards disputed this. She refused to obey Tom Edwards's command to "get him something to eat." She was no more willing to take orders than he was. Perhaps she, too, had paraded around the overseer's house that week behind the Spencer rifle.

Blocked from voting, women focused on the courts. By going to the Bureau—suing and being sued—women gave a clear public declaration of their rights and assumed their place as citizens. They claimed their civil rights. A citizen in their eyes included the sum of her parts—neighbor, mother, worker, kin. Women called for a social citizenship based on a relational identity—one that encompassed not just the individual but everything that made up an individual.[54]

African-American men and women expressed their rights differently. Men represented their households in crop disputes and in contests over property. Women, by and large, represented their households in cases of assault. Both freedmen and freedwomen claimed rights in relation to their households, but they expressed distinct visions of those rights. Men often claimed rights based on their position as the heads of their households—on their mastery over male-headed nuclear households. If married, women seem to have accepted men's right to represent them in crop disputes. Women, however, fought for recognition of their rights and authority over their own labor and over their children regardless of family structure. Rights, according to freedwomen, did not rest on the marriage covenant alone. Rights rested on individual freedom and on the responsibility of a mother, sister, aunt, grandmother to protect (and control) her family. In other words, women pressed the case for the alternative household. With or without husbands, they claimed that they still had rights over themselves and their families.

Southerners' responses to free labor, then, revealed distinct understandings of household rights and obligations. In claiming rights, planter men, planter women, freedmen, and freedwomen each expressed his or her unique definition of citizenship.

For planter men, rights rested in landownership. White men claimed the privileges of the past. The plantation, in their eyes, was still their private domain and subject to their rule. Looking back, one common thread ran through planters' contradictory reactions to African-American households: the belief that all property—both the land and the cotton produced on that land—properly remained concentrated in their hands. Encouraging a male-headed nuclear family proved critical to that end. Planters could better control labor by contracting primarily with African-American married men. By privileging the male-headed nuclear family, planters could squeeze alternative households off the land and reduce freedpeople's independent production of goods. Many planters, using contracts, employed property rights to construct a new foundation for mastery.

Planter women, supporting their men, assumed new rights to maintain family privilege under the Married Women's Property Act. Rather than challenge their husbands' authority, planter-class women worked to preserve entitlements based on race and class distinctions. Yet by opening the door to women's rights (and consequently the rights of dependents), the conservative legislature took a gamble. Under Radical Reconstruction poorer women, both black and white, attempted to claim rights, not as women alone, but as citizens.

Likewise, African-American men fought back. They claimed independence. As heads of their households, they asserted their rights to their wages, the crop, and their families. As men, they poised themselves to compete as equals with white men for full citizenship.

African-American women, by and large, ceded this ground to freedmen. Yet many disputed the sharp distinction between independence and dependence that the marriage relation implied. Household rights, from their perspective, promised more than manhood rights. Upholding the values of alternative households, they argued that all persons, whatever their status—married or unmarried, rich or poor, man or woman—deserved citizenship. In pressing their cases, they pushed the state to recognize and endorse the ties between kin, neighbors, man, woman, and child regardless of formal bonds.

Policing the boundaries of their households as they defined them, southerners laid claim to political and civil rights. Citizenship began at home and on the field of labor. Yet the questions remained: Which articulation of citizenship would Mississippi and the United States uphold? How would the politics of the household be represented by the state? To answer these questions, men and women in the Delta carried the household from the plantation to the public sphere. Their next battle centered on Reconstruction party politics.

7

❧

Legislating Rights

Citizens, "Legal Voters," and the Boundaries of the Household

*I*N 1867 AFRICAN-AMERICAN men voted for the first time in the state of Mississippi. The ramifications registered throughout every family. Universal manhood suffrage promised to disrupt racial hierarchies. Race and property no longer marked the free from the less free—the independent from the dependent. All men, as heads of their households, were created equal. Or were they? The household remained the seat of power in the Mississippi Delta. Yet it was by no means clear which households would be accorded power and on what terms. In 1871 Susan Dickerson took her stand. Dickerson, the daughter of a former slave and a former slaveholder, sued her white relatives to claim her father's property.

Susan Dickerson's father, L. P. Dickerson, died on February 2, 1871, leaving a large estate in Coahoma County in the western Delta. When he died, his brother W. N. Brown inherited his property. At this point Susan and her brother, Oliver, took Brown to court. They claimed that the 1869 Mississippi constitution made them the rightful heirs—that with freedom and with full citizenship, mixed-race families (including families created by slaveholders and slaves) had the legitimate right to their fathers' estates.

As the Dickersons' lawyers stated, Mary Ann and L. P. Dickerson never married "because at the time their intercourse commenced, marriage between a white man and a colored woman was prohibited by law." However, Susan and Oliver argued that "their father loved their mother devotedly, and that they were married in heart and by the laws of nature and love." Moreover, they claimed that the 1869 constitution legalized their parents' marriage. "The law, in its highest type," declared the Dickersons, "pronounced words more potent than those of any priest and made them flesh of one flesh."[1]

Brown's lawyers disagreed. They stated that L. P. and Mary Ann "knowingly

Fig. 12. Freedmen and freedwomen participated in politics, often expressing gendered definitions of citizenship. ("Electioneering," *Harper's Weekly*, 1868.)

and willfully chose to live together . . . in a state of fornication and concubinage,
as a roue and mistress, and not as a husband and wife." To declare such a relationship a marriage was absurd, Brown's attorneys submitted, because "he lived
with her as master while she a slave in concubinage." Regardless of the law, they
declared, marriage between black and white, master and slave was unthinkable:
"their disparity of rank and the degradation involved rebut any such presump-
tion, if not forbidden even by law." In other words, from Brown's perspective,
the laws of the state of Mississippi could not, and should not, be evenly applied
to all citizens.

The Dickersons countered. "Indeed there are no black and no whites in this
State, in contemplation of the law," they argued. "The State only knows its
citizens, as her children, and recognizes no difference between them." The
Mississippi Supreme Court justices agreed: "the law recognizes no distinction
on the account of color. Neither can the amount of property involved enter
at all into consideration. . . . Matters of taste and propriety, like this, the people
must determine for themselves within the established laws."[2]

Aghast, the white conservative press reported, "The decision throws the sanctity of the marriage tie around the beastly degradation of concubinage and says with King Lear, 'let copulation thrive.'" The jurists, according to the *Weekly Clarion,* were madmen by permitting "the alleged illegitimate offspring of a colored woman [to become] . . . the legitimate heirs of a white man."[3]

Dickerson v. Brown highlighted the place of the household in the reconstruction of rights in the postemancipation Delta. As the case made clear, Mississippians debated the basic rules by which citizenship could be guaranteed. First, could the state write and enforce laws that citizens and jurists would respect and obey? Second, could Mississippi create a legal system protecting everyone's rights equally, regardless of race? And third, would the interests of all people, regardless of class and property holdings, be represented by the state? The answer to each question circled back to whose household would be protected and on what terms.

Dickerson v. Brown threatened white conservatives' understanding of the household. For conservatives, the household was sacrosanct—a seat of private privilege. Power, in their minds, rested on the ability to command resources—which, after emancipation, meant the command of one's wife, children, and property. From their perspective, property and marriage were deeply enmeshed. A family could secure property only if it could successfully pass that property undisturbed from generation to generation. *Dickerson v. Brown* upset that flow of property by permitting children born outside of marriage— and, as conservatives stated, outside of the white race—to inherit wealth. The law placed whiteness, bloodlines, and class privilege at risk.[4] Conservatives declared any law that disturbed the boundaries between races, and to a lesser degree between classes, to be an unjust interference by the state in a private matter. To protect and perpetuate their rights as citizens and heads of their households, conservatives declared themselves above the law.

Radicals, by and large, also connected marriage with rights. In their view, however, rights originated with the individual, not with the family. A man, whatever his family's status or race, had the right to marry any unmarried woman. This right permitted him to pass property to his children. Moreover, radicals believed that all rights of property, of whatever size, should be protected by the state. Equality between men, they argued, rested on this principle.

Both the conservative and radical readings of citizenship ignored the alternative family structures that spanned sweethearting, taking up, extended families, and households based on friendships. To win her rights, Susan Dickerson had to "legitimate" her parents' marriage. She could not argue her case based on an alternative reading of household rights. Her case, therefore, marked a departure from the cases freedwomen filed with the Freedmen's Bureau in 1867 and 1868.

Alternative relationships disrupted the connection between property, marriage, and citizenship. By sweethearting, taking up, quitting, and forming single-sex households, many freedpeople recognized a wide range of dependencies. Articulating what can be termed "social citizenship," they understood that each person is dependent upon another.[5] A head of household, after all, is dependent on others both within and outside his home. The freedwomen who filed complaints with the Bureau defended the unfixed nature of identity—that one could be both subordinate to some and in a position of dominance to others. They contested a definition of rights based on a false dichotomy between independent and dependent.

This chapter explores how, from 1867 to 1875, the politics of the state restricted citizens' interpretations of the politics of the household. What was the basis for rights? What separated an independent person from a dependent person? Planters believed that independence lay in white manhood and landed property. Planter women, for the most part, agreed, understanding that their privilege and authority rested on preserving family ties. African-American men, by and large, believed that independence lay in their manhood—their ability to provide for and protect their families. Many freedwomen supported that position. Susan Dickerson, for example, defended her inheritance by supporting her father's right to provide for her. Other African-American women and men eschewed the distinction between independence and dependence. Defending the principles of the alternative households, they argued that each person, regardless of status, deserved protection and representation by the state. Of course, these issues were by no means clear in 1867. This chapter explores how each definition took on different shapes as the struggle for households entered the legislature and the courts.

"Give Justice to All Loyal Citizens": Congressional Reconstruction and Dissent to Conservative Rule

In March 1867, Congress stripped Mississippi of its sovereignty and placed the state under the military command of General Edward O. C. Ord.[6] Congress commanded Ord to prepare the state for a constitutional convention and to register African-American men to vote for the first time. Workers and planters understood that everything rested on the convention. The new constitution would determine who would write the labor laws and who would have access to the courts. At issue was the question of household and property.

With so much at stake, electoral politics turned brutal.[7] In January two Bureau agents had been murdered in Grenada and Greenville, setting the tone for the year.[8] Determined to keep black men from voting, Delta planters attacked emissaries from the federal government. By keeping registrars and Freedmen's Bureau agents away from their plantations, conservatives hoped that African-Americans would remain ignorant of their newly won rights. These actions demonstrated planters' blindness to the political momentum that had developed within freedpeople's households.

African-Americans already knew their rights. After two years of constant struggle for workers' rights, many freedpeople had sharpened their understanding of what was necessary. From April 1865 through March 1867, freedpeople had been denied wages, stripped of their share of the crop, and been beaten and robbed. They had responded by trying to sue their employers, strengthen their households, and carve out space for personal autonomy.

Yet often isolated, miles from any town and far removed from any form of protection, freedpeople risked their lives to register their men. Many planters fired any man or woman leaving the plantation to attend political meetings, and some planters threatened to shoot them. Freedpeople responded by reporting employers to the Bureau. In a complaint, five men from Yazoo County described their ordeal: "We live twenty miles from [Yazoo City] in the interior and we would state that we in many ways oppressed not being able to exercise the rights of Freemen," they explained. In July a Freedmen's Bureau agent had visited the plantation to inform freedmen of their right to vote. The men stated, "After his representation we wished to Register and we men informed by him that the Registers would be in Yazoo City. . . . We expressed our desire to Col Gilmor. . . . He refused permission." Gilmore, their employer, not only refused but also threatened to fine anyone who left the plantation. Furthermore, Gilmore warned that if the workers left the plantation "to attend politics or voting he would be prepared for us and would shoot the last one of us." Nonetheless, the men left the plantation the next day. Petitioning the federal government, they begged for the "promised protection of the military."[9]

Despite persistent violence, 60,167 blacks registered to vote in the state of Mississippi. Marching to the polls in November, close to 10,000 Delta freedmen elected at least five African-Americans to represent them in the 1868 constitutional convention.[10] For freedpeople, government was no longer an abstraction.

Equal Rights for Men: The Colorblind Household and the Extension of Patriarchy

The 1868 convention was responsible for framing Mississippi's second Reconstruction government. By order of the United States Congress, African-American and white men now shared full political rights, at least in theory. At issue was the practice of those rights. Would planter men be able to maintain their privileged position in the face of equal rights? Or would African-American representatives claim equal power? And how would equality be expressed? To answer these questions, representatives turned to their households to uphold their vision of manly authority as the basis for rights. Implicitly, legislators argued that citizenship began at home with a man's authority over his household.

From 1868 to 1874, four subjects dominated the discussion of male citizenship: property, marriage, interracial sexual relations, and school integration. By and large, African-American men worked to secure equal rights by extending the privileges of marriage and property rights to all men. Whether one was a former slave, a former slaveholder, a man who owned land, or a man who owned only the shirt on his back, basic property and marital rights should be respected. Men could then meet in public as equals, secure in their mastery over what they defined as basic rights—a family and property.

White conservatives countered by shifting the focus to race and the preservation of property. While they might be required to grant black men the right to head a black household, conservatives would make sure that the black household remained separate and apart from their own. Strong borders, they believed, would halt the flow of property and power from the white household to the black. The white, propertied household could be maintained if households and races never merged through intermarriage. Conservatives therefore consistently issued strong statements concerning sexual promiscuity, interracial sex, and—what they saw as the seedbed of race mixing—school integration.

Of the 100 delegates to the 1868 constitutional convention, 17 of the 71 Republicans were African-American. Five of the seventeen black men represented the Delta: Doctor Stites and William Combash from Washington County,

William Leonard from Yazoo County, and Thomas W. Stringer and Albert Johnson from Warren County.[11]

Together, Stringer and Stites pressed for legislation legitimating the African-American nuclear family. In the struggle over the boundaries of male citizenship, they ignored the alternative household. One of Stringer's first acts as a delegate was to restate Mississippi's commitment to recognizing slave marriages. He introduced a resolution stating: "All persons who are now, and have heretofore lived and cohabitated together as husband and wife, shall be taken and held, in law, as legally married and their issue shall be . . . held as legitimate."[12] The legal recognition of slave marriages accorded men rights as heads of household. The marriage contract also gave women and children legal rights to a deceased husband's property. As Jarrit Ware recalled, marriage was important to African-American men "so that should they die the wife and children could come in for their money."[13]

While supporting marriage, Stringer condemned informal relationships. His resolution stated that "concubinage and adultery are prohibited." In many ways, Stringer's prohibition of adultery and concubinage was pro forma. The antebellum marriage law used similar wording to the same effect. Yet Stringer's words carried additional meaning. When Stringer denounced "concubinage," he was denouncing "taking up" and "sweethearting"—relationships with a long history and a degree of legitimacy for most of his African-American constituents. As an A.M.E. minister, Stringer disapproved on religious grounds.[14] As a politician, he understood that alternative households left all African-Americans vulnerable to charges of immorality.

African-American households faced stinging condemnations in this period, especially from Freedmen's Bureau agents. In 1867 agent J. D. Webster in Rosedale reported, "The marital relations of the freedpeople are very loose. Marriages are infrequent and they 'take up' with each other and cohabit during mutual good pleasure." Agents charged freedpeople with "immoral" and "uncivilized" behavior, which marked African-Americans as a degraded "race of mankind." As legal historian Katherine Franke argues, these charges raised the question of whether African-Americans could be fit citizens. Stringer attempted to firmly answer these charges by raising the question himself and publically condemning alternative households.[15]

White conservatives went even further. Not all marriages were equal, they declared. The races must be kept separate. They demanded that all interracial marriages be outlawed. In pressing their position, white conservatives focused on "natural" differences. George Stovall, representing the conservatives, asserted, "The fact has been demonstrated by physiologists and long since settled as an axiom of science that the progeny resulting from an intermarriage between the white and black races, are very liable to a character of hereditary diseases." Interracial marriage, according to Stovall, was "destructive to human life." Therefore, he reasoned, "all good men of both races, who desire the perpetuation and prosperity of their respective races" should vote to outlaw interracial marriage. Essentially, Stovall represented African-Americans and European-Americans as separate species. Black and white men might share rights, but, in Stovall's mind, natural law barred any assumption that they were alike.[16] Equality was a man-made conceit.

Interracial marriage endangered the synthesis between whiteness and privilege. The issue placed whiteness, status, and property at risk. If women married outside their race and class, a family's property, accumulated over generations, might be dispersed. Worse, whiteness itself would be erased. Interracial marriages threatened to invade the seat of white men's dominion in every sphere—family, land, and race privilege. To be sure, the conservative 1865 legislature had paved the way for this loosening of men's authority within their household. The 1867 Married Women's Property Act, one of the last acts of that conservative lawmaking body, weakened white men's patriarchal privileges—their ultimate control over property—by granting new authority to their wives. Yet conservatives never intended to extend this privilege to all men and to all marriages, particularly interracial ones.

African-American legislators offered a complex response to the Stovall resolution. Several African-American delegates supported the law banning interracial marriage. They pointedly amended the Stovall resolution, however. They argued that interracial marriages *and relationships* should be outlawed. And they raised the punishment for such crimes. Matthew Newsom, an African-American representing Claiborne County, introduced the amendment. He asked that both "concubinage and miscegenation" be made illegal and that any man found guilty of either should be stripped of his citizenship. Newsom, in essence, forced white men to officially recognize, and then criminalize, the practice of having sexual intercourse with African-American women. Newsom pushed the idea of manhood equality to its logical conclusion.

At this point Doctor Stites, an African-American from Washington County, objected. A marriage between a white woman and a black man, he argued, could not be equated with the sexual relationship between a white man and a black woman. According to Stites, the white man committed a graver crime. Stites stated that "white men living with and cohabitating with females of color, except under and by virtue of the rights of marriage, are guilty of a greater crime than that of adultery."[17] Stites proposed that such a crime should "disqualify [white men] from the rights of citizenship." Stites did not elaborate. White men's actions could be considered a greater trespass on several levels. First, not all African-American women consented to these relationships. Was Stites representing their rights? Second, by labeling these acts a "greater crime than that of adultery," Stites drove home the point that these men did not intend to marry their sexual partners and accept the responsibilities of a head of household. Finally, these acts could be considered criminal because these men, by not marrying, were not legally bound to take responsibility for their children or leave them portions of their estate. While it remains unclear whether Stites was referring to one or all three of the above interpretations, his meaning apparently rang clear to the men who witnessed his speech. Stites's proposal killed Stovall's conservative resolution. Every African-American delegate, except for Newsom, changed his vote. They defeated the amendment. Interracial marriages would be legal under the 1868 constitution.[18] Manhood rights rested on marriage, not race.

Susan Dickerson would use the final outcome of this act to lay claim to her white father's property. She rightfully claimed that the common-law marriage between a slaveholder, her father, and a slave, her mother, became legally binding when both long-term relationships and interracial marriages became recognized by law. Property, under this law, could descend to all children.

Attacking the issue of property head on, Charles Caldwell, an African-American delegate from Hinds County, worked to secure assets freedpeople had acquired during slavery. Under antebellum law, no slave could legally own property. Yet both masters and slaves informally recognized that enslaved African-Americans owned property ranging from livestock and personal possessions to cotton and other commodity crops. Caldwell declared that after the Civil War "[g]reat frauds have been committed in this way by evil-disposed white persons, in seizing and taking away, and appropriating to themselves said property without regard to right and justice." Caldwell called on the Constitutional Convention to recognize former slaves' rights to property acquired after the Emancipation Proclamation, and asked the courts to "mete out equal and exact justice to said colored persons in protecting them in their lawful rights." The convention agreed, requesting that the commanding general of Mississippi issue a special order commanding that freedpeople be compensated for their stolen property.[19]

In many ways, the Caldwell amendment represented the alternative economy established largely by freedwomen during the Civil War. The property that Caldwell referred to in his resolution—cotton, corn, horses, cows, pigs, chickens—had served as a cornerstone of freedom. By relying on the expansion of their own property, members of the fluid and flexible households that developed on the plantations had managed to avoid wage work, to some degree. Planters' usurpation of that property at the war's end had forced freedpeople to depend heavily on wages and had helped push flexible households off the land.

Yet the Stringer amendment tempered the far-reaching effects of Caldwell's resolution. Stringer's amendment condemning informal relationships permitted marriage to trump women's property rights. By converting informal households into legal households, the Stringer amendment placed women under the authority of their husbands. By law, husbands subsumed freedwomen's legal identity in ways that sweethearts could not. Marriage restricted women's property rights. The black household benefited (property would be protected), but it was primarily the male-headed nuclear household that reaped these advantages.

Continuing to push the issue of property, Republican delegates encouraged the state to broaden the Homestead Act to protect working families. The question centered on whether the "poor of this State should be afforded the same relief from debt as their more wealthy neighbors." Republicans proposed that "each and every head of family" be able to keep 160 acres of land, his or her home, five hundred dollars of personal property, and "the wearing apparel of each and every member of the family." Should a crop fail, working men and women would not be stripped of all their worldly possessions. This amendment significantly broadened the Homestead Act. Even landless people could claim rights to property. To further protect workers, the delegates stipulated: "No property shall be exempt from execution for . . . the wages of the laborer." In other words, even if it meant the loss of land, employers must pay workers.[20] Once again the new Homestead Act did not protect married women who could lose their homes should their husbands fall into debt.

In one of the last acts of the convention, William Stringer offered an amendment regarding public schools. Stringer asked the convention to consider four months of mandatory schooling for every child under the age of fifteen. Compulsory schooling would assure that every child learn the basic reading and mathematical skills required to negotiate business transactions and become an informed citizen. Stovall, a white conservative, immediately countered with an amendment to Stringer's resolution. Stovall agreed to compulsory education "*Provided* That separate schools for white and colored children be maintained in each district." The African-American delegates agreed, voting in a group to pass the resolution. Stovall, however, along with thirty-three other delegates, voted to drop the resolution, and it failed.[21] Conservatives apparently had hoped that the issue of segregation would divide Republicans. When their tactic failed, they quashed the bill. School would not become compulsory in Mississippi for another fifty years.

Throughout the 1868 Constitutional Convention, George Stovall raised the issue of race to polarize black and white Republicans and to galvanize Democrats. Stovall's resolutions repeatedly warned that interracial politics would lead to interracial sexual relationships. If black and white children attended school together, he feared, the color line would dissolve. Whites and blacks would learn to respect each other and possibly marry. Cultures and bloodlines would merge. Stovall, in other words, believed that political rights could not be separated from the intimate relations of the household. This was the lesson of his youth, after all. Raised in the antebellum South, Stovall had learned that his privileged position as a white man stemmed from his domestic authority over others—male and female, black and white. By 1867, however, black men shared manhood rights and obligations with white men, and Stovall served with them as equals at the Constitutional Convention. Household authority no longer set white men apart from all others, only whiteness did. And, as Stovall understood, whiteness could be an ephemeral category unless ruthlessly policed.

The Politics of Whiteness: Ratification of the 1868 Constitution

White conservatives interpreted the 1868 constitution as a direct assault upon their political rights. Their task lay in persuading all white men that privileges based on whiteness were at risk.

Planters, however, feared that the boundaries of whiteness were unclear. The 1868 constitution, after all, benefited all poorer Mississippians, regardless of color. Conservatives could not be certain that white men would vote along the color line. To unite white men, planters had to redefine the politics of household.

To appeal to white workingmen, conservatives abandoned property as a qualification for political rights. Instead they spoke of whiteness as the marker of freedom. Centering their argument on "whiteness," conservatives attempted to supplant mastery with race. Before the war, in times of crisis, the planter elite had employed "mastery" to build consensus among white men. They had reminded poorer white men that they—as heads of their households—stood apart from all others as the masters of women, children, and slaves.[22] Whiteness was part of this equation. After all, southern laws denied citizenship to all black men, whether slave or free.

By 1868, however, the call to mastery worked against the elite. Suddenly black men were masters, full citizens, and enfranchised voters. Planter men discovered that if they maintained mastery as the basis for privilege, then white men would be outnumbered. Mastery, moreover, offered limited appeal to white workingmen. According to antebellum law and the conservative Black Codes, laborers and the landless did not enjoy full legal privileges. The laws classified them as dependent men, beholden to their employers and therefore subject to an employer's private regulation.

To build a new foundation for political privilege, Democratic party leaders dropped the language of dependency based on social relations—which had formerly included workers, women, and slaves—to emphasize a biological dependency based on blackness and gender. At a convention of the ultraconservative Democratic White Man's Party, members declared that the Republican Party's "nefarious design . . . [is to] degrade the Caucasian race as the inferiors of the African race." This convention called "upon the people of Mississippi to vindicate alike the superiority of their race over the negro and their political power to maintain constitutional liberty."[23] Conservatives rallied white men around the issue of Article 7, Section 5 of the 1868 constitution, which disenfranchised some former Confederates.[24] Democrats argued that Article 7 revealed an intent to disenfranchise all white men while empowering black voters. African-Americans, according to the conservatives, were not "the people of Mississippi." Meeting in April, the Democrats declared the 1868 Constitutional Convention unconstitutional because "the delegates [were] not . . . elected by qualified voters of the state but by negroes destitute alike of moral and intellectual qualifications." Moreover, the Democrats declared, the Constitutional Convention "wickedly conspir[ed] to disenfranchise and degrade the people, and rob them of their liberty and property, to destroy their political and social status, and finally, to place them under the yoke of negro government." Likening themselves to Revolutionary War heroes, the Democratic Party encouraged the formation of "committees of correspondence" and "vigilance committees" to ensure white liberty. Conservatives called on all white men to join "White Men's Clubs for the purpose of adopting and recommending to the White Man of Mississippi, the best plans and means to defeat the Radical Constitution."[25] Issuing a solemn warning, the Democratic Executive Committee declared: "Freedmen of Mississippi, look before you leap. There is an awful gulf yawning before you. . . . If you abandon the people with whom you have ever lived and who invite you to their protection in the future, you cast your destiny with an enemy between whom and us there is eternal war."[26]

Obliterating the boundaries between public and private, the Ku Klux Klan targeted any white man or black who spoke out. Representatives from the 1868 Constitutional Convention were marked as the enemy and persecuted. D. N. Quinn, a white delegate, returned home from the convention to find that all of his mail had been opened and those constituents to whom he had written had been forced out of the county. His letters were then read at an open forum "in order to excite the public mind against me."[27] As it turned out, this was a relatively mild response.

Seizing command, conservatives rejected the authority of the law, the state, and the federal government. Legal authorities had no control. In Yazoo County, L. Galinger hurriedly reported, "Kidnappers & possible murderers of freedmen at large. Sheriff . . . unable to reach them because of overflow." When Bureau agents attempted to help the freedpeople, they faced retribution. Allen Huggins, in Greenwood, traveled to John Pollard's plantation after being summoned by a freedman, Jim Pate. As Huggins tried to register Pate's complaint, Pollard "struck me in the face twice with his fist and then caught me by the throat and choked me down. As I lay on the [office] floor. he stamped my person." Huggins concluded his report by stating very matter-of-factly, "it seems to be a very difficult matter to convince these (*people*) that I possess any authority whatever." In a later report, Huggins declared: "I wish to break up this brute force, one-man-law-making power."[28]

According to Bureau agents stationed throughout the Delta, the Democratic Party's combined tactic of race baiting and terror worked to mobilize white voters. White southerners, regardless of class, responded to the call of whiteness. "Three murders of Freedmen . . . one committed by . . . the so called Ku Klux . . . also a great number of whippings, all more or less traceable to political differences" had occurred, according to Bureau agent William Wedemeyer.

There was, he continued, "a sistematic persecution of the colored people on account of political creed." The political creed, however, was whiteness. Wedemeyer believed that race outweighed any differences among white Mississippians. "Against the freedmen," Wedemeyer reported, "the majority of the whites are a Unit and even honorable men otherwise will vouch for persons of . . . doubtful character."[29] In attempting to dominate public and private spaces by any means necessary, many white men acted on the stated principles of the Democratic Party. They dismissed any government that included African-American citizens.

African-Americans, however, refused to renounce their citizenship or to concede public space to white terrorists. Together, African-American men and women asserted their right to political space. To recruit members and get out the vote, Republicans organized lively parades with brightly colored banners, flags, and marching bands that traveled from town to town. In Yazoo City, white southerners fiercely attacked these marchers, murdering one young man and wounding dozens. In self-defense the marchers began carrying guns, which sent the white community into a frenzy. Whites, an observer recalled, threatened a "wah [sic] of races."[30]

Despite the level and intensity of violence in the Delta, the region approved the 1868 constitution by a vote of 8,611 to 3,557.[31] The state, however, rejected ratification by 7,629 votes. As a result, Mississippi reverted to military rule under the leadership of General Alvan Gillem, a Democratic sympathizer. The national election, however, placed Republican Ulysses S. Grant in the presidency, and one of his first acts was to replace Gillem with General Adelbert Ames, a staunch Republican.

In the fall of 1869, a revised version of the Mississippi State Constitution was placed on the ballot, stripped of the clause disenfranchising former Confederates. The revised constitution was easily "ratified by a vote of 113,735 to 995."[32] Mississippi rejoined the Union. Republicans, moreover, controlled the legislature.

Gendered Rights: Legislation and the Courts, 1870–1874

The Republican legislature, building on the agenda established by the 1868 Constitutional Convention, pushed to protect property rights while privileging marriage. In doing so, lawmakers struggled with an inherent contradiction. Many workers were married women. Could wives, as workers, have rights, independent of their husbands? If so, could marriage be maintained as the foundation of social order? Wrestling with these questions, lawmakers rewrote the laws of the state. The result was the 1871 Revised Code.

The Revised Code extended workers' rights by strengthening the lien laws, the Homestead Act, and the Married Women's Property Act. First, the 1871 Code upheld the existing lien laws. Employers, by law, had to pay their workers before paying off other creditors. Second, the Homestead Exemption Act was carried over from the 1867 legislative session. Householders could not lose their homes if they fell into debt. Moreover, the loose terminology of "householder" protected both male-headed and female-headed households. Finally, the legislators expanded the Married Women's Property Act to protect wives' rights to real and personal property acquired before or during a marriage. For the first time in Mississippi history, the act stipulated that a married woman had the right to the "fruits of her personal service"—a language vague enough to suggest that married women might have the right to their own wages. Technically, rich and poor families could use these acts to protect their wages, their homes, and some capital assets from seizure should a husband fall into debt.[33] The 1871 Code thus expanded both workers' and married women's rights.

The Code, however, protected only certain workers and certain households. The law protected wage workers, but remained suspicious of the independent poor. In particular, lawmakers heavily regulated hawkers and peddlers. Licenses to sell goods on foot or from a wagon cost between ten and fifty dollars. The state imposed a hundred-dollar fine for selling without a license, and fined people ten dollars for not carrying the license with them. To secure an independent livelihood, many poorer African-American women had relied on selling pies and cakes as well as garden produce. Few managed to secure licenses for these businesses, and the Revised Code made them extremely vulnerable to law enforcement.[34]

Moreover, the lawmakers discouraged the alternative households that had provided another mainstay for nonelite single women. According to the 1871 Code, the marriage relation was the only legitimate relationship between a man and woman. First, legislators reminded citizens that all "persons who were living together as husband and wife, (although not married), at the time of the adoption of the present constitution" were legally married and could not remarry without a divorce. Second, anyone ignoring this law and marrying another without a divorce would be tried as a bigamist and harshly punished. Finally, any man and woman cohabiting would be charged with fornication. In other words, the state outlawed alternative households based on sweethearting and taking up.[35] The Revised Code expanded rights for married men and women while leaving people who were outside the marriage relation vulnerable.

Unwilling to accept this narrow construction of rights, some women, black and white, pushed Mississippi to recognize their full rights as citizens regardless of gender or household structure. The dynamic interplay between the courts and the legislature worked to rapidly expand workers' and women's rights.

In 1871 Josephine Thoms tested the gender-neutral language of the Homestead Act. Josephine Thoms and Henry A. Thoms had an acrimonious marriage, made even worse by failing finances. When it became clear to Henry Thoms that he was on the verge of bankruptcy, he sold the Thoms house to his brother. Then Henry filed for bankruptcy. Finding herself abandoned by her husband and evicted by her brother-in-law, Josephine filed suit against her husband and claimed that Henry had no right to sell their family home. She called on the Homestead Act to represent her interests. The 1867 Homestead Act protected the home of anyone "male or female, being a householder and having a family" from bankruptcy sale. While Josephine did not own the house, she claimed that she became the householder when Henry abandoned her. His lawyers protested, "But there cannot be two heads to the family of H. A. Thoms." The judge concurred. By law, a wife could not claim her home as her property as long as her husband was alive. Yet Josephine Thoms's case caught the attention of the court. Judge C. J. Simrall urged the state legislature to act to broaden married women's rights.[36]

The people and the legislature responded. In 1873 voters went to the polls again and elected a more radical Republican legislature.[37] Heeding Judge Simrall, the new legislature revised the Homestead Act and changed its language to specifically protect women's rights. In 1871 the law had protected "householders." In 1873 the legislators chose the explicit wording "That it shall not be lawful for a married man to sell or otherwise dispose of his homestead without the consent of his wife."[38] By taking her case to court, Josephine Thoms earned married women the right to keep their homes. Husbands still acted for the family, but wives now had a limited legal right to intervene in family affairs.

In the same legislative session, Mississippi lawmakers strengthened the Married Women's Property Act. The 1871 law protected a woman's rights to the "fruits of her personal service," but the language was vague. In 1873 legislators changed the law to refer directly to wages. They wrote that "the wages and compensation of married women for services and labor done and performed by them shall be free from the debts and control of their husbands."[39] For the first time, married women legally owned their own wages and could rightfully sue employers in their own name. Of course, in 1867 and 1868 many African-American women had done exactly that. Yet, in 1873 they had the legal right to do so.

The expansion of women's rights culminated in a recognition of women's citizenship and their active participation, at least in part, in local government. In 1874 the state passed the Vinous and Spirituous Liquors Law, which gave women the right to help regulate liquor consumption in their neighborhoods. The law stated that no one could be granted a license to sell liquor without the approval of a majority of the citizens. For the first time in Mississippi history, women were explicitly included in the category "citizen." A licensee needed the "genuine signatures, or . . . genuine marks of . . . the majority of male citizens over twenty-one years of age and a majority of the female citizens over eighteen years of age."[40] This far-reaching legislation made women instrumental in either granting or denying liquor licenses. As a Republican newspaper declared, "Here we have . . . a very distinct recognition of female suffrage."[41]

Initially, conservatives met the law with relative silence.[42] When the law came up for a vote in the Mississippi Senate, one senator pressed to change the term "female citizen" to "female resident." Yet this amendment never came up for a vote. In Congress, Representative Mosely was more explicit. He declared, "I vote no, because I believe it unjust for women to control men, and as I was created first, women have no right to say what man shall do or what he shall not do." Still, the bill passed.[43]

Unable or unwilling to defeat the bill in Congress, Democrats took their case to court. *John J. Rohrbacher v. Mayor and Aldermen of the City of Jackson* tested the constitutionality of the temperance law. Rohrbacher, a hotel owner, filed suit against the city for refusing to accept his petition for a liquor license. Along with his license application, Rohrbacher had submitted a list of only male citizens' signatures. Based on the new law, the city denied his application. Rohrbacher claimed that the law was unconstitutional because, first, the law was passed illegally and, second, the law granted women suffrage rights. The courts upheld the law on both the local and Supreme Court level. Several attorneys, however, went on record expressing disapproval of the rulings. By giving a voice to women, lawyer Frank Johnston wrote, "the act gives to females (minor females) the right of voting, and it violates the constitution. It gives them a controlling voice in this great question of domestic policy." Judge Jonathan Tarbell agreed. He wrote that "the legislature of Mississippi in submitting the granting or refusing of license to females was attempting . . . to delegate its authority to a 'new agency.'" He declared that the legislators created a new class of voters to do their bidding, thereby circumventing "the legal voters, the people." Women were not legal voters, nor were they, in Tarbell's mind, included in the phrase "the people." He cast them out of the body politic.[44] The law, however, held firm. The Republicans' construction of woman's citizenship remained in place.

The Vinous and Spirituous Liquors Law upheld women's citizenship. Yet by connecting women's rights with temperance, the law reinforced women's rights within a language of dependency. Judge Simrall, defending the law, argued that women should be granted this right to limit alcohol consumption, not as genderless citizens, but as relatively defenseless dependents. He stated, "Females who participate [in regulating alcohol] have attained a marriageable age, and are profoundly concerned that those with whom their future may be linked be surrounded with influences that contribute to sobriety, thrift and prosperity."[45] The law, in other words, granted women this right—and this right alone—because of their unique status within marriage.

The reinforcement of dependency carried long-term consequences for women of both races and for African-Americans regardless of gender. The implications became immediately evident in the courts and the legislature. In 1875, in a landmark case cited by generations of future lawyers, Mary Garland filed suit against her husband, William H. Garland, testing the limits of both the Homestead Act and the Married Women's Property Act. The Garlands married in 1855. In 1867 they separated. Later they resumed conjugal relations, then finally separated again in 1871. William disappeared. Mary remained in the family home (as guaranteed by the new Homestead Act) and took in boarders. However, Mary could not support herself and their two daughters on this limited income. Calling for justice, Mary asked the courts to give her William's land so that she could maintain her family. There was only one problem. Mary was not covered by the Married Women's Property Act. Mary never held any property in her own name. The court could not simply give her William's property. Moreover, as a married woman, she could not sue her husband. She was a *feme covert*—a legal nonentity.

The presiding judge, Tarbell, faced a bitter truth. Quoting Judge Mills, the Mississippi justice wrote that "it is clear that a strong moral obligation must lie on every husband, who has abandoned his wife, to support her. . . . To fail to do so is a wrong acknowledged at common law." Yet "the law knows no remedy, because there the wife cannot sue her husband." Establishing a precedent that still holds today, Judge Tarbell granted Mary (and all women unwillingly abandoned by their husbands) the status of a *feme sole*. By regaining her legal independence, Mary could sue William for support. She had no claim to his property, but Judge Tarbell ruled that she had a right to demand the "enforcement of the marriage contract . . . to the extent of maintenance."[46]

If a husband reneged on his duty as the head of the household, a wife could step in and take his place. *Garland v. Garland* moved married women's rights beyond property rights. The court fully emancipated Mary Garland. A married woman could head a household, though only in a time of extreme duress and then only if her reputation was beyond reproach.[47]

The court protected Mary Garland, not as a citizen, but as a vulnerable woman. The emphasis on reputation threatened the sanctity of the household. Only certain households deserved rights and protection from the state. Others became susceptible to outside intrusion.

Violet Maples, an African-American mother, discovered this in 1873 when she sued her father. That winter, her fifteen-year-old son Boss Maples left her home in Alabama and moved in with his grandfather, Ambrick Maples, in Mississippi. Violet protested. She believed that her father, Ambrick, was holding Boss against his will. So she filed suit to free her son and have him returned to her. The DeSoto County Chancery Court ruled in Violet's favor.

At that point, Ambrick Maples appealed to the Mississippi Supreme Court. Reversing the lower court's judgment, Judge Tarbell focused on Violet's private life. "Violet Maples," he wrote, "is the mother of seven children by different fathers. . . . her position, her employment [as a cook], and character, offer no guarantee of proper care." He continued, "Ambrick Maples, the grandfather, is apparently a respectable farmer." Tarbell rejected Violet's suit because he did not regard her household as legitimate.[48] It is by no means clear that Violet's neighbors would have made the same judgment. Violet Maples's perception of household clashed with the court's. She lost. The court intruded into her household and turned her son over to her father. The court deemed Maples an undeserving woman.

Because she had children by several men, Violet Maples lost custody over her son. Sexual propriety served as a keyword, separating the deserving from the undeserving. Yet the emphasis on respectability does not tell the whole story. Violet Maples lost custody for another reason as well. The court pointed to the fact that Violet was a cook while her father, Ambrick, was a "respectable farmer." As a domestic worker, the court classified Violet as a dependent person, undeserving of even the most basic right to her child. Not all workers were equal.

Neither, apparently, were all dependent people. The definition of dependency shifted under Republican rule, reflecting a complex reordering of the household. On one hand, household dependents gained rights, something that would have been unthinkable in a slave society. Married women won the right to their wages and the right to head a household in the case of abandonment. Both rights upset a man's undisputed mastery over his wife. Without slavery, the need to protect a husband's ultimate authority within his household weakened. On the other hand, as the case of Violet Maples demonstrates, dependents outside the marriage relation remained vulnerable and without rights. With property Ambrick Maples won custody, but without property Violet Maples was judged as having and deserving little. Still, in taking her case to court, Maples did not see herself as a woman without rights. Citizenship, in her mind, did not rest in property or marriage.

Thus by 1873, the open debate between citizens and the legislature and the courts gave rise to competing visions of rights. Women, including Josephine Thoms, Mary Garland, Violet Maples, and temperance activists, stepped into the public forum and effected change for better and worse. To halt the promiscuous mixing of voices and visions, Democrats launched a conservative revolution.

Maintaining Whiteness: The Conservative Revolt

Rallying under the banner of the white family, unreconstructed southerners launched a violent overthrow of the government in 1873. They asked white Mississippians to lend them full support by rejecting democratically elected officials. If whites failed to act, conservatives warned, the white family would cease to exist.

To appeal to white men and women alike, conservatives argued that Republicans threatened the sanctity of the home. After all, the legislature had recognized women as citizens, emancipated married women at least in part, and legalized common law marriages. In other words, the rights of household had been extended indiscriminately while the power of the head of the household had been reduced. By opening the household to state control, Republicans had endangered the family. Nowhere, conservatives argued, was this more apparent than in the 1873 Civil Rights Act. Slipping easily from the question of moral fitness to the issue of white supremacy, conservatives racialized the question of household.

In 1873 the Mississippi House passed a civil rights bill prohibiting "proprietors of hotels, theatres, or other places of amusement, common carriers, etc., from making any distinction on account of color." Conservatives labeled the bill perverse. "It is an attempt to compel association between races," a newsman opined, "in violation of natural laws, and in disregard of peace and good order. ... its authors ... insist on legislating colored people into association unnatural with whites."[49] That "unnatural association," conservatives feared, would lead to integrated schools and, as a consequence, interracial marriage. "I have silently looked on and watched the manoevering of the Black and Tan public school system," reported a Lee County resident, "which alone is enough to make a decent devil blush."[50] The *Weekly Clarion* stated, "They would rather see their children grow up in ignorance. [Integrated schools] would break down every public institution of learning in the country, and create a hatred between the races that will end in the extermination of the colored race." In another piece the editors warned, "It is the very thing to create 'agitiation' and destroy 'peace.' Our people ought not, and will not tamely submit to it."[51]

Conservatives simultaneously attacked on three fronts. They attempted to overthrow democratic elections, reduce access to the courts, and drive citizens from the polls. First, they contested the 1873 local election with a show of force. In Yazoo County, an armed mob prevented the newly elected sheriff, A. T. Morgan, from taking office. For conservatives, Morgan represented the social dangers of Republican rule.

Morgan had arrived in the Delta as a Union officer and settled in Yazoo County after the war. He had supported the education of freedpeople, opening schools on his plantation and contributing lumber to build others throughout the community. In 1870, he had cemented his close bond with the Yankee schoolteachers in his community by marrying Carrie Highgate, an African-American teacher from Syracuse, New York.[52] In January 1874, Morgan "made a formal demand ... for the Sheriff's office." Francis P. Hilliard, the standing sheriff, "declined to surrender it." The next day, Morgan appeared at the courthouse to assume his new office. He informed former deputy Frank Dyer "that I had my certificate of election to the office ... had given bond, and was recognized by the Board of Supervisors as the lawful sheriff." Dyer left the office and sounded the courthouse bell. At that moment, Hilliard and "25 or 30 of his friends" arrived outside the courthouse. Outnumbered, Morgan ran around the side of the building while Hilliard and his men "threw themselves with great force against the [courthouse] door, breaking it open. The deputies inside fired, and Hilliard received two wounds, one fatal." At that point, Morgan surrendered himself to the mayor and was jailed for murder. In a letter to the governor from the Yazoo County jail, Morgan wrote, "My colored friends are true as steel. They watch the street corners and by ways, and even guard the jail to prevent assassination." A lynch mob was fully expected, but the Republicans stood their ground. Morgan was found not guilty, but still feared for his life. "Let me beg you to send some sort of relief to Yazoo at once. Should these demons get once at it the lives of my wife and children would be sacrificed beyond a doubt."[53]

Morgan was right to fear for his family and other citizens. The Yazoo City *Banner* sounded a familiar tone: "Mississippi is a white man's country, and by Eternal God we'll rule it."[54] He understood that the 1870 riots in Meridian and Grand Parish could be repeated in Yazoo. "[C]an you not see, Governor," he pleaded, "that these men are but preparing for such another slaughter?"[55] Yazoo was spared in 1874, but would not be so lucky in 1875.

Second, the Democrats targeted the court system. To limit poor people's access to justice, Washington County Democrats attempted to block the creation of additional county courts. Mob action was not an option. Unlike Yazoo, Washington County had a large black majority. So rather than taking up arms, its Democrats tried to use the political process to block Republican reforms. From 1869 to 1874, four African-American men served in prominent law enforcement positions in Washington County. John Harris and Oliver Winslow acted as justices of the peace, John Werles served as district attorney, and J. Allen Ross and Winslow both served terms as sheriff. In February 1874, Sheriff Ross proposed instituting a county court in Greenville. For generations, the citizens of Greenville were forced to make the long trek upriver to Friars Point to try their cases. The trip was expensive. Consequently, many civil cases fell beyond the reach of the less well off. A local court would bring justice closer to home. Democrats organized to crush the proposal. They ostracized, humiliated, and intimidated white Republicans, hoping to drive them into the Democratic Party. Their efforts failed, and the court bill passed.[56]

Whites, however, had been warned. Colonel James Lusk remarked, "No white man can live in the South in the future and act with any other than the Democratic party unless he is willing and prepared to live a life of social isolation."[57] The *Hinds County Gazette* made voters' options clear: "All other means having been exhausted to abate the horrible condition of things, the thieves and robbers and scoundrels, white and black, deserve death and ought to be killed."[58]

Finally, conservatives launched a civil rebellion, driving citizens from the polls. Mississippi's governor, Adelbert Ames, observed, "The old rebel forces are being re-organized, not under the name of the Ku Klux but as the White League." He continued, "The White Leaguers or White Man's Party are emboldened by a belief amounting to a conviction that they will not be interfered with by the National Government lest their deeds be ever dark."[59]

In the Delta, white conservatives tested the strength and determination of the state government by invading Coahoma County. Unlike Tallahatchie County to its east, Coahoma had a large black majority. This situation, along with Coahoma's relatively strong Republican party, posed a threat to white citizens of Tallahatchie.[60] Thus when two black men attempted to register to vote in Tallahatchie, they were greeted by armed members of the Democratic Party who chased them into Coahoma. Thereupon, the Tallahatchie [County] Democratic Party "committed other illegal and outrageous acts upon the citizens of Coahoma County irrespective of color." Fearing reprisal, the Tallahatchie men returned home and gathered "white citizens of this and adjoining counties to the number of five hundred, armed . . . to force their way into Coahoma and 'kill every negro on 20 miles square.'" The sheriff of Coahoma County wrote to Ames "earnestly request[ing] assistance of the government and that very speedily as all order is overthrown." [61]

By 1875 a black man risked his life if he attempted to vote in the Delta. In Yazoo County, freedman Houston Burris wrote the governor, "They have hung six men since the killing of Mr. Fawn. They won't let the Republicans have know ticket they will not print any at all. For they plan to have a war tomorrow the Democrats are going to vote themselves and tell the Republicans they shant vote Now they are going to have a war here tomorrow—Send Help . . . help—help—help—soon as you can." Burris closed, "Send help—Troops—I would telegraph you but they wont let Mr. Richman go in the office."[62]

Ames had no troops to send. In one of his final speeches to the Legislature, he remarked that "the evil is attributed to a race question. . . . How far this effort has resulted in the virtual disenfranchisement of one race, and revolutionized the state government is worthy of inquiry. . . . our government proves unequal to its pretensions . . . unless every class of Citizens be thoroughly protected in the exercise of all their rights and privileges."[63] The rest of the nation, and the South in particular, watched Mississippi with great interest. To usher in a ninety-year rule of white party politics, Democrats across the South imitated the violent tactics of the Mississippi conservatives. They labeled their actions the Mississippi Plan.

Reinscribing Household Authority: Race and Respectability

Democrats soundly defeated Republicans through force and violence during the 1875 elections. Yazoo County, with an African-American majority, recorded only seven votes for Republicans. A former state representative from Yazoo, James M. Dixon, reported that he was "warned by armed Democrats not to campaign for the Republican Party." James G. Patterson did not heed that warning. White Leaguers murdered Patterson in Yazoo County while he still held the office of state representative. Noah Parker, a standing justice of the peace and Republican organizer in Issaquena County, also lost his life. Countless other political activists fled the region. In the Delta, only three African-Americans won office in the Mississippi Congress, compared with eighteen in 1873.[64]

Almost immediately the courts began to test the application of the laws passed by Republican lawmakers from 1870 to 1874. The Mississippi Supreme Court turned its back on workers, women, and mixed-race families. Asserting the power of manhood and whiteness, the court used the language of the household to reinscribe boundaries between classes and races.

In 1877 the court tested a working woman's right to "the fruits of her labor" as protected by the 1871 and 1873 Married Women's Property Acts. In 1877 a woman, N. E. Booth, sued W. F. Hamilton, the sheriff of Carroll County, for taking a cotton crop that, she claimed, belonged to her. During the year in question, the Booths were tenant farmers. Mr. W. A. Booth rented the land in his name, but he counted on his two teenaged sons, Mrs. Booth, and a sharecropper to help him make a crop. Almost all of the family's financial assets belonged to Mrs. Booth. She had some money and two mules. Mr. Booth bought supplies with Mrs. Booth's money through June. Then the money ran out. So Mr. Booth borrowed money, using the crop as collateral. At the end of the year, they could not pay off their debts. After paying the sharecropper his share, Hamilton confiscated the Booths' cotton crop.

The sharecropper's right to his wage was protected by Mississippi law. If an employer fell into debt, the worker had the first claim. After the wages were paid, the rest of the crop went to the creditors.

Mrs. Booth protested. She argued that the crop was hers and not her husband's. The cotton, she insisted, could not have been produced without the mules, which belonged to her. Moreover, the crop was partly financed by her, and, equally important, the crop could not have been produced without her labor. As Mrs. Booth pointed out, Mississippi statutes entitled a married woman to "the fruits of her own labor." Therefore, the cotton belonged to her. The lower court agreed.

The Supreme Court, however, reversed the judgment. Judge J. Chalmers pronounced that Mrs. Booth had no legal title to the crop. "It belongs to the husband," Chalmers declared, "because [it was] grown on his land." Chalmers then spelled out the legal ramifications of a patriarchal household. Mrs. Booth, he reasoned, had a right to the fruits of her labor, but if she worked her husband's land, then she produced property for him and not in her own right. Nor did the Booths' minor sons have a right to the crop because, as the head of the household, Booth claimed their earnings and labor. If he had "emancipated" them, they could have earned separate wages. But Booth had not emancipated his sons. Chalmers concluded that Mr. Booth, as the head of his household, legally owned the family's crop and their labor. To permit Mrs. Booth's claim to the crop based on her mules, her cash, and, most important, her labor would "alter this manliest legal consequence." By so firmly upholding Mr. Booth's status as the undisputed head of his household, Chalmers permitted the Booths' creditors to take everything. Apparently the Married Women's Property Act did not protect a married woman's right to the property her labor produced. Working families could not shelter family assets under a wife's right to compensation.[65]

The Supreme Court's verdict in *W. F. Hamilton v. N. E. Booth* mirrored planters' responses to the African-American household on their plantations. Both the court and planters strictly enforced a patriarchal family structure to the detriment of the working family's property interests. Unlike planters, working people could not avoid creditors by distributing property to different family members. Consequently, poorer households were much more vulnerable to intrusion by outsiders. Nonelite families did not have a safety net—a loophole—to legally escape creditors' control.

The Married Women's Property Act functioned in large part as class legislation. The courts protected a married woman's right to specific kinds of property—land, buildings, tools, and cash gifts—but made it difficult for her to claim wages, especially wages paid in cotton. In essence the court ruled that not all forms of property were created equal. Land outranked cotton; real property took precedence over wages. That is, landholding families had a better chance to hold on to property than working-class families.

Tightening control over marriage laws, the Democratic legislature worked to ensure that only certain men might have manhood rights. One had to fall within new standards of respectability, which did not include alternative households or, it appears, mixed-race households. In 1878 the lawmakers ruled that a person could be convicted of fornication for "a single act of adultery." Anyone "convicted of cohabitating or living together as man and wife" without a marriage license could serve up to ten years in the penitentiary.[66] Almost immediately a Hinds County sheriff arrested H. W. Kinard, a white man, and an unnamed African-American woman. The lower court convicted them of unlawful cohabitation and sentenced them to jail time. Kinard appealed his case to the Supreme Court. Kinard testified that their relationship constituted a marriage under the 1869 constitution. They had lived together since 1868. For ten years they had shared a one-room house and a bed, and they had three sons together. They lived, his lawyer stated, in "the open assumption of the forms and rights of matrimony . . . [holding] each other out to the world as husband and wife." They were legally married and could not be convicted of fornication.

Thomas C. Catchings, attorney general for the state, disagreed. Kinard, he believed, needed a lesson in whiteness. Catchings argued that the 1869 constitution "was designed to protect innocent persons, who, by reason of their former condition, had not been legally married." The law, Catchings continued, "had not the effect to unite those who were living together, as master and servant." In other words, the constitution formalized marriages between African-Americans but not between the races or, in Catchings's words, between "master and servant."

His logic is hard to follow. The 1869 statute recognized *all* relationships between "persons who have not been married, but who are living together, cohabitating as husband and wife." Catchings clearly read the law to refer to common-law relationships between African-Americans alone. From his perspective, the law did not apply to mixed-race couples even though Mississippi had legally recognized mixed-race marriages. Catchings believed that the only proper relationship between a white man and an African-American woman was as master and servant. Acting married was not enough. The hierarchies of race, from Catchings's perspective, undermined any claim of marriage.

Supreme Court Justice J. Chalmers agreed. In a bizarre ruling, Chalmers wrote: "The doctrine enunciated is that clandestine acts of sexual intercourse, no matter how often repeated do not constitute lawful cohabitation . . . but whenever secrecy is abandoned and the concubinage is open, the offense is complete." In other words, if the Kinards kept their relationship secret, it would not have been illegal. But since they "openly and notoriously live[d] together . . . habitually assuming and exercising . . . the rights belonging to the matrimonial relationship," they had transgressed. Chalmers called for harsher laws: "In the interest of morality, it is perhaps to be regretted that a more rigorous doctrine cannot be deduced from our present statute."[67] Despite the law, Chalmers made it clear that the blending of races suggested by the Civil Rights Act would not occur. Neither households nor the power they secured would be shared.

Maintaining an Alternative Body Politic

Planter Frederick Metcalfe, in Washington County, closely monitored the political activities of the freedpeople on the Newstead plantation during these years. His plantation journals record the black southerners' responses to the harsh realities of political life under the Mississippi Plan. In 1875 he remarked that "all the hands on this place . . . voted." By 1876, however, only "some went to . . . register." Metcalfe, by this time, had joined both the Democratic Party and the Vigilance Committee in Greenville.[68] His increasing political involvement was in direct contrast to his workers' withdrawal from formal politics.

Even though freedmen no longer voted in great numbers, both men and women still regularly left the plantation for political rallies. Yet even these actions became dangerous. When John R. Lynch, an African-American Republican candidate for Congress, spoke on October 11 in Greenville, Metcalfe reported "No work done." Whites responded quickly to this show of political force by rioting. Metcalfe calmly noted "several colored people arrested." The message was clear. Not surprisingly, few freedmen from the Newstead plantation cast ballots in the 1876 election. Metcalfe found "election day quiet." In 1876 Metcalfe went into Greenville to vote for the first time since 1868. While freedmen had been voting, Metcalfe and other whites in his neighborhood had set up an alternative polling booth to avoid having to vote side by side with former slaves. In 1876, however, Metcalfe proudly returned to Greenville to cast his ballot.[69] Greenville was once again the political territory of white Democrats.

By 1877 Democrats had effectively halted the black political franchise. "Nov.

6, 1877—election day—more quiet than in past 16 years—scarcely any negroes vote." November 1880: "Election day. Quiet." November 1882: "Election Day ... didn't vote because none of the candidates suited me."[70] In four short years, Metcalfe felt secure enough to not even bother voting. Whites had effectively blocked all opposition to Democratic rule.

Freedmen and Republicans were literally shut out of the political system. Yet Metcalfe's diaries demonstrate that all was not forgotten, much less forgiven. Every election day, freedmen and women refused to work. Metcalfe routinely remarked: "Election Day ... negroes out of the field." And many Washington County blacks still attended public meetings. In 1880 all workers left Metcalfe's plantation for a school meeting. Later in the year, all went to Greenville to hear a political debate between J. R. Chalmers and J. R. Lynch. Most freedmen did not dare vote, but they still formed a large political presence at town meetings.[71] In essence, they let Democrats know they were listening.

Many voted with their feet: they moved to Kansas between 1878 and 1882. According to a migrant, S. M. Cole, most of the Mississippians leaving for Kansas came from the Delta—from Washington, Issaquena, and Warren Counties. "A few families from my section, near delta, and between Greenville and Vicksburg, went to Kansas and wrote back to their friends of the glorious country and how easy it was to make a living out there."[72] Ben Scott on Metcalfe's plantation heard the call and left for Kansas in search of land and personal and political autonomy. Dorcas Anderson remembered that "we started for this place [Kansas] and it took us over two years to get up here. We would come a little way and stop and make a little money and come to another place and make a little more money and that is the way we got here. There were a great many coming North."[73]

The Metcalfe journals also reveal another pattern of protest. In 1876 women on the Newstead plantation withheld their labor. Since the end of the war, Metcalfe had anxiously watched the freedwomen living on his plantations. Each day he meticulously recorded the name of every woman who chose to stay at home rather than work in the fields. Before 1876, women withdrew their labor, for the most part, on an individual day-to-day basis. Metcalfe struggled with particular women, especially Minerva Branch, who chose to stay in the quarters rather than do field work. After 1876, however, women were regularly, and as a group, refusing to labor. Their withdrawal from the field followed a pattern. Almost every spring and late summer "women refuse[d] to work." In September 1878, Metcalfe fired two women for "disobeying orders." He fired three more in December. By 1880 he had given up. Occasionally he would refuse women rations for not working, but for the most part he numbly recorded their resistance to field labor.[74]

So why did women refuse to work? Perhaps women were asserting the rights of household in the face of a full-scale attack on men's political privileges. The Mississippi Plan attempted to block freedmen's access to the polls. In doing so, the Plan stripped black men of one of the principal rights of manhood. Women responded to this assault by asserting their rights of womanhood—their right to labor for their family first and the landlord second. They refused to relinquish the philosophy that undergirded the alternative economies established during the war. Landlords could strip them of gardens, livestock, and chickens. Employers could contract with male-headed nuclear families alone. Yet they could not force women to work or force freedpeople to place planter-class interests above their own households. Unable to assert autonomy through the right to vote, black southerners forced planters to face the politics of household on their plantations.

Long after the Mississippi Plan blocked African-American political suffrage, the politics of the household remained on the land. "The household," after all, meant different things to different people, expressing a broad spectrum of competing worldviews. For white conservatives, the household secured property rights and protected the privileges of whiteness. Conservatives' power lay in maintaining closed households at all costs. For African-Americans, on the other hand, the household represented at least two competing political philosophies. The first fought for equal rights by asserting the essential equality of all men based on the marriage relation. The second questioned individualism by pushing forward the interdependent relationships of the alternative household. Freedpeople continued to press for an acknowledgment that all people, regardless of status, relied on others, and that those ties should be respected and upheld. All Mississippians, then, regardless of race, gender, or class, continued to connect domestic relations with public power.

Yet from 1865 to 1875, only a small portion of these households—these expressions of political consciousness—entered Reconstruction politics. The politics of the alternative household never received a hearing in the statehouse. When freedwomen filed cases with the Freedmen's Bureau from 1867 to 1868, many tenaciously pressed for a recognition of social citizenship. Yet Mississippi's representative government and its courts consistently rejected a broader reading of rights in favor of a strict definition of independence and dependence as framed by the marriage relation. By placing marriage at the center of rights, legislators and the laws secured individualism on its seeming opposite—one's ties, connections, or, as many freedwomen understood, one's interdependence on others.

Individualism belied what every southerner in the Delta understood—that no person stood alone. No one could compete for political and economic power as an individual divorced from connections. Yet the legal system framed dissent. One could fight for oneself and others only through the myth of individualism. Remember the case of Susan Dickerson. The daughter of a slave and a slaveholder, Dickerson went to court to claim her inheritance. In order to do so, she had to first construct a legitimate household—a male-headed nuclear family. She could not argue her case as a child of an alternative household within a web of complex relationships. The laws, privileging independence grounded on the marriage relation, restricted her expression. Rights, as defined by the state, could not speak to African-Americans' expressions of freedom.

Afterword

*I*N 1968, MORE THAN one hundred years after emancipation, the Memphis sanitation workers took to the streets carrying placards that declared "I *AM* A MAN." Using the language of the household, African-American men demanded rights *and* respect. As historian Laurie Green eloquently argues, African-American women closely identified with the slogan. Women, too, demanded respect—to be treated as adults and given the full privileges that come with maturity. As Green argues, civil rights were not enough. After all, by 1968 the United States Congress had granted African-Americans full voting rights and had passed the Civil Rights Act guaranteeing equal access to schools, businesses, and employment. Rights, however, did not ensure respect. Rights did not reflect the fullest meaning of citizenship embedded within many African-Americans' political consciousness.[1]

In many ways, African-Americans in Memphis demanded the formal political recognition of social citizenship. Rights—defined by the state—did not produce freedom. Rights permitted the continued discrimination between the "deserving" and the "undeserving" poor, the "independent" and the "dependent" races, the industrial and the service worker. By declaring "I *AM* A MAN," African-American men and women demanded that the City of Memphis demolish the false boundaries that permitted a person to work full time as a service worker and still qualify for food stamps. Further, city workers criticized Memphians for chastising and labeling them as "dependent" on both counts, either as domestic laborers or as welfare recipients. The Memphis sanitation workers strike struck a chord in Memphis, in the Delta, in the mind of Martin Luther King Jr., and in the Southern Christian Leadership Conference. People immediately recognized what "I *AM* A MAN" expressed. The phrase signaled more than manhood. It spoke to the politics of the alternative households in which people had lived daily. It spoke to the belief that a person was deserving because of, not in spite of, the relationships he or she had formed.

Still, few historians recognize the radical power of the politics of household. Instead those debating the southern household generally take one of two positions. Many historians argue that the household was a social reality, and therefore relatively uncontested. Other historians counter that southerners recognized its hegemonic power and contested its authority over them.[2] The debate, then, divides southerners into two groups—the powerful and the powerless—with the powerful upholding the household in law, politics, the church, and the economy, and the powerless contesting the household through individual action. Yet neither people nor the household can be so easily categorized.

Despite the constraints of household, people could, and did, envision rights within it. The politics of household reflected southerners' belief that individualism exists only in theory. Few people can live without being dependent on others. Human beings are social creatures and can rarely live in complete isolation. Southerners, even at the moment of emancipation, did not turn to individualism. Instead, to relocate a sense of self, they turned to one other. They did not have the social vocabulary to conceive of themselves or their society in any other terms.[3] The challenges came, instead, from within.

Framing freedom in the patriarchal language of household could, and did, lead to abuse. By establishing marriage as the foundation for rights, the South and the nation created a barometer against which deserving and less deserving citizens could be measured. The politics of household conjoined freedom and domestic hierarchies, opening the door to exclusions based on gender, respectability, property rights, and whiteness. A man could beat his wife, a mother could beat her child, and an employer could murder his employee, all in the name of liberty.

Yet the politics of household also produced a continued political consciousness that kept a vision of social citizenship alive. The tension between these two expressions of the household remind us that while dissent can carry with it the habits of oppression, it also carries seeds of change.

Southerners, white and black, clung to the household because it was what they knew. The household became imprinted in people's minds and on the landscape of the Delta. Southerners hotly debated the meaning of household, but they structured their dissent to slavery, emancipation, free labor, and

Reconstruction within the institution they knew best. Household was their inheritance and they would not—they could not—discard the familiar. The household was deeply ingrained within them, and they carried it with them into the future.

Abbreviations

AC	Records of the Assistant Commissioner for the State of Mississippi (Freedmen's Bureau)
Duke	William R. Perkins Library, Duke University, Durham, N.C.
LC	Manuscript Collection, Library of Congress, Washington, D.C.
LR	Letters Received
LS	Letters Sent
MDAH	Mississippi Department of Archives and History, Jackson
MGP	Mississippi Governors' Papers, Mississippi Department of Archives and History, Jackson
NA	National Archives, Washington, D.C.
Pensions	Pension Case Files of the Bureau of Pensions and the Veterans Administration
RC	Register of Complaints (Freedmen's Bureau)
RG 15	Records of the Veterans Administration, National Archives
RG 94	Records of the Adjutant General's Office, National Archives
RG 105	Records of the Bureau of Refugees, Freedmen, and Abandoned Lands, National Archives
RG 159	Records of the Office of the Inspector General, National Archives
RG 217	Records of the United States General Accounting Office, National Archives
RG 366	Records of the Civil War Special Agencies of the Treasury Department, National Archives
RLR	Registered Letters Received
SAC	Records of the Subassistant Commissioner (Freedmen's Bureau)
SCC	Southern Claims Commission

SFO   Subordinate Field Office (Freedmen's Bureau)

SHC   Southern Historical Collection, University of North Carolina, Chapel Hill

ULR   Unregistered Letters Received

UT   Center for American History, University of Texas, Austin

WDM   Western Division—Mississippi (Freedmen's Bureau)

Notes

Introduction. Framing Dissent: Household(s) in Black and White

1. Garner, *Reconstruction in Mississippi*, 269–70; Wharton, *The Negro in Mississippi*, 146.

2. Inaugural Address, March 10, 1870, James Lusk Alcorn Papers, MDAH.

3. Quotation cited in J. R. Johnson to Col. S. P. Lee, June 1, 1866, in Berlin, Reidy, and Rowland, *The Black Military Experience*, 672. See Edwards, "Marriage Covenant" and "Politics of Marriage."

4. The literature on the southern household includes: Fox-Genovese, *Within the Plantation Household*; MacLean, *Behind the Mask*; McCurry, *Masters of Small Worlds*; Bardaglio, *Reconstructing the Household*; Van Tassel, "Only the Law"; K. Brown, *Good Wives*; Edwards, *Gendered Strife*; O'Donovan, "Transforming Work"; Kierner, *Beyond the Household*; K. Wood, "Fictive Mastery"; Frankel, *Freedom's Women*; Kaye, "The Personality of Power"; Franke, "Becoming a Citizen"; Dailey, *Before Jim Crow*.

5. McCurry, *Masters of Small Worlds*; Edwards, *Gendered Strife*; Bardaglio, *Reconstructing the Household*; Bynum, *Unruly Women*; Fox-Genovese, *Within the Plantation Household*; Bercaw, *Southern Body Politic*; Dailey, Gilmore, and Simon, *Jumpin' Jim Crow*.

6. Edwards, *Gendered Strife*; Bardaglio, *Reconstructing the Household*; Gross, *Double Character*; Genovese, *Roll, Jordan, Roll*, 25–49; Morris, *Slavery and the Law*; Oakes, *Slavery and Freedom*; Tushnet, *American Law of Slavery*.

7. Recent literature examining the role of domestic relations in the transition to capitalism in regions outside the South includes: Stanley, *From Bondage to Contract*; Stansell, *City of Women*; Grossberg, *Governing the Hearth*; Tomlins, *Law, Labor, and Ideology*; S. Alexander, "Women, Class and Sexual Differences"; E. Foner, *Story of American Freedom*, 69–94; Fox-Genovese, "Gender, Class and Power"; Baron, *Work Engendered*; Boydston, *Home and Work*; Davidoff and Hall, *Family Fortunes*; Fraser, *Unruly Practices*; Pateman, *The Sexual Contract*; Landes, *Women and the Public Sphere*; Smith-Rosenberg, *Disorderly Conduct*; Ryan, *Cradle of the Middle Class*; Joan Scott, *Gender and*

the Politics of History; Hunt, *Family Romance*; Kerber, *Women of the Republic*; Nicholson, *Feminism/Postmodernism*.

8. For the uses of household in the transition to freedom, see Edwards, *Gendered Strife*; Frankel, *Freedom's Women*; Bardaglio, *Reconstructing the Household*; Kaye, "The Personality of Power"; Franke, "Becoming a Citizen"; Van Tassel, "Only the Law"; Saville, *The Work of Reconstruction*; Schwalm, *Hard Fight*; O'Donovan, "Transforming Work."

9. Hudson, *To Have and to Hold*; Stevenson, *Life in Black and White*; Malone, *Sweet Chariot*; Berlin, *Many Thousands Gone*; Olwell, "'Loose, Idle, and Disorderly'" and *Masters, Slaves, and Subjects*; B. Wood, *Gender, Race, and Rank* and *Women's Work, Men's Work*; Genovese, *Roll, Jordan, Roll*; P. Morgan, "Work and Culture"; Armstrong, "From Task Labor to Free Labor."

10. In the National Archives, in Military Pension Claims (hereafter referred to as Pensions), RG 15, see: Deposition C, Charity Smith, November 16, 1899, Samuel Bugg claim, Wid. Cert. 527482; Affidavit, Cary Adams, March 9, 1889, Pleasant Adams claim, Cert. 1031897; Exhibit, Courtney Burton, November 9, 1883, Philip Burton claim, Mother's App. 203450; Deposition C, Roxie Passmon, June 30, 1899, Charles Willis claim, Wid. Cert. 483850; Deposition A, Maria Bell, September 9, 1890, Daniel Bell claim, Cert. 421529; Deposition, Martha Willis, December 12, 1922, George Willis claim, Wid. Cert. 928295; Deposition E, Emiline Farley, April 8, 1898, Gabriel Davis claim, Wid. App. 393852. Also see Frankel, *Freedom's Women*; Stevenson, *Life in Black and White*; Kaye, "The Personality of Power"; Franke, "Becoming a Citizen."

11. E. Brown, "Uncle Ned's Children"; Penningroth, "Slavery, Freedom, and Social Claims"; Stevenson, *Life in Black and White*; Kaye, "The Personality of Power."

12. Frankel, *Freedom's Women*; Stevenson, *Life in Black and White*; Kaye, "The Personality of Power"; Franke, "Becoming a Citizen"; Edwards, *Gendered Strife*; Schwalm, *Hard Fight*; E. Brown, "Uncle Ned's Children."

13. In Pensions, RG 15, see: Affidavit, Samuel White, August 22, 1885, Lewis Carroll claim, Wid. Cert. 226914; Affidavit, Cyndia Kimbraugh, August 21, 1888, Lewis Carroll claim, Wid. Cert. 226914; Deposition W, Willis Henderson, July 21, 1894, Daniel Bell claim, Cert. 421529; Deposition AA, Ada Burton, January 19, 1904, Peter Burton claim, Wid. Cert. 572446; Deposition A, Susan Linsey, September 1, 1896, Wesley Bradford claim, Wid. App. 440505; Deposition A, Mary Jane Kelley, October 3, 1890, Silas Clear claim, Wid. Cert. 560243; Deposition E, Matilda Anderson, July 22, 1900, Judson Burris claim, Wid. Cert. 706569; Affidavit, Robert Hudson, February 4, 1920, Robert Hudson claim, X.C.2.656–260.

14. Penningroth, "Slavery, Freedom, and Social Claims"; Stevenson, *Life in Black and White*; Frankel, *Freedom's Women*; Kaye, "The Personality of Power"; Franke, "Becoming a Citizen"; Edwards, *Gendered Strife*; Schwalm, *Hard Fight*; E. Brown, "Uncle Ned's Children."

15. Schwalm, *Hard Fight*; Joyner, *Down by the Riverside*; E. Foner, *Nothing but Freedom*; Saville, *The Work of Reconstruction*; Kerr-Ritchie, *Freedpeople in the Tobacco South*; W. Williams, *Slavery and Freedom in Delaware*; Jenkins, *Seizing the New Day*; Fields, *Middle Ground*; Rose, *Rehearsal for Reconstruction*; Reidy, *Slavery to Agrarian Capitalism*.

Recent published work on the Old Southwest during the Civil War and Reconstruction includes: Finley, *From Slavery to Uncertain Freedom*; Frankel, *Freedom's Women*; R. Davis, *Good and Faithful Labor*; Wayne, *Reshaping of Plantation Society*; Rosen, "Not That Sort"; Moneyhon, *Impact*; Tunnell, *Crucible of Reconstruction*; Powell, *New Masters*.

Recent work on the nineteenth-century Delta includes: Brandfon, *Cotton Kingdom*; Cobb, *Most Southern Place*; Woods, *Development Arrested*; Willis, *Forgotten Time*; J. Williams, "Civil War and Reconstruction"; Giggie, "God's Long Journey"; Kaye, "The Personality of Power."

16. Population figures are based on the 1850 and 1860 U.S. Census. Population Schedules of the Eighth Census of the United States, Mississippi, 1860, and Population Schedules of the Eighth Census of the United States, Mississippi, 1860, (Slave Schedules) for Bolivar, Coahoma, DeSoto, Issaquena, Tunica, Warren, and Yazoo Counties. The rolls for Sunflower and Washington Counties are missing. Population Schedules of the Seventh Census of the United States, Mississippi, 1850, and Population Schedules of the Seventh Census of the United States, Mississippi, 1850, (Slave Schedules) for Sunflower, Yazoo, Coahoma, Tunica, Issaquena, and Washington Counties. I examined the pension applications for 345 former Union soldiers or their widows. In all those applications, not one single person who was eighteen years old in 1861 had been born in the Delta. See Delta Database in possession of the author. Also see Olmsted, *Journey*, 72–81.

17. F. Smith, *The Yazoo River*, xiv.

18. Ibid., 45.

19. Brandfon, *Cotton Kingdom*; Cobb, *Most Southern Place*; Willis, *Forgotten Time*.

20. In 1850, fifteen men (10 percent of the white population) controlled 54.4 percent of the wealth. By 1860, thirty-eight men (10 percent of the white population) managed 79.8 percent of the Delta's resources. See Population Schedules of the Seventh Census (1850) and the Eighth Census (1860) for Sunflower, Yazoo, Coahoma, Tunica, Issaquena, and Washington Counties, Mississippi.

21. Absentee ownership was calculated by comparing the 1850 Slave Census, the 1850 Population Census, and the 1848 Land Taxes for Sunflower, Yazoo, Coahoma, Tunica, Issaquena, and Washington Counties. There are 997 names that appeared on both the land tax rolls and the slave census rolls. Of those, 645 (55 percent) lived in the county where they owned land and slaves in 1850, while 352 resided elsewhere. Fewer than half of the absentee owners (140 out of 352) lived in Mississippi. See, for the six named counties, the Population Schedules of the Seventh Census of the United States, NA, the Slave Schedules of the same, and the 1848 Land Taxes, County Records, MDAH; Jackson

and Teeples, *Mississippi 1850 Census Index*; Gillis, *Mississippi 1850 Census: Surname Index.*

Also see, in Pensions, RG 15, accounts by former slaves including: Deposition W, Willis Henderson, July 21, 1894, Daniel Bell claim, Cert. 421529; Deposition A, Susan Linsey, September 1, 1896, Wesley Bradford claim, Wid. App. 440505; Deposition, Gus Bell, June 13, 1890, William Brooks claim, Wid. App. 417996; Deposition A, James Chaplain, April 11, 1885, Edward Brown claim, Wid. Cert. 316462; Exhibit, Courtney Burton, November 9, 1883, Philip Burton claim, Mother's App. 203450; Deposition C, Peter Ellis, July 21, 1910, Judson Burris (Jared Barnes) claim, Wid. Cert. 706569; Deposition, Harrison Willis, Charles Willis claim, Wid. Cert. 483850.

22. Amanda Worthington Journal, March 15, 1862, Worthington-Stone Family Papers, MDAH. Also see ibid., April 12, 1862; Louisa Burrus to Sister La Elleray, September 3, 1848, John C. Burrus Family Papers, MDAH; Bazil to My Dear Wife, September 1848, Kiger Family Papers, Natchez Trace Collection, UT; Martha to Mother and Father, January 25, 1849, Blanton-Smith Letters, MDAH; James T. Rucks to Father, October 14, 1846, Rucks-Valliant Family Papers, MDAH.

23. Bazil Kiger to Caroline, June 5, 1853, Kiger Family Papers, UT; Plantation Journals, March 5, 1856, F. T. Leake Papers, SHC.

24. William Gale to Mother, February 4, 1844, Gale and Polk Family Papers, SHC; Annie E. Jacobs, "The Master of Doro Plantation," unpublished manuscript, MDAH; Mary Bolton to Richard, June 3, 1842, and Edwin Bolton to Brother, n.d. [ca. 1840], Edwin C. Bolton Papers, MDAH.

25. In Chamberlain-Hyland-Gould Papers, UT, see Ellen to Father, May 2, 1848; Susan to Ellen, February 10, 1852; Ellen to Mary C. Hutchins, February 2, 1858. In Kiger Family Papers, UT, see Bazil to Caroline, January 1, 1852; Aleck Gwin to Caroline, July 30, 1852; Aleck Gwin to Caroline, October 23, 1852; Caroline to Bazil, March 31, 1854; Bettie Martin to Brother, June 15, 1861.

26. Janie to Hannah, March 16, 1858, Matthews Family Papers, MDAH.

Scholars who downplay the Delta's antebellum history include Cobb, *Most Southern Place*; Willis, *Forgotten Time*; and Brandfon, *Cotton Kingdom*. More recently, scholars have begun to study the region's antebellum and Civil War history. See especially Kaye, "The Personality of Power," and J. Williams, "Civil War and Reconstruction."

For the Delta's large African-American population in 1850, see census rolls listed in note 16.

27. Affidavit, James Henry Clay, April 1, 1896, James Henry Clay claim, Invalid Cert. 1019911, Pensions, RG 15.

28. January, February, and March 1859, Panther Burn Plantation Account Book, MDAH; Newstead Plantation Diary, 1857–60, SHC; Plantation Account Books, 1849–57, 1860, Kiger Family Papers, UT.

29. Joyner, *Down by the Riverside*; E. Foner, *Nothing but Freedom*; Saville, *The Work of Reconstruction*; Schwalm, *Hard Fight*.

30. In Pensions, RG 15, see: Exhibit, Courtney Burton, November 9, 1883, Philip Burton claim, Mother's App. 203450; Deposition C, Roxie Passmon, June 30, 1899, Charles Willis claim, Wid. Cert. 483850; Deposition A, Maria Bell, September 9, 1890, Daniel Bell claim, Cert. 421529; Deposition, Martha Willis, December 12, 1922, George Willis claim, Wid. Cert. 928295; Deposition E, Emiline Farley, April 8, 1898, Gabriel Davis claim, Wid. App. 393852. Also see Kaye, "The Personality of Power"; Stevenson, *Life in Black and White*; Malone, *Sweet Chariot*; Hudson, *To Have and to Hold*.

31. J. Williams, "Civil War and Reconstruction," 39–62; Miers, *Web of Victory*; Carter, *The Final Fortress*; Connelly, *Army of the Heartland* and *Autumn of Glory*.

32. Fields, "Ideology and Race"; Hale, *Making Whiteness*; Jacobson, *Whiteness of a Different Color*; Lott, *Love and Theft*; Saxton, *White Republic*; Roediger, *The Wages of Whiteness*; Smith-Rosenberg, *Disorderly Conduct*; Joan Scott, *Gender and the Politics of History*; Dollimore, *Sexual Dissidence*; Butler, *Gender Trouble*; Stallybrass and White, *Transgression*; Garber, *Vested Interests*.

Chapter 1. The Foundation of Our Rights? Emancipation, Marriage, and African-American Households

1. In the National Archives, in the Southern Claims Commission records (hereafter cited as SCC), RG 217, see Claim Form, December 1874, and Deposition, William H. Wallace, December 1874, Allowed Claims, Mississippi, Washington Co., Irene Smith and Alexander Bullet claim, No. 18473.

2. For Delta African-American slave households, see Kaye, "The Personality of Power," 112–72. For postemancipation Mississippi, see Frankel, *Freedom's Women*, 79–159. For the South more generally, see Stevenson, *Life in Black and White*, 206–57, and "Distress and Discord"; Hudson, *To Have and to Hold*; Malone, *Sweet Chariot*; Edwards, *Scarlett Doesn't Live Here*, 52–55.

3. Kaye, "The Personality of Power," 36–111.

4. Ibid.; Penningroth, "Slavery, Freedom, and Social Claims;" Edwards, "Law, Domestic Violence"; Hudson, *To Have and to Hold*; Stevenson, *Life in Black and White*; E. Brown, "Uncle Ned's Children."

5. Kaye makes the critical distinction between neighborhood and community in chapter 1, "Neighborhoods," in "The Personality of Power," 49, 55, 58–59, 62, 90. Kaye's argument revises the literature on the slave community. See, for example, Blassingame, *The Slave Community*; Gutman, *Black Family*; Joyner, *Down by the Riverside*; Abrahams, *Singing the Master*. In many ways, Kaye's distinction between neighborhood and community refines Eugene Genovese's contention that the conditions of slavery in the U.S. South stymied class consciousness among slaves. See Genovese, *Roll, Jordan, Roll*.

6. Frankel, *Freedom's Women*, 28–55; Schwalm, *Hard Fight*, 88–97; Glymph, "'This Species of Property.'"

7. Both Leslie Schwalm and Lawrence Powell have noted that women made up the majority of wartime free laborers. See Powell, *New Masters*, 109; Schwalm, *Hard Fight*, 90.

8. Edwards, "Politics of Marriage," 9.

9. Quotation cited in J. R. Johnson to Col. S. P. Lee, June 1, 1866, in Berlin, Reidy, and Rowland, *The Black Military Experience,* 672. See Edwards, "Marriage Covenant" and "Politics of Marriage."

10. Jonathan Pearce to James A. Seddon, November 3, 1863, in Berlin et al., *The Destruction of Slavery,* 775–76; Robert R. Shotwell to Lt. Col. Lamar, July 5, 1863, ibid., 801–2; John W. Boyd to Pettus, August 1, 1862, Administration of John J. Pettus, Roll 38, MGP; Statement of Plantations Leased, Assistant Special Agent up to March 9, 1864, Reports of A. McFarland, Skipwith's District, Second Special Agency, Civil War Special Agencies, RG 366; W. B. Farr, Provost Marshall of Freedmen, to Col. Thomas, Asst. Provost Marshall, July 1865, RLR, AC, RG 105; Petition, W. B. Farr, L. T. Wade, et al. to Col. Samuel Thomas, July 17, 1865, RLR, AC, RG 105.

11. J. Williams, "Civil War and Reconstruction," 39–62; Miers, *Web of Victory*; Carter, *The Final Fortress*; Connelly, *Army of the Heartland* and *Autumn of Glory.*

12. In Pensions, RG 15, see: Deposition of Ailsey Tyler, August 22, 1901, George Buckner claim, Wid. App. 736402; Deposition E, Emiline Farley, April 8, 1898, Gabriel Davis claim, Wid. App. 393852; Deposition E, Isiah Kelley, September 16, 1890, Silas Clear claim, Wid. Cert. 560243; Affidavit, Julia Anderson, October 15, 1906, John Anderson claim, B. Cert. 632823.

13. Frankel, *Freedom's Women,* 28–55; in Pensions, RG 15, under Daniel Bell claim, Cert. 421529, see: Deposition C, William Fletcher, July 7, 1894; Deposition X, Harrison Henderson, July 21, 1894; Deposition V, Sanford Taylor, July 21, 1894.

14. Lorenzo Thomas to Hon. H. Wilson, May 30, 1863; Brig. Gen. Elias S. Dennis to Col. John A. Rawlins, June 6 and 12, 1863, in Berlin, Reidy, and Rowland, *The Black Military Experience,* 532–34; Cornish, *The Sable Arm,* 144–45; Glatthaar, *Forged in Battle,* 130–35.

15. Deposition, Boss B. Becker, November 20, 1903, and Deposition, Turner Holts, November 21, 1903, John Ben claim, B. Cert. 564628, Pensions, RG 15.

16. Deposition E, Kinchen Cook [aka Nub Templeton], August 29, 1903, Washington Foster claim, Wid. Cert. 965465, Pensions, RG 15; Deposition B, Nelson Colbert, May 12, 1905, Samuel Hayden claim, Wid. App. 729789, Pensions, RG 15.

17. Deposition, Gus Bell, June 13, 1890, William Brooks claim, Wid. App. 417996, Pensions, RG 15.

18. In Pensions, RG 15, see: Deposition E, Kinchen Cook, August 29, 1903, Washington Foster claim, Wid. Cert. 965465; Deposition B, Nelson Colbert, April 12, 1905, Samuel Hayden claim, Wid. App. 729789; Deposition C, John W. Hill, Invalid Cert. 496047; also see Deposition, Boss B. Becker, November 20, 1903, John Ben claim, B. Cert. 564628; Deposition, Turner Holts, November 21, 1903, John Ben claim, B. Cert. 564628; Deposition C, Peter Ellis, July 21, 1910, Judson Burris claim, Wid. Cert. 706569; Deposition D, Willis Reed, October, 1896, Wesley Bradford claim, Wid. App. 440505; Deposition A,

Minerva Butler Divine, Anthony Butler claim, Cert. 700–941; Deposition, Gus Bell, June 13, 1890, William Brooks claim, Wid. App. 417996; Franklin Canady to Commissioner of Pensions, July 15, 1910, James Buckner claim, Wid. Cert. 963405; Deposition F, Harrison Templeton, August 5, 1903, Washington Foster claim, Wid. Cert. 965465.

19. Howard W. Wilkinson to Pettus, January 1, 1862[3], Administration of John J. Pettus, roll 39, MGP.

20. Jonathan Pearce to James A. Seddon, November 3, 1863, in Berlin et al., *The Destruction of Slavery,* 776; Robert R. Shotwell to Lt. Col. Lamar, July 5, 1863, ibid., 801–2; William S. Hyland to Dear Child, June 23, 1861, and William Hyland to Pattie Hyland, September 14, 1862, Chamberlain-Hyland-Gould Papers, UT; Charles B. Allen to Father and Mother, June 4 and October 17, 1864, James and Charles Allen Papers, SHC. Also, in the Administration of John J. Pettus papers, MGP, see: E. L. Acee to Pettus, July 29, 1862, roll 38; W. Cooper to Pettus, August 8, 1862, roll 38; W. Henry Calhoun to Pettus, December 23, 1862, roll 40; Thomas S. Goff to Pettus, August 30, 1861, roll 34; Girard Stiles to Pettus, November 27, 1861, roll 36; B. S. Bowles to Pettus, July 28, 1862, roll 38; J. T. Simms and Samuel N. Delancy to Pettus, July 29, 1862, roll 38; W. W. Fall to Pettus, July 11, 1862, roll 38.

21. Affidavit of Geo. Gorman, June 6, 1866, in Berlin et al., *Wartime Genesis,* 671–73. Also, from note 10, see: John W. Boyd to Pettus, Administration of John J. Pettus, roll 38, MGP; Statement of Plantations Leased, Assistant Special Agent up to March 9, 1864, Reports of A. McFarland, Skipwith's District, Second Special Agency, Civil War Special Agencies, RG 366; W. B. Farr, Provost Marshall of Freedmen, to Col. Thomas, Asst. Provost Marshall, July 1865, RLR, AC, RG 105; Petition, W. B. Farr, L. T. Wade, et al. to Col. Samuel Thomas, July 17, 1865, RLR, AC, RG 105.

Noralee Frankel writes a wonderful analysis on the meaning of home in *Freedom's Women,* 19–25.

22. In Pensions, RG 15, under Peter Burton claim, Wid. Cert. 572446, see: Deposition AA, Ada Burton, January 19, 1904; Deposition B, Sam Burton, January 19, 1901; Deposition C, Cornelia Moore, January 19, 1901; Deposition E, Nathan Blackburn, April 23, 1904; Deposition J, Charles Coleman, April 24, 1904.

23. The most complete account of slave property in the Delta is chapter 3, "Labor, Exchange, and Property," in Kaye, "The Personality of Power," 173–263. Also see accounts kept with slaves in Kiger family plantations books, 1852, 1849–57, 1860, Kiger Family Papers, UT; Panther Burn Plantation Account Book 1859–62, Panther Burn Collection, MDAH; Rear Adm. David D. Porter to Gen. Lorenzo Thomas, October 21, 1863, in Berlin et al., *Wartime Genesis,* 746–49; Testimony of Maj. Gen. Samuel R. Curtis, March 19, 1863, Court of Inquiry, 1:21–22, and Exhibit J, S. N. Wood to Col. Myers, August 11, 1862, Court of Inquiry, 1:195, RG 159; and, in Rawick, *The American Slave,* interviews with Mark Oliver, 7:1659–71, and Prince Johnson, 7:1167–79.

For other regions of the South, see Penningroth, "Slavery, Freedom, and Social

Claims"; Reidy, *Slavery to Agrarian Capitalism,* 61–62, 101–7; Hudson, *To Have and to Hold,* 16–20; Olwell, "'Loose, Idle, and Disorderly'"; B. Wood, *Women's Work, Men's Work*; P. Morgan, "Work and Culture."

24. See, for example, in RG 159: Testimony of M. G. Miles, May 11, 1863, Court of Inquiry, 2:300; Testimony of W. E. Henderson, Quartermaster, 13th Illinois Volunteers, April 6, 1863, Court of Inquiry, 1:251; Testimony of Maj. Gen. Samuel R. Curtis, March 19, 1863, Court of Inquiry, 1:19.

25. Rear Adm. David D. Porter to Gen. Lorenzo Thomas, October 21, 1863, in Berlin et. al., *Wartime Genesis,* 746. See also Testimony of Maj. Gen. Samuel R. Curtis, March 19, 1863, Court of Inquiry, 1:22, and Exhibit J, S. N. Wood to Col. Myers, August 11, 1862, Court of Inquiry, 1:195, RG 159.

26. Gerteis, *From Contraband to Freedmen*; Rose, *Rehearsal for Reconstruction,* 141–241; Berlin et al., *Wartime Genesis,* 85–113, 347–77, 621–50; R. Davis, *Good and Faithful Labor.*

27. For the gender division of labor in the Delta, see Kaye, "The Personality of Power," 193–98; Newstead Plantation Diary 1857–1861, M-2339, SHC; Panther Burn Plantation Journals 1859–1860, MDAH; Plantation Journals, 1856–1859, F. T. Leak Papers, SHC; Olmsted, *Journey,* 72–81; Frankel, *Freedom's Women,* 4–6; Sydnor, *Slavery in Mississippi,* 10, 21.

More generally, see Schwalm, *Hard Fight,* 19–72; Robertson, "Africa into the Americas?"; Cody, "Cycles"; Bush, "Hard Labor"; B. Wood, *Men's Work, Women's Work,* 16–19; Jacqueline Jones, *Labor of Love,* 17; Fox-Genovese, *Within the Plantation Household,* 141, 172–73.

28. Testimony of Sam Washington, June 27, 1863, 2:561, Court of Inquiry, RG 159. Also in Court of Inquiry on the Sale of Cotton, RG 159, see: Willis Scott, June 27, 1863, 2:562–63; Lt. Col. S. N. Wood, 6th Missouri Cav., to Col. Myers, Asst. Quartermaster, August 11, 1862, 1:195–96; Gen. Curtis, May 25, 1863, 2:414–15; David Haywood, Pvt., Co. A, 1st Regt. Missouri Infantry (Colored), June 27, 1863, 2:558–61; Exhibit A: Statement of Cotton Received, Sold, and Transported at the Depot of Memphis during the Month of Jan.-May, 1863, 2:365–83.

29. "Tobacco Sold to the Negroes Oct. 20th 1850," in Plantation Book, 1849–57, Kiger Family Papers, UT; Panther Burn Plantation Account Book 1859–62, Panther Burn Collection, MDAH. Also see, as in note 23, Adm. Porter to Gen. Thomas in Berlin et al. *Wartime Genesis,* 746–49; Testimony of Gen. Curtis; Wood to Col. Myers, Court of Inquiry, RG 159. Also see Kaye, "The Personality of Power," 237–43.

30. Wood to Col. Myers, Court of Inquiry, 1:195, RG 159.

31. Ibid.; Exhibit A: Statement of Cotton Received, Sold, and Transported at the Depot of Memphis during the Month of Jan.-May, 1863, 2:365–83, Court of Inquiry on the Sale of Cotton, RG 159; William and Emily Sykes et al. to Gen. W. W. Orme, June 15, 1865, Correspondence of W. Orme, Second Special Agency, RG 366.

32. Testimony of Maj. W. D. Greene, May 4, 1863, Court of Inquiry, 2:99, RG 159. For

African-American statements to the contrary, see Testimony of Maj. Gen. Samuel R. Curtis, March 19, 1863, 1:21–22, and April 25, 1863, 2:70–71; Testimony of Lt. John Guilee, March 23, 1863, 1:37–39; Testimony of Maj. W. D. Greene, May 4, 1863, 2:99; Testimony of John H. Morse, April 13, 1863, 1:341–42, 345. For a thorough discussion of changing military policies toward freedpeople's claims to cotton in the Delta, see Hess, "Confiscation and the Northern War Effort."

33. For an excellent survey of U.S. government policy in the Mississippi Valley, see "The Mississippi Valley" in Berlin et al., *Wartime Genesis,* 621–50.

34. Lorenzo Thomas to Hon. H. Wilson, May 30, 1863; Brig. Gen. Elias S. Dennis to Col. John A. Rawlins, June 6 and 12, 1863, in Berlin, Reidy, and Rowland, *Black Military Experience,* 532–34; Cornish, *The Sable Arm,* 144–45; Glatthaar, *Forged in Battle,* 130–35.

35. In Pensions, RG 15, see: Deposition A, Belle Harris, November 15, 1899, Samuel Buggs claim, Wid. Cert. 527482; Affidavit, Ellen Suggs, September 2, 1904, John Anderson claim, Wid. App. 540765; Deposition C, Adam Metcalfe, October 3, 1890, Silas Clear claim, Wid. Cert. 560243; Deposition AA, Ada Burton, January 19, 1904, Wid. Cert. 572446; Deposition A, Minerva Butler Divine, September 11, 1900, Anthony Butler claim, Cert. 700–941; Deposition, Ann Davis, April 7, 1897, Gabriel Davis claim, Wid. App. 393852; Deposition, Eliza Turner, December 30, 1897, Charles Campbell claim, Minor App. 671857; Deposition W, Henderson Willis, July 21, 1894, Daniel Bell claim, Cert. 421529.

For recruitment policies in the Delta, see Berlin, Reidy, and Rowland, *The Black Military Experience,* 9. For black enlistment in the Lower Mississippi Valley and in the South more generally, see *The Black Military Experience,* 1–34, 116–22; Frankel, *Freedom's Women*; Cornish, *The Sable Arm,* 29–78, 112–31; Glatthaar, *Forged in Battle,* 61–80.

For the Delta, see General-in-Chief H. W. Halleck to Maj. Gen. U. S. Grant, March 31, 1863, in *The Black Military Experience,* 143–44; Harry Beard to Caroline Beard, April 22 and August 10, 1863, and Harry Beard diaries, April 3–May 25, 1863, Family Correspondence—Harry Beard, Daniel C. Beard Papers, LC; John G. Jones to Family, May 29 and June 9, 1863, John Griffith Jones Papers, LC; Samuel D. Barnes Journal, March 16–April 24, 1864, Samuel D. Barnes Diaries, LC; Deposition of Edmund Wynn, October 28, 1872, Deposition of Altmore Young, September 12, 1876, Allowed Claims, Mississippi, Washington Co., Mary B. Phelps claim, No. 9509, SCC, RG 217; Depositions of Joseph Wilson, David Lowry, Frances Stampley, August 21, 1875, Allowed Claims, Mississippi, Washington Co., Martha L. Knox claim, No. 2296, SCC, RG 217; Deposition of Martha Willis, December 12, 1922, George Willis claim, Wid. Cert. 928295, Pensions, RG 15; Affidavit, Samuel White, August 22, 1885, Lewis Carroll claim, Wid. Cert. 226914, Pensions, RG 15.

36. Testimony of Isaac McLean, July 11, 1874 (for a similar account see John Lewis, July 11, 1874), Allowed Claims, Mississippi, Washington Co., Henry J. Irish file, No. 6676, SCC, RG 217; Berlin, Reidy, and Rowland, *The Black Military Experience,* 116–22, 1–34; Cornish, *The Sable Arm,* 29–78, 112–31; Glatthaar, *Forged in Battle,* 61–80.

37. Deposition, Ailsey Tyler, August 22, 1901, George Buckner claim, Wid. App. 736402, Pensions, RG 15.

38. Fiske, "Diary of James Oliver Hazard Perry Sessions."

39. A. W. Harlan to Maj. W. G. Sargent, February 5, 1864, in Berlin et al., *Wartime Genesis*, 787.

40. Adj. Gen. Lorenzo Thomas to Edwin M. Stanton, August 23, 1863, Ira Berlin et al., *Destruction of Slavery*, 309–10; Acting Asst. Quartermaster B. O. Carr to Capt. F. S. Winslow, July 24, 1862, in Berlin et al., *Wartime Genesis*, 659; Chaplain Samuel Sawyer to Maj. Gen. Samuel Curtis, January 26, 1863, ibid., 674–76; Capt. G. L. Fort to Brig. Gen. M. C. Meigs, September 9, 1862, ibid., 666; Chaplain J. B. Rogers to E. L. Stanton, September 19, 1862, ibid., 667–70; Brig. Gen. N. B. Buford to Lt. Col. H. Binmore, October 10, 1863, ibid., 735–37.

41. Eaton, *Grant, Lincoln and the Freedmen*; Wm. P. Mellen to Hon. S. P. Chase, March 29, 1864, in Berlin et al., *Wartime Genesis*, 66, 798–99.

Percentages are based on the reports of A. W. Harlan to Maj. W. G. Sargent, February 5, 1864, ibid., 786–87, and John Eaton Jr. to Lt. Col. Jno. A. Rawlins, April 29, 1863, ibid., 684–97. In contrast, women made up 46 percent of the adult work force in the Delta during slavery. The counties included in this statistic are Bolivar, Coahoma, Issaquena, Sunflower, Tunica, Washington, and Yazoo. See 1860 census figures in *Statistics*, 267–68.

42. Testimony of Gen. Wadsworth before the American Freedmen's Inquiry Commission, January 1864, in Berlin et al., *Wartime Genesis*, 501. For similar examples, see Brig. Gen. Wm. Sooy Smith to Lt. Col. Binmore, March 23, 1863, in Berlin et al., *Destruction of Slavery*, 303; Gen. Thomas to Stanton, August 23, 1863, ibid., 308.

43. Testimony of Gen. Wadsworth before the American Freedmen's Inquiry Commission, January 1864, in Berlin et al., *Wartime Genesis*, 501. Also see, for example, John Eaton Jr. to Colonel, February 14, 1863, and John Eaton Jr. to Henry Wilson, February 1863, ibid., 677–80; George B. Field to E. M. Stanton, March 20, 1863, ibid., 681–83; James Bryan to Edwin M. Stanton, July 27, 1863, ibid., 715–18; Brig. Gen. Jas. S. Wadsworth to Adj. Gen. Lorenzo Thomas, December 16, 1863, ibid., 761.

44. Testimony of Gen. Wadsworth before the American Freedmen's Inquiry Commission, January 1864, in Berlin et al., *Wartime Genesis*, 501.

45. J. S. Herrick, Chaplain, Superintendent of Freedmen, Helena, to Sir, January 1, 1864, Applications to Lease Lands, District of Helena, Records of the Second Special Agency, RG 366; Lease between William P. Mellen, Supervising Special Agent of the Treasury Department, First Agency, and George W. Perry and Washington J. Warwick, February 16, 1864, Leases of Plantation Lands to Freedmen (1864), District of Helena, Second Special Agency, RG 366; Josua Culverson, Willis Culverson, Lee Whaley, James Houston, Manuel Johns, and Nathan Buckner to George B. Fields, Commissioner of Leasing, January 11, 1864, Vicksburg District, Second Special Agency, RG 366; Plantations Leased by A. W. McFarland, January 1864, WDM, AC, RG 105.

For leases to freedpeople, see, in Second Special Agency, RG 366: Leases of Plantation Lands to Freedmen (1864), District of Helena; Agreements of Registry for Plantations, District of Helena; Reports of A. McFarland (1864), Assistant Special Agent, Skipwith District; Correspondence Received by George B. Field, Vicksburg District. See also Registers of Leased Plantations (1863–65) and Applications for Lease of Abandoned Plantations (1863–65), SFO–Vicksburg, SAC, RG 105; Monthly Land Reports, WDM, AC, RG 105. For examples of freedmen subletting a plantation, see Memorandum of Agreements of Registry for Plantations, District of Helena, Second Special Agency, RG 366.

46. See Schwalm, *Hard Fight,* 199, 238–50; Powell, *New Masters,* 84; Stanley, *From Bondage to Contract,* 122–28, 187–90; Glymph, "'This Species of Property,'" 70; Frankel, *Freedom's Women,* 44–55.

47. Maj. Gen. W. T. Sherman to Maj. J. A. Rawlins, August 14, 1862, in Berlin et al., *Destruction of Slavery,* 291; Sherman to Thomas Hunton, August 24, 1862, ibid., 294; General Order 67, ibid., 289–91; Maj. Gen. S. A. Hurlbut to the President, March 27, 1863, ibid., 304–7; Brig. Gen. C. C. Washburn to Hon. E. M. Stanton, September 6, 1862, in Berlin et al., *Wartime Genesis,* 665. Also see Frankel, *Freedom's Women,* 44–55; Schwalm, *Hard Fight,* 90, 94, 103; Glymph, "'This Species of Property,'" 62–63.

48. See, for example, Col. Saml. Thomas to Col. John Eaton Jr., March 14, 1864, in Berlin et al., *Wartime Genesis,* 811; Lt. Col. Jno. Phillips, "Consolidated Report," ibid., 821; Brig. Gen. John P. Hawkins to Hon. Gerritt Smith, October 21, 1863, ibid., 745; Maj. W. G. Sargent to Col. John Eaton Jr., March 1, 1864, ibid., 737; James E. Yeatman, *A Report on the Condition of the Freedmen of the Mississippi, Presented to the Western Sanitary Commission, December 17th, 1863* (St. Louis, 1864), quoted in *Wartime Genesis,* 781.

49. Maj. Julian E. Bryant to Captain, October 10, 1863, in Berlin et al., *Wartime Genesis,* 729; Brig. Gen. John P. Hawkins to Hon. Gerritt Smith, October 21, 1863, ibid., 743–45.

50. See A. A. Swayze, Adams Place, Yazoo Co., July 18, 1865, Labor Contracts, AC, RG 105, M826, roll 44; Hudson, *To Have and To Hold*; also in Labor Contracts, AC, RG 105, M826, see: M. Morrisy and Milan Forman and other Freedmen, January 1, 1865, Washington Co.; James Valliant and John A. Biddle and Freedmen, April 10, 1865, Washington Co.; Jones and Boyd and Freedmen, January 1, 1865, Sunflower Co.; Woodland Plantation, January 15, 1866, Issaquena Co.; H. P. Duncan and Freedmen, January 1, 1865, Issaquena Co.; Mary A. Billington and Freedmen, July 7, 1865, Yazoo Co.

51. Maj. Julian E. Bryant to Captain, October 10, 1863, in Berlin et al., *Wartime Genesis,* 730; Chaplain John Eaton Jr. to Lt. Col. Jno. A. Rawlins, April 29, 1863, ibid., 694; A. McFarland to William Mellen, March 11, 1864, ibid., 796; H. Wilson to C. A. Montross, March 7, 1864, ibid., 825; M. D. Landon to William Mellen, May 12, 1864, ibid., 827.

52. M. Morrisy and Milan Forman and other Freedmen, January 1, 1865, Washington County; James Valliant and John A. Biddle and Freedmen, April 10, 1865, Washington County; Jones and Boyd and Freedmen, January 1, 1865, Sunflower County; Woodland

Plantation, January 15, 1866, Issaquena County; H. P. Duncan and Freedmen, January 1, 1865, Issaquena; and Mary A. Billington and Freedmen, July 7, 1865, Yazoo, in Labor Contracts, AC, RG 105, M826.

53. Isaac Shoemaker Diary, April 2, 1864, Duke; A. G. Swain to AC, September 8, 1865, ULR, WDM, RG 105.

54. Testimony of Isaac McLean, July 11, 1874, Allowed Claims, Mississippi, Washington Co., Henry Irish file, No. 6676, SCC, RG 217; *Allen Walker v. John A. Miller,* September 7, 1867, RC, SFO–Greenville, Mississippi, AC, RG 105.

55. Isaac Shoemaker Diary, April 2 and 5, 1864, Duke.

56. Forty-three percent of the contracts in the Delta permitted the use of land for the independent production of food, cotton, rice, and livestock. For example, in Labor Contracts, 1865, AC, RG 105, M826, roll 43, see William H. Fulgate and Freedmen, January 1, 1865, which stated that the freedmen could "cultivate as much land on their own account as they may desire." John H. Woolfolk and Freedmen, June 26, 1865, allowed freedpeople as "much land as they can cultivate on Saturday." Benjamin Roach of Prairie Plantation permitted "as much land as they can cultivate and support themselves and make use of their own horses and mules and oxen." The standard phrase in the 1865 contracts read "as much crops or patches as desired."

57. T. P. Anderson to J. H. Weber, Acting AC, September 23, 1865, ULR, WDM, RG 105; C. A. Montross, "Statement of Plantations," March 1, 1864; Plantations Leased, March 1864, Vicksburg, Second Special Agency, RG 366; and, in Report of the Court of Inquiry on the Proceeding of the Sale of Cotton, RG 159: Testimony of Maj. Gen. Samuel R. Curtis, March 19, 1863, 1:8–22, 69–71; Testimony of Lt. John Guilee, March 23, 1863, 1:37–39; Testimony of Willis Scott, June 27, 1863, 2:562–63; Testimony of Gideon Pillow, July 2, 1863, 2:580–81, 683–84.

58. Testimony of Charles Dana before the American Freedmen's Inquiry Commission, January 4, 1863, in Berlin et al., *Wartime Genesis,* 769; M. D. Landon to Wm. P. Mellon, May 12, 1864, ibid., 829; Maj. Julian E. Bryant to Captain, October 10, 1863, ibid., 733; Rear Adm. David D. Porter to Gen. Lorenzo Thomas, October 12, 1863, ibid., 747; Maj. Gen. W. T. Sherman to Maj. Gen. J. B. McPherson, September 1, 1863, ibid., 721; Special Orders No. 45, August 18, 1863, ibid., 720; Maj. Gen. W. T. Sherman to W. H. Hill, Esq., September 7, 1863, ibid., 722; Adj. Gen. L. Thomas to Hon. Edwin M. Stanton, October 15, 1863, ibid., 739; Brig. Gen. John P. Hawkins to Hon. Gerritt Smith, October 21, 1863, ibid., 743; Brig. Gen. Jas. S. Wadsworth to Adjutant General U.S. Army, December 16, 1863, ibid., 760.

59. W. T. Sherman to W. H. Hill, September 7, 1863, ibid., 722.

60. Isaac Shoemaker Diary, April 4, 13, 16, and 20, 1864, Duke.

61. Testimony of Madison Sharp, August 21, 1875, Allowed Claims, Mississippi, Washington Co., Martha Knox claim, No. 2296, 6776, SCC, RG 217. Also see Main, *Colored Cavalry.*

62. "A Brothers' War: Black Soldiers and Their Kinfolk," in Berlin, Reidy, and Rowland, *The Black Military Experience*, 658–59; 1st Lt. Robt. M. Campbell to Col. H. Scofield, July 18, 1863, ibid., 149; James Herney to Secretary Stanton, May 15, 1866, ibid., 779; Capt. T. A. Walker to Capt. J. S. Lord, January 24, 1865, ibid., 720; Circular, Office of Supt. Freedmen West Tenn., April 4, 1864, in Berlin et al., *Wartime Genesis*, 820.

63. Maj. Gen. S. A. Hurlbut to the President, March 27, 1863, in Berlin et al., *Destruction of Slavery*, 304.

64. 1st Lt. Robt. M. Campbell to Col. H. Scofield, July 18, 1863, in Berlin et al., *The Black Military Experience*, 149; James Herney to Secretary Stanton, May 15, 1866, Berlin et al., *The Black Military Experience*, 779; Capt. T. A. Walker to Capt. J. S. Lord, January 24, 1865, in Berlin et al., *The Black Military Experience*, 720; Circular, Office of Supt. Freedmen West Tenn., April 4, 1864, in Berlin et al., *Wartime Genesis*, 820.

65. For conflicts between the military and its chaplains, see, for example, monthly reports in the journal of George North Carruthers, Chaplain, 51st U.S. Colored Infantry, George North Carruthers Collection, LC, and General Order 41, 60th U.S. Colored Infantry, February 3, 1865, in Berlin, Reidy, and Rowland, *The Black Military Experience*, 709. The army's hostility toward the black family is recorded in just about every regimental record book; for example, in Regimental Records, RG 94, see: General Order 34, Acting Asst. Adj. Gen. Peter Karberg, August 8, 1864, 3d USCC Order Book; General Order 9, Col. H. Scofield, September 30, 1863, 47th USCI General Order Book; General Order 3, Lt. Col. Ferd. Peebles, January 6, 1865, 47th USCI General Order Book.

66. Chaplain James Peet to Brig. Gen. Lorenzo Thomas, September 30, 1864, in Berlin, Reidy, and Rowland, *The Black Military Experience*, 604–5; General Order 41, 60th U.S. Colored Infantry, February 3, 1865, ibid., 709.

67. Col. F. W. Lister to Brig. Gen. W. D. Whipple, December 14, 1865, and George Buck Hanon to Gen. Thomas, November 19, 1865, in Berlin et al., *The Black Military Experience*, 713–15. Also see Lt. Robert M. Campbell to Col. H. Scofield, July 18, 1863, ibid., 148–49; Capt. T. A. Walker to Capt. J. S. Lord, January 24, 1865, ibid., 719–20; monthly reports for August and November 1864 in Journal of George North Carruthers, Chaplain, U.S. Colored Infantry, 108–9, 113–17, George North Carruthers Collection, LC.

68. Noralee Frankel studies the nuances of black households in Mississippi after the war with her excellent analysis of military pension records in *Freedom's Women*. These relationships are more fully explored in chapter 4.

69. Lt. Col. John Foley to Lt. Col. T. Harris, January 11, 1865, in Berlin, Reidy, and Rowland, *The Black Military Experience*, 720; General Order 34, Acting Asst. Adj. Gen. Peter Karberg, August 8, 1864, 3d USCC Order Book, and General Order 9, Col. H. Scofield, September 30, 1863, 47th USCI General Order Book, Regimental Records, RG 94. Also, in Pensions, RG 15, see: Deposition C, Adam Metcalfe, October 3, 1903, and Deposition A, Mary Jane Kelley, October 3, 1903, Silas Clear claim, Wid. Cert. 560243; Deposition B, Laura Dickerson, July 16, 1901, Henry Bush claim, Invalid Cert. 745220.

70. Affidavits of Milton Brown and Courtney Burton, March 29, 1880, Philip Burton claim, Mother's App. 203450, Pensions, RG 15.

71. In Pensions, RG 15, see: Deposition, Dorcas Anderson, February 3, 1892, Isaac Anderson claim, Wid. Cert. 327221; Deposition B, Haynes Sharkey, April 11, 1895, Jefferson Boose claim, B. App. 400738; Deposition A, Hester Speed, April 8, 1910, John Divine claim, Cert. 700541; Deposition S, Hester Green, July 27, 1894, Daniel Bell claim, Cert. 421529; Deposition, Ellen Ben, November 20, 1903, John Ben claim, B. Cert. 654628; Deposition D, Willis Reed, October 5, 1896, Wesley Bradford claim, Wid. App. 440505; Deposition A, Mary Jane Clear, August 28, 1908, Silas Clear claim, Wid. Cert. 560243; Deposition C, Adam Metcalfe, October 3, 1890, Silas Clear claim, Wid. Cert. 560243; Deposition A, Minerva Butler Divine, July 11, 1900, Anthony Butler claim, Cert. 700–941; Deposition, Martha Willis, December 12, 1912, George Willis claim, Wid. Cert. 928295.

72. Deposition B, Haynes Sharkey, April 11, 1895, Jefferson Boose claim, B. App. 400738, and Deposition A, Hester Speed, April 8, 1910, John Divine claim, Cert. 700541, Pensions, RG 15.

73. Deposition S, Hester Green, July 27, 1894, Daniel Bell claim, Cert. 421529; Deposition, Ellen Ben, November 20, 1903, John Ben claim, B. Cert. 654628; Deposition D, Willis Reed, October 5, 1896, Wid. App. 440505; Deposition A, Mary Jane Kelley, August 28, 1908, Silas Clear claim, Wid. Cert. 560243; Deposition C, Adam Metcalfe, October 3, 1890, Silas Clear claim, Wid. Cert. 560243; Deposition A, Minerva Butler Divine, July 11, 1900, Anthony Butler claim, Cert. 700–941; and Deposition, Martha Willis, December 12, 1912, George Willis claim, Wid. Cert. 928295, Pensions, RG 15, NA.

74. Samuel Sawyer, Pearl P. Ingall and J. G. Forman to Maj. Gen. Curtis, December 29, 1862, in Berlin et al., *Wartime Genesis*, 675–76; Chaplain Samuel Sawyer to Maj. Gen. Samuel R. Curtis, January 26, 1863 (with enclosure), ibid., 674–77; from Regimental Records., RG 94, see: General Order 34, Acting Asst. Adj. Gen. Peter Karberg, August 8, 1864, 3d USCC Order Book; General Order 9, Col. H. Scofield, September 30, 1863, 47th USCI General Order Book; General Order 3, Lt. Col. Ferd Peebles, January 6, 1865, 47th USCI General Order Book. Also see Deposition C, Adam Metcalfe, October 10, 1903, Silas Clear file, 560243; Deposition A, Mary Jane Kelley, October 10, 1903; Silas Clear file, 560243; and Deposition B, Laura Dickerson, July 16, 1901, Henry Bush file, 745220, Pensions, RG 15.

75. General Order 75, Head Quarters District of Memphis, July 17, 1863, and editor's endnote in Berlin et al., *Wartime Genesis*, 714–15. For report of similar order in Natchez see Supt. of Freedmen Geo. W. Young to Brig. Gen. L. Thomas, March 31, 1864, ibid., 815–16.

76. In Pensions, RG 15, see: Deposition, Ellen Ben, November 20, 1903, John Ben claim, B. Cert. 654628; Deposition A, Hester Speed, April 8, 1910, John Divine claim, Cert. 700541; Questionnaire, Listfield Carter, September 8, 1897, Jonas Carter claim,

Wid. Cert. 582312; Jarrit Ware to Pension Examiner, June 13, 1890, and Deposition, Richard Chapman, June 13, 1890, William Brooks claim, Wid. App. 417996; Jefferson Willis and Mary Jane Griffin, Marriage Certificate, March 28, 1864, Jefferson Willis claim, Wid. Cert. 366054; Deposition A, Jane Boose, April 10, 1895, Jefferson Boose claim, B. App. 400738. Also see Frankel, *Freedom's Women*, 40–44.

77. Jarrit Ware to Pension Examiner, June 13, 1890, William Brooks claim, Wid. App. 417996, Pensions, RG 15.

78. Frankel, *Freedom's Women*, 43; Col. F. W. Lister to Brig. Gen. W. D. Whipple, December 14, 1865, in Berlin, Reidy, and Rowland, *The Black Military Experience*, 713–15. Also see Lt. Robert M. Campbell to Col. H. Scofield, July 18, 1863, ibid., 148–49; Capt. T. A. Walker to Capt. J. S. Lord, January 24, 1865, ibid., 719–20; Monthly reports for August and November 1864 in Journal of George North Carruthers, Chaplain, U.S. Colored Infantry, 108–9, 113–17, George North Carruthers Collection, LC.

79. General Order No. 41, Headquarters 60th U.S. Colored Infantry, February 3, 1865, in Berlin et al., *The Black Military Experience*, 709; and Col. F. W. Lister to Brig. Gen. W. D. Whipple, December 14, 1865, ibid., 713–15.

80. John Higgins to Hon. E. M. Stanton, May 28, 1866, in Berlin et al., *The Black Military Experience*, 474–75; and General Court Martial Order 12, Headquarters, Department of the Mississippi, November 11, 1865, ibid., 475–76.

81. Capt. O. J. Wright to Gen. Lorenzo Thomas, November 11, 1864, in Berlin et al., *The Black Military Experience*, 504; Lt. Col. David Brabson to Lt. Col. Irwin, July 7, 1864, ibid., 505. For fatigue duty, also see, for example, Adj. Gen. Lorenzo Thomas to Edwin M. Stanton, November 11, 1864, ibid., 169–72; Chaplain Samuel L. Gardner to Gen. Ullman, December 19, 1864, ibid., 417–18.

82. General court-martial case of Pvt. John Mitchell, June 15, 1864, in Berlin et al., *The Black Military Experience*, 449–52. Also see Register of Deaths and Deserters, Descriptive Roll, Descriptive Books for Companies A-F and G-M, 3d U.S. Colored Cavalry, Regimental Records, RG 94. Also useful are the descriptive books for the 5th U.S. Colored Heavy Artillery and the 47th U.S. Colored Infantry, Regimental Records, RG 94.

83. Price Warefield et al. to Hon. E. M. Stanton, February 20, 1865, in Berlin et al., *The Black Military Experience*, 459; David Washiton to Mr. A. Lincoln, November 26, 1864, ibid., 455; John Higgins to Hon. E. M. Stanton, May 28, 1866, ibid., 474–75; Capt. M. Mitchell to Major, December 20, 1865, ibid., 671; George Buck Hanon to "Genel thoms," November 19, 1865, ibid., 715.

84. Deposition of Ailsey Tyler, August 22, 1901, George Buckner claim, Wid. Cert. 736402; Deposition E, Emiline Farley, April 8, 1898, Gabriel Davis claim, Wid. Cert. 393852; Deposition E, Isiah Kelley, September 16, 1890, Silas Clear claim, Wid. Cert. 560243; and Affidavit, Julia Anderson, October 15, 1906, John Anderson claim, B. Cert. 632823, Pensions, RG 15.

Chapter 2. Locating Authority: Planter Women and the Shattering of the Plantation Household

1. Ann Matthews to Gov. Pettus, October 21, 1862, Records of the Administration of John J. Pettus, Roll 38, MGP. See also Mrs. L. E. Nicholson to Gov. Pettus, December 17, 1862, Roll 39, MGP.

2. Robinson, "Day of Jubilo"; Faust, "Altars of Sacrifice"; Rable, *Civil Wars,* 59–63.

3. See Fox-Genovese, *Within the Plantation Household,* 109–29; 163–65; 203–6; Edwards, *Scarlett Doesn't Live Here,* 15–31; McCurry, *Masters of Small Worlds*; Faust, *Mothers of Invention*; Cashin, *A Family Venture,* 99–121; Weiner, *Mistresses and Slaves*; Bynum, *Unruly Women.*

4. The study of race as a social construction has a long history in southern scholarship, including Jordan, *White Over Black*; E. Morgan, *American Slavery, American Freedom*; Fields, "Ideology and Race." Among more recent works, see K. Brown, *Good Wives*; Dailey, *Before Jim Crow;* Rosen, "The Gender of Reconstruction."

The study of whiteness as a race has come relatively late to southern history. See Hale, *Making Whiteness*; Helper, "Whole Lot of Shakin'"; Brattain, *The Politics of Whiteness*; Watkins, "Locating the Self"; Watts, "Imagining a White South"; Spear, "'Whiteness and the Purity of Blood.'"

Also see Morrison, *Playing in the Dark*; Roediger, *The Wages of Whiteness* and *Abolition of Whiteness*; Lipsitz, *Possessive Investment in Whiteness*; Crenshaw, *Critical Race Theory*; Haney López, *White by Law*; Back and Solomos, *Race and Racism.*

5. Faust, "Man's Business."

6. Faust, "Creation of Confederate Nationalism" and *Creation of Confederate Nationalism*; Thomas, *The Confederate Nation*; Escott, *After Secession*; Beringer et al., *Why the South Lost.*

7. Bettie Morton to My Dear Brother, June 15, 1861, Kiger Family Papers, UT; Ed. T. Worthington to My Dear Cousin, October 4, 1861, Worthington-Stone Papers, MDAH.

8. In the *Weekly Panola (Miss.) Star,* see: "Slave Tamperers," December 20, 1860; "No Cause for Alarm," December 27, 1860; "The Republic of Miss.," January 18, 1861; "Synopsis of Lincoln's Inaugural," March 7, 1861; "Peach Creek, January 18, 1861," January 24, 1861; "Patrols," June 18, 1861. See also Ellen Hyland to Pattie Hyland, April 14, 1861, Chamberlain-Hyland-Gould Family Papers, UT; in Administration of John J. Pettus, MGP, see: Joseph T. Tolbert to Gov. Pettus, September 2, 1861, roll 35; B. A. Smith to Gov. Pettus, December 11, 1862, roll 38; Augustus A. Montgomery to General, May 26, 1862, roll 40.

9. Kate S. Sperry Diary, August 23, 1861, Virginia State Library, quoted in Rable, *Civil Wars,* 265.

10. Ellen M. Hyland to Mary, May 25, 1861, Chamberlain-Hyland-Gould Family Papers, UT; Susie to Mother, March 1862, Downs Family Papers, MDAH; Rebecca to My Dear Sister, June 26, 1861, Downs Family Papers, MDAH; Ann Hardeman Journal, Janu-

ary 10, 1861, Mayes-Dimitry-Stuart Papers, MDAH. Also see Faust, "Altars of Sacrifice"; Rable, *Civil Wars*, 59–63.

11. Jim to My dear mother, June 5, 1861, Downs Family Papers, MDAH.

12. "The Military Spirit of Our People" and "To the Lady Readers of the *Star*," January 24, 1861; "A Few Words to Those Who Need Them," May 2, 1861; and "An Accusation against Women," 15 August 1861, *Weekly Panola Star*.

13. Faust, "Man's Business," 198. As Stephanie McCurry argues, gender was central to the southern construction of mastery and the politics of slavery before the war. By 1830 marriage, and the role of wives in particular, assumed a prominent position in the proslavery argument. Marriage, according to proslavery ideology, provided proof of a universal, transhistorical hierarchy between man and his dependents, be they his wife, children, or slaves. Slavery, the argument ran, was like marriage a "natural dependency," a compact between the strong and the weak. A wife's voluntary submission to her husband proved that hierarchy was fitting and natural, and slavery was merely a logical extension of this relationship—familiar, affectionate, and based on differences grounded in nature. Gender, according to McCurry, was pivotal in the construction of mastery, whiteness, and citizenship. See McCurry, "The Two Faces of Republicanism."

The tension between bourgeois political economy and women's subordinate position in the household is discussed in Kerber, *Women of the Republic*; Fox-Genovese, "Property and Patriarchy"; Stanley, "Conjugal Bonds and Wage Labor." For the northern emphasis on motherhood and the southern emphasis on the marriage relation, see Kerber, *Women of the Republic*, 269–88, and McCurry, "Two Faces," respectively. Petitions to the Mississippi governors appear to corroborate Kerber's and McCurry's conclusions. When petitioning the governor, northern women emphasized their authority as mothers while southern women pointed to their dependency as wives. See, for example, two petitions surrounding the case of Thomas Hutchinson: "Matrons and Daughters of Washington, Pa. to the Governor of Mississippi," July 1832, and "Female Petitioners of Vicksburg to Governor Abram M. Scott," July 25, 1832, Administration of Abram M. Scott, MGP.

14. "Stand Firm," May 23, 1861; "Letter from the Vindicators" and "Southern Literary Messenger," February 20, 1862, *Weekly Panola Star*.

15. See Faust, "Altars of Sacrifice."

16. Mrs. C. A. V. Deason to Gov. Pettus, August 17, 1861, Administration of John J. Pettus, roll 35, MGP; Ann Hardeman Journal, June 8, 1861, Mayes-Dimitry-Stuart Family Papers, MDAH. Also see Rebecca to My Dear Sister, June 27, 1861, Downs Family Papers, MDAH.

17. "A few Thoughts for Govr Pettus," anonymous, n.d., Administration of John J. Pettus, roll 41, MGP.

18. Mrs. A. L. Coverly to Gov. Pettus, November 9, 1861, Administration of John J.

Pettus, roll 36, MPG; see also Hannah Brown to Gov. Pettus, July 8, 1861, roll 38; M. J. Reynolds to Gov. Pettus, November 26, 1861, roll 36, administration of John J. Pettus, MGP.

19. A. L. Coverly to Gov. John J. Pettus, November 9, 1861, roll 36; Hannah Brown to Gov. Pettus, July 8, 1862, roll 38; H. M Shoemaker to Gov. Pettus, September 10, 1861, roll 35; Mary A. Harper to Gov. Pettus, October 8, 1862, administration of John J. Pettus, roll 38, MGP, MDAH.

20. Ann Hardeman Journal, February 27, April 26, September 6, 15, and 18, 1861, Stuart Family Papers, MDAH.

21. On the substitution of spiritual hierarchy for corporal hierarchy, see Faust's introduction, "Macaria, A War Story for Confederate Women," to Evans, *Macaria,* xxiii–xxiv. On white women's participation in the southern church, see Heyrman, *Southern Cross*; Mathews, *Religion in the Old South,* 101–24, 169; McCurry, "Defense of Their World," 212–14, 242–319; Beringer et al., *Why the South Lost,* 82–102, 336–67. As Elizabeth Fox-Genovese has suggested, planter women understood and constructed criticism in the ideological, structural, and spiritual frameworks provided by their class and race. I agree with Fox-Genovese that planter women never created a separate political consciousness which would have placed them in opposition to slavery and the men of their class. However, I disagree with Fox-Genovese's conclusion that the absence of planter women's political consciousness was rooted in their immersion in "subjective" versus "objective" thinking. See her *Plantation Household,* 334–71. Also see Lebsock, *Free Women of Petersburg,* 241–44, and de Lauretis, "Eccentric Subject."

22. Ann Hardeman Journal, April 21, June 9, and August 22, 1861, Stuart Family Papers, MDAH. See also Faust, introduction to Evans, *Macaria,* as in note 21, and Ownby, "Patriarchy."

23. McPherson, *Ordeal by Fire,* 181–82.

24. Petition to Gov. Pettus signed by Malissa F. Mayfield et al., June 31, 1862, Administration of John J. Pettus, roll 38, MGP; Petition regarding Richard Carter, October 25, 1862, roll 38, MGP; see also Ann Matthews to Gov. Pettus, October 21, 1862, roll 38, MGP; Mrs. L. E. Nicholson to Gov. Pettus, December 17, 1862, roll 39; Lydia Hodges to Gov. Pettus, January 26, 1863, roll 39, MGP.

25. Ann Eliza Hurst to Gov. Pettus, September 30, 1862, roll 38, MGP. See also Martha Dillahanty to Gov. Pettus, November 5, 1862, roll 39, MGP.

26. Edwards, "Law, Domestic Violence"; Bynum, *Unruly Women.*

27. Minerva Cook Journal, October 3, 1856, January 1, 1857, and January 28, 1857, Mrs. Jared Reese Cook Collection, MDAH.

28. See Chamberlain-Hyland-Gould Family Papers, UT; James Trooper Armstrong Papers, SHC; Kiger Family Papers, UT; Matthews Family Papers, MDAH.

29. L[ouisa] Burrus to Lizzie and Katie Burrus, January 4, 1858; S. M. T. to Lizzie and Kate, March 15, 1858; L. B. to Lizzy, June 1, 1858; M. L. B. to Lizzie, September 30, 1855; Mother to Lizzie, April 1, 1855, John C. Burrus Family Papers, MDAH. For supplies,

many Delta planters had to rely upon steamboats if their gardens failed. Taking advantage of a captive market, steamboats traveling from Vicksburg to Memphis hawked cotton seed, groceries, and dry goods on "trading boats." Also see Mary E. Bateman Diary, March 14, April 8, May 8 and 20, 1856, SHC. A daguerreotype boat made quite a stir stopping at Argyle plantation and ended up staying three days to assure that each family member got just the right "likeness" taken; see Bateman Diary, 1–3 April, 1856. The Burruses objected to this trade, perhaps because of high prices, but often they had no choice.

30. Ellen to Father, May 2, 1848, Chamberlain-Hyland-Gould Papers, UT.

31. Minerva Cook Journal, January 1, 1858, Mrs. Jared Reese Cook Collection, MDAH.

32. For uses of gender in class analysis see Silverblatt, *Moon, Sun, and Witches,* xix–xxxi, and "Women in States"; Fox-Genovese, "Placing Women's History in History" and "Gender, Class, and Power"; Stansell, *City of Women*; McCurry, "Two Faces"; Flax, "Postmodernism and Gender Relations"; Fraser and Nicholson, "Social Criticism without Philosophy"; Spivak, "Subaltern Studies"; MacCabe, foreword to *In Other Worlds*; O'Hanlon, "Recovering the Subject"; Gramsci, *Prison Notebooks,* 55–63, 323; Laclau and Mouffe, *Hegemony and Socialist Strategy*; Hall, "Signification, Representation, Ideology."

33. Minerva Cook Journal, December 29, 1856, and January 26 and 30, 1857, Mrs. Jared Reese Cook Collection, MDAH.

34. Minerva Cook Journal, December 29, 1856, and January 26, 1857, Mrs. Jared Reese Cook Collection, MDAH.

35. Edwards, *Gendered Strife*; Bardaglio, *Reconstructing the Household*; Bynum, *Unruly Women.*

36. Mary E. Bateman Diary, February 19, March 4, May 8, 22, and 23, and June 23, 1856, SHC.

37. Mary E. Bateman Diary, February 14, 22, and 23, March 19, August 24, and September 7, 1856, SHC.

38. Mary B. Carter to Gov. Pettus, March 14, 1863, Administration of John J. Pettus, roll 40, MGP. See, for example, Mrs. H. C. Heed to Gov. Pettus, January 7, 1863, roll 39; Mrs. T. N. Davis to Gov. Pettus, March 3, 1863, roll 40; Mary B. Carter to Gov. Pettus, March 14, 1863, roll 40; Letitia A. Andrews to Gov. Pettus, March 28, 1863, roll 40; E. M. Godwin to Gov. Pettus, April 28, 1863, roll 40; Mrs. Thos. E. Clarke and Mrs. C. V. Miller to Gov. Pettus, June 25, 1862, roll 38, Administration of John J. Pettus, MGP.

39. Berlin et al., *Wartime Genesis,* 621–900; Hess, "Confiscation."

40. Richard Winters to Gov. Pettus, September 24, 1863, roll 41; Rufinia A. Lawrence to Gov. Pettus, February 17, 1863, roll 40; Charles F. Howde to Gov. Pettus, August 23, 1862, roll 38, Administration of John J. Pettus, MGP.

41. Mrs. L. E. Nicholson to Gov. Pettus, December 17, 1862, roll 39; Lydia Hodges to Gov. Pettus, January 26, 1863, roll 39; Jane E. C. Pattison to Gov. Pettus, February 23, 1863,

roll 40, Administration of John J. Pettus, MGP; G. L. Blythe to Gov. Charles Clark, February 3, 1864, Administration of Charles Clark, MGP. Confederate companies, guerrillas, and outlaws proved to be a more visible threat to plantations than African-Americans. At least one gang of outlaws disguised themselves as blacks. In Administration of Charles Clark, box 56, MGP, see: W. E. Montgomery to Gov. Clark, November 25, 1863, and January 24 and 26 and August 7, 1864; Petition from the Citizens of Warren County to Gov. Clark, March 1865; Citizens of Bolivar County to Gov. Clark, February 20, 1864.

42. See, for example, Mary M. Smith to Gov. Pettus, June 30, 1863, roll 41; Mollie Shunnamaker to Gov. Pettus, n.d., roll 41; M. E. Fisher to Gov. Pettus, n.d., roll 41; Emily T. Stafford to Gov. Pettus, n.d., roll 41, Administration of John J. Pettus, MGP.

43. Robert Hudson to Gov. Pettus, August 20, 1861, roll 35, Administration of John J. Pettus, MGP.

44. Eugene Genovese grounds slaves' respect for powerful planters in their "admiration for aristocratic life" and in a need for security; see *Roll, Jordan, Roll*, 113–23. He is more explicit about planters' control of resources as the explanation for general consent to their domination in "Yeoman Farmers."

45. Lucie Armstrong to J. Y. Armstrong, November 22, 1861, James Trooper Armstrong Papers, SHC.

46. Samuel Magruder to Gov. Pettus, January 8, 1863, roll 39; Sallie B. Harris to Gov. Pettus, January 18, 1863, roll 39; Mrs. E. L. Greenwood to Gov. Pettus, June 30, 1862, roll 38; J. M. Holman to Gov. Pettus, June 30, 1862, roll 38, Administration of John J. Pettus, MGP.

47. Petition, Citizens of Canton to Governor Charles Clark, n.d.; Robert J. Hudson to Gov. Clark, October 6, 1864, Administration of Charles Clark, MGP.

48. W. H. Powell to Gov. Pettus, January 12, 1863, roll 39; G. W. Humphrey to Gov. Pettus, December 16, 1862, roll 39; E. A. Prince to Gov. Pettus, July 10, 1862, roll 38, Administration of John J. Pettus, MGP.

49. Emma S. Crutcher to William O. Crutcher, undated and January 6 and 14, 1861 [1862], Crutcher-Shannon Papers, UT.

50. Lezinka White to Annie E. "Bettie" Stuart, Yazoo City, August 15, 1863, Mayes-Dimitry-Stuart Family Papers, MDAH; "Ladie" Armstrong to J. A. Armstrong, August 24, 1864, James Trooper Armstrong Papers, SHC. Also see, among others, Mrs. H. Heed to Gov. Pettus, January 7, 1863, roll 39; F. Russel, E. H. Anderson, et al. to Gov. Pettus, January 12, 1863, roll 39; Mrs. I. N. Davis to Gov. Pettus, March 3, 1863, roll 40; Mary B. Carter to Gov. Pettus, March 14, 1863, roll 40, Administration of John J. Pettus, MGP.

51. Miss Mollie Colbert to Gov. Pettus, September 2, 1861, roll 35, among others, Administration of John J. Pettus, MGP.

52. Mrs. Almeria L. McGee to Gov. Pettus, October 26, 1861, roll 37; A. H. Raymond to Gov. Pettus, August 20, 1861, roll 35; W. McWillie to Gov. Pettus, September 3, 1861, roll 35; William A. Camfield to Gov. Pettus, September 12, 1861, roll 35; L. B. McLaurin to Gov.

Pettus, October 22, 1861, roll 37, Administration of John J. Pettus, MGP; also, from the *Weekly Panola Star*: "Communications," September 5, 1861; "Public Meeting," February 20, 1862. Almost half of the letters written from Ladies Aid Societies were authored by men. Keeping within their sphere, planter women enlisted the help of men to transact their business.

53. Emma S. Crutcher to William O. Crutcher, December 23, 1861, Crutcher-Shannon Papers, UT.

54. Bynum, *Unruly Women*, 111–57, and "War Within a War"; Rable, *Civil Wars*, 106–11; Faust, *Creation of Confederate Nationalism*, 52–56.

55. Emma to Will, December 29, 1861, and January 6, 14, and 20, 1861 [1862], Crutcher-Shannon Papers, UT.

56. Emma to Will, January 20, 1861 [1862], Crutcher-Shannon Papers, UT.

57. Ibid.

58. Ibid.; Emma to Will, January 12 and April 5 and 7, 1862, Crutcher-Shannon Papers, UT. Also see Saxton, *White Republic*; Roediger, *The Wages of Whiteness* and *Abolition of Whiteness*; Bynum, *Unruly Women*; Edwards, *Gendered Strife*; McCurry, *Masters of Small Worlds*.

59. Emma to Will, November 18 and December 29, 1861; February 7, 1862; March 27 and April 15, 1861 [1862]; June 22, 1862, Crutcher-Shannon Papers, UT.

60. Emma to Will, January 20, 1861 [1862]; see also Emma to Will, December 23 and 29, 1861; January 6 and 14, 1861 [1862]; March 6, 1862, Crutcher-Shannon Papers, UT.

61. Will to Emma, January 12, 1862, Crutcher-Shannon Papers, UT.

62. Will to Emma, October 29, 1861; February 2, 1862; Emma to Will, March 21, 1862; March 27, 1861 [1862]; April 9, 1862, Crutcher-Shannon Papers, UT.

63. Emma to Will, January 2, 1862, Crutcher-Shannon Papers, UT.

64. Emma to Will, December 29, 1861, Crutcher-Shannon Papers, UT.

65. Emma to Will, February 7, 1862, Crutcher-Shannon Papers, UT.

66. Emma to Will, January 2, 1862; January 14, 1861 [1862]; March 23, 1862, Crutcher-Shannon Papers, UT.

67. Emma to Will, undated; January 6, 1861 [1862]; January 14, 1861 [1862], Crutcher-Shannon Papers, UT.

68. Emma to Will, January 6, 1861 [1862], Crutcher-Shannon Papers, UT.

69. Emma to Will, undated, Crutcher-Shannon Papers, UT.

Chapter 3. The Perversion of Defeat: The Crisis of White Manhood

1. George Torrey to Gov. Humphreys, March 29, 1866, Administration of Benjamin G. Humphreys, MGP.

2. Anne Shannon Martin to Emma Shannon Crutcher, August 8, 1863, Crutcher-Shannon Papers, UT; Capt. W. E. Montgomery to Gov. Clark, November 23, 1863, Administration of Charles Clark, MGP; in the *Memphis Daily Appeal*: "Miscegenation,"

July 30, 1868; "Brownlow on the Carpetbaggers," September 28, 1868; "An Atrocious Transaction," September 27, 1867; "Shall the Negroes Have the Vice-Presidency?—Why Not?," September 28, 1867; "The Negro Mania," October 12, 1867; "Social Equality," December 11, 1867; "A Curious Story—Miscegenation, Superstition and Crime," August 14, 1868; "The Avengers of Blood," August 20, 1868; in the *Weekly Panola Star*: "A Negro Homicide in Rutherford, Tennessee," May 12, 1866; "Attempt to Kill Colonel Galloway," September 1, 1866; "Miscegenation—A Mixture of the Races," October 6, 1865; in the *Coahomian* of Friars Point, Miss.: "The Work Goes Bravely On," October 6, 1865.

3. McCurry, *Masters of Small Worlds* and "Two Faces"; Edwards, *Scarlett Doesn't Live Here*, 32–47; Stanley, *From Bondage to Contract*; Bynum, *Unruly Women*; Bardaglio, *Reconstructing the Household*.

4. Garner, *Reconstruction in Mississippi*, 123.

5. Bardaglio, *Reconstructing the Household;* Dailey, *Before Jim Crow*; Edwards, *Gendered Strife*; Waldrep, *Roots of Disorder*.

6. Anne Shannon to Emma, June-July 1863, Crutcher-Shannon Papers, MDAH. Christopher Waldrep also describes this incident in *Roots of Disorder,* 85.

7. Capt. W. E. Montgomery to Gov. Clark, November 23, 1863, Administration of Charles Clark, MGP. Curry's Gang was one of the many groups of bandits plaguing the Delta during and after the war. Hiding out in swamps or on islands, these men raided plantations and smuggled cotton, timber, and livestock. See Testimony of G. Gordon Adam, "Testimony Taken by the Joint Select Committee to Inquire into the Condition of Affairs in the Late Insurrectionary States. Mississippi, Vol. 1," *U.S. Senate Reports,* no. 41, pts. 11–12, serials 1494–95, 60–63; Capt. Scott Ewing, 49th USCI, Bolivar, to Capt. J. H. Weber, Acting AC of Freedmen Dist. West. Miss., September 30, 1865, RLR, AC, RG 105; Richard Harris, "Condition of the Colored People in Miss.," January 24, 1866, RLR, AC, RG 105; W. R. Barksdale to Gov. B. G. Humphreys, March 18, 1866, Administration of Benjamin G. Humphreys, MGP; Capt. W. E. Montgomery to Gov. Clark, January 26, 1864, Administration of Charles Clark, MGP; Citizens of Warren County to the General Commanding the Department of Ala., Miss., and East La., March 26, 1865, Administration of Charles Clark, MGP; A. B. Bradford to Gov. Clark, 27 August 1864, Administration of Charles Clark, MGP.

8. "The Arming of Negroes," *Memphis Daily Appeal,* July 2, 1863. Also in the *Appeal,* see: "Anarchy in the North," July 20, 1863; "The Destiny of the Negro," November 9, 1865; "Alabama and Mississippi," November 22, 1865; "Sensational Rumors," November 30, 1865; "Condition of the South," December 17, 1867; "Women in Distress," February 17, 1866. See also "We Have Warned the Frozen Vipers and They Now Seek to Destroy Us," *Weekly Panola Star,* December 14, 1867.

9. For bestiality, see "Whether ferocity, folly or beastly vulgarity," *Memphis Daily Appeal,* September 12, 1863. The language of bestiality continued after the war; in the *Appeal* see: "Planters and the Freed Man," November 15, 1865; "The Colored People,"

January 18, 1866; "The Cunning Plunderers," December 7, 1867; "Brownlow on the Colored Man," September 28, 1868.

10. In Administration of Charles Clark, MGP, see: R. S. Hudson to Clark, June 25, 1864; Hudson to William H. Mangum, May 24, 1864; Citizens of Warren County to the Department of Ala., Miss., and East La., March 25, 1865.

11. R. S. Hudson to Gov. Clark, May 24, 1864, and R. S. Hudson to William H. Mangum, May 24, 1864, Administration of Charles Clark, MGP; Judge Robert Hudson to Jefferson Davis, November 1864 in Robert Scott, *Official Records of the Union and Confederate Armies,* ser. 1, vol. 32, pt. 3, 625–27. Also see McCurry, "Citizens, Soldiers' Wives."

12. Faust, "Altars of Sacrifice," "Man's Business," and *Mothers of Invention*; Whites, *Crisis in Gender*; Rable, *Civil Wars*.

13. Sarah F. Buckner to Judge Sharkey, June 27, 1865, Administration of William L. Sharkey, MGP. Also see Summary Report, Claim of Malinda Williams, n.d.; Malinda Williams Testimony, 26 April 1875, Malinda Williams claim no. 19843, Mississippi—Bolivar Co., SCC, RG 217.

14. J. A. Hawley, Report of Tour, July 4, 1865, RLR, AC, RG 105.

15. As historian Laura Edwards recently argued in "The Problem of Dependency," the Black Codes built upon antebellum labor laws granting heads of household the right to oversee the labor and domestic life of their employees. In other words, the laws inscribed workers within the household as dependents. Also see Tomlins, *Law, Labor, and Ideology*; Woodman, *New South, New Law*; Stanley, *From Bondage to Contract*; Harris, *Presidential Reconstruction in Mississippi,* 121–53; Garner, *Reconstruction in Mississippi,* 75–121; Wharton, *The Negro In Mississippi,* 80–105; Waldrep, *Roots of Disorder,* 105–19.

16. E. Foner, *Reconstruction,* 216–80; Harris, *Presidential Reconstruction in Mississippi*; Wharton, *The Negro In Mississippi,* 90–97; Garner, *Reconstruction in Mississippi,* 147–55.

17. Amanda Worthington Journal, October 6 and August 7, 1865, Worthington Family Papers, MDAH.

18. See notes 13, 14, and 17; also, in the *Memphis Daily Appeal,* "Testimony Against the South," March 14, 1866, and "Speak Gently," March 18, 1866. Also see Silber, *The Romance of Reunion*; Faust, *Mothers of Invention*; Whites, *Crisis in Gender*.

19. *Statistics,* 267–68; Harris, *Presidential Reconstruction in Mississippi,* 121–53; Garner, *Reconstruction in Mississippi,* 75–121; Wharton, *The Negro In Mississippi,* 80–105.

20. Genovese, *Roll, Jordan, Roll,* 25–49; Tushnet, *American Law of Slavery*; Sydnor, "Southerner and the Laws"; Higginbotham, *Matter of Color*; Fox-Genovese and Genovese, "Slavery, Economic Development, and the Law"; Bynum, *Unruly Women,* 59–110; Bardaglio, *Reconstructing the Household*; Ayers, *Vengeance and Justice*.

21. Ann Red to Ophelia, February 18, 1879, Lockhart-Weir Collection, MDAH; Katie Burrus to Johnnie, February 27, 1883, John C. Burrus Family Papers, MDAH.

22. Edward Stuart to Father, October 19, 1863, John Bull Smith Dimitry Collection, Duke; Edward Stuart to Annie, March 6, 1868, Mayes-Dimitry-Stuart Papers, MDAH.

23. A. L. Hardeman to Adelaide, December 9, 1867, Mayes-Dimitry-Stuart Papers, MDAH; Edward Stuart to Father, October 19, 1863, John Bull Smith Dimitry Collection, Duke.

24. "Young Men," *Weekly Panola Star,* February 24, 1866; "The Southern People," *Coahomian,* October 6, 1865; "The Mississippi Valley," November 10, 1865.

25. Caroline Kiger to William Kiger, November 27, 1870, Kiger Family Papers, UT; Willie Kiger to My Dear Beloved Mother, December 28, 1868, and October 16, 1871, Kiger Family Papers, UT.

26. J. A. Hawley, Report of Tour, 4 July 1865, RLR, AC, RG 105.

27. Jean Smith to Martha Blanton and Sister, January 20, 1870, Blanton-Smith Letters, MDAH.

28. Wyatt-Brown, *Southern Honor;* also as in note 20.

29. Wharton, *The Negro in Mississipp*i, 149.

30. Testimony of William Davis, Colored, August 9, 1865, RLR, SFO–Yazoo City, SAC, RG 105; Lt. Col. R. S. Donaldson, Acting Asst. Comm., District of Northern Mississippi, to Lt. Stuart Eldridge, Acting Asst. Adj. Gen., October 4, 1865, RLR, AC, RG 105.

31. Lt. Col. R. S. Donaldson to Capt. J. H. Weber, Acting Asst. Adj. Gen., November 6, 1865, RLR, AC, RG 105; Pvt. Calvin Holly to Maj. Gen. O. O. Howard, December 16, 1865, in Berlin, Reidy, and Rowland, *The Black Military Experience,* 754–56; Asst. Insp. Gen. T. Sargent Free to Col. Samuel Thomas, Asst. Comm. of Freedmen, "Report of Tour of Northern Mississippi," September 9, 1865, RLR, AC, RG 105; also Sub-Comm. O. B. Foster, Skipwith's Landing, to Maj. T. S. Free, Insp. Gen., Freedmen's Bureau, Mississippi, December 12, 1865, Narrative Reports, AC, RG 105, M826, roll 30.

32. This is fully explored in chapter 4.

33. O. B. Foster to Maj. F. L. Free, December 12, 1865, Narrative Reports, AC, RG 105.

34. Sub-Comm. Thomas Smith, Chaplain, to Capt. E. Bamberger, Freedmen's Bureau, RLR, AC, RG 105.

35. Dean, *Shook over Hell*; Faust, "Christian Soldiers: The Meaning of Revivalism in the Confederate Army," in *Southern Stories,* 107–9; Wilson, *Baptized in Blood.*

36. R. S. Donaldson, Acting Asst. Comm., to Lt. Stuart Eldridge, October 5, 1865, and Agent J. H. Weber to Lt. Stuart Eldridge, December 31, 1865, RLR, AC, RG 105.

37. Testimony of G. Gordon Adam, "Testimony Taken by the Joint Select Committee to Inquire into the Condition of Affairs in the Late Insurrectionary States. Mississippi, vol. 1," *U. S. Senate Reports,* no. 41, parts 11 and 12, serials 1494 and 1495, 60–63.

38. Capt. Scott Ewing, 49th USCI, Bolivar, to Capt. J. H. Webber, Acting AC of Freedmen Dist. West. Miss., September 30, 1865, RLR, AC, RG 105; Richard Harris, "Condition of the Colored People in Miss.," January 24, 1866, RLR, AC, RG 105; W. R. Barksdale to Gov. Humphreys, March 18, 1866, Administration of Benjamin G. Humphreys, MGP.

39. In RLR, AC, RG 105, see Agent J. B. Webster, Sub-District Rosedale, to Captain, October 20, 1867; also see Sub-Asst. Comr. D. M. White to A. W. Preston, May 5, 1867; Sub-Asst. Comm. James H. Shepley to Preston, June 30, 1867; Sub-Asst. Comm. W. S. Myers to Maj. Gen. Thos. J. Wood, January 17, 1867; S. K. Ingram to General Ord, September 12, 1867; Agent C. T. Lawson to Acting Asst. Adj. Gen. Merritt Barber, November 15, 1867.

40. Allen P. Huggins to Maj. Gen. S. C. Greene, May 12, 1868, RLR, AC, RG 105; "Testimony Taken by the Joint Select Committee to Inquire into the Condition of Affairs in the Late Insurrectionary States. Mississippi, vol. 1," *U.S. Senate Reports,* no. 41, parts 11 and 12, serials 1494 and 1495; Trelease, *White Terror,* 272–301; Fitzgerald, *Union League Movement,* 50–57, 224–26.

41. Kantrowitz, "One Man's Mob," 70.

42. Richard Harris to Maj. Gen. C. B. Fisk, January 24, 1866, RLR, AC, RG 105; Deposition of Charles Coe, September 8, 1868, County of Shelby, State of Tennessee, RLR, AC, RG 105. The countless complaints registered with the Freedmen's Bureau graphically illustrate that most violent acts occurred without masks in broad daylight. Masked raids generally occurred against independent freedpeople—those without employers. Perhaps white southerners cloaked themselves to harm those who did not "belong" to them or any other white man. In some ways they were stepping outside the bonds of mastery into the realm of the "slave patroller."

43. Trelease, *White Terror,* 16–21; MacLean, *Behind the Mask.*

44. Wilson, *Baptized in Blood*; Silber, *The Romance of Reunion*; Foster, *Ghosts of the Confederacy.*

45. "Our Fate in Case of Failure," *Memphis Daily Appeal,* September 7, 1863. Also see, for example, "Letter From Morton, Mississippi," *Memphis Daily Appeal,* August 20, 1863, and, in the *Weekly Panola Star*: "A Declaration," February 7, 1861; "The Yanks Coming," June 25, 1862; "The Future of the Southern States," June 22, 1865.

46. On transgression as empowering, see Dollimore, *Sexual Dissidence*; Butler, *Gender Trouble*; Stallybrass and White, *Transgression*; Burke, *Popular Culture*; Garber, *Vested Interests.*

47. "The Colored People," *Memphis Daily Appeal,* January 18, 1866.

48. Dailey, *Before Jim Crow,* 85–87, 132–54; Edwards, *Gendered Strife,* 7–10, 24–31.

49. "Our Planters are the Freedmen," *Memphis Daily Appeal,* November 15, 1865. Also see "The Nigger in Everything," *Weekly Panola Star,* August 18, 1865, and, in the *Coahomian*: "Negro Equality," September 22, 1865; "Voodooism in Mobile," October 13, 1865; "The Situation—Negro Testimony," October 27, 1865. Slaveholders flirted with the biological justification for racially based slavery before the war. Josiah Nott, most notably, from his laboratories at the University of Pennsylvania attempted to prove a biological distinction between African- and European-Americans by studying cranial measurements.

50. In the *Memphis Daily Appeal,* see: "Culture of Cotton by Free Labor," August 29, 1863; "Whether ferocity, folly or beastly vulgarity," September 12, 1863; "Our Planters are the Freedmen," November 15, 1865; "The Colored People," January 18, 1866; "Cunning Plunderers," December 12, 1867; "Brownlow on the Colored Man," September 28, 1868. In the *Coahomian,* see: "Voodooism in Mobile," October 13, 1865; "The Columbus (Miss.) Index Says," October 27, 1865.

51. "Miscegenation," *Memphis Daily Appeal,* July 30, 1868. Also see, for example, in the *Appeal:* "Brownlow on the Carpetbaggers," September 28, 1868; "An Atrocious Transaction," September 27, 1867; "Shall the Negroes Have the Vice-Presidency?—Why Not?," September 28, 1867; "The Negro Mania," October 12, 1867; "Social Equality," December 11, 1867; "A Curious Story—Miscegenation, Superstition and Crime," August 14, 1868; "The Avengers of Blood," August 20, 1868; also, in the *Weekly Panola Star,* "A Negro Homicide in Rutherford, Tennessee," May 12, 1866, and "Attempt to Kill Colonel Galloway," September 1, 1866; also, in the *Coahomian,* "Miscegenation—A Mixture of the Races" and "The Work Goes Bravely On," October 6, 1865.

52. Dailey, *Before Jim Crow;* Edwards, *Gendered Strife;* Hale, *Making Whiteness.*

53. "An Atrocious Transaction," *Memphis Daily Appeal,* September 27, 1867. Also in the *Appeal,* see: "The Negro Again," March 13, 1866; "Shall the Negroes Have the Vice-Presidency," September 28, 1867; "Negro Mania," October 12, 1867; "Social Equality," December 11, 1867; "Miscegenation," July 30, 1868; "A Curious Story: Miscegenation, Superstition and Crime," August 14, 1868; and, in the *Coahomian:* "A Dream on a Piece of Bride's Cake—And Its Result," January 19, 1866, and "Friendly Feelings in the South," February 9, 1866.

54. "The Mobile *Register,*" *Memphis Daily Appeal,* August 20, 1863.

55. "A Dream on a Piece of Bride's Cakes—And Its Result," *Coahomian,* January 19, 1866; "We Need a Male School," *Weekly Panola Star,* March 31, 1866; "Wanted," *Weekly Panola Star,* March 20, 1869; "Shame, Shame," *Memphis Daily Appeal,* August 4, 1868; "Our Colored Rulers," *Memphis Daily Appeal,* September 19, 1868; "A Tennessee Lady Makes 'Her Mark,'" *Memphis Daily Appeal,* January 23, 1866.

Chapter 4. Husbands, Wives, and Sweethearts: Gender Relations within African-American Households

1. Deposition B, Silas Clear, October 3, 1890, Silas Clear claim, Wid. Cert. 560243, Pensions, RG 15.

2. Deposition A, Mary Jane Kelley, October 3, 1890; Deposition A, Mary J. Clear, August 28, 1903, Silas Clear claim, Wid. Cert. 560243, Pensions, RG 15.

3. Deposition A, Mary Jane Kelley, October 3, 1890; Deposition C, Adam Metcalfe, October 3, 1890, Silas Clear claim, Wid. Cert. 560243, Pensions, RG 15.

4. As in note 2.

5. Edwards, *Gendered Strife*, "Marriage Covenant," and "Politics of Marriage"; Dailey, *Before Jim Crow*, 89–94; Franke, "Becoming a Citizen."

6. McClintock, "Civil War Pensions"; Franke, "Becoming a Citizen"; Kaye, "The Personality of Power," 112–72; Frankel, *Freedom's Women*, 79–159.

7. Franke, "Becoming a Citizen"; Kaye, "The Personality of Power," 112–72; Frankel, *Freedom's Women*, 79–159.

8. I have been influenced greatly by Elsa Barkley Brown's argument that the historian "can only unravel the threads of the community by seeing community not as a static structure but as a historical process." She emphasizes that, as historians, we need to explore "the ways in which diversity and collectivity *simultaneously* wove community and the ways in which events could lead individuals *simultaneously* closer to and further away from community"; see "Uncle Ned's Children," 575–76. Also see her "Public Sphere," 111–41.

9. See chapter 1 of this work; Frankel, *Freedom's Women*, 40–46.

10. See chapter 1 of this work; Frankel, *Freedom's Women*, 28–55.

11. Agreement with Freedmen, E. P. Brickell, July 14, 1865, Labor Contracts, AC, RG 105, M826, roll 43; in Pensions, RG 15, see: Deposition, Dorcas Anderson, February 3, 1892, Isaac Anderson claim, Wid. Cert. 327211; Affidavit, Julia Anderson, October 15, 1915, John Anderson claim, B. Cert. 632823; Deposition A, Minerva Butler Divine, July 11, 1900, Anthony Butler claim, Cert. 700–941; Deposition A, Mary Jane Kelley, October 3, 1890, Wid. Cert. 560243; Deposition, Ellen Ben, November 20, 1903, John Ben claim, B. Cert. 654628; Deposition, Martha Willis, December 12, 1922, George Willis claim, Wid. Cert. 928295; Deposition C, Roxie Passmon, June 30, 1899, Charles Willis claim, Wid. Cert. 483850; Affidavit, Milton Brown, March 29, 1880, Philip Burton claim, Mother's App. 203450.

12. Edwards, "The Problem of Dependency."

13. In ULR, WDM, AC, RG 105, see: T. P. Anderson to J. H. Weber, AAC, September 23, 1865 and W. S. Myers, Subcommissioner, Greenville, to Capt. J. H. Weber, November 26, 1865; in Labor Contracts, AC, RG 105, M826, roll 44, see: Contract, A. A. Swayze, Adams Place, Yazoo Co., July 18, 1865, and Contract, William B. Johnson, Yazoo Co., July 31, 1865.

14. Morris, *Slavery and the Law*; Edwards, *Gendered Strife*; Genovese, *Roll, Jordan, Roll*, 25–49; Tushnet, *American Law of Slavery*; Sydnor, "Southerner and the Laws"; Higginbotham, *Matter of Color*.

15. McCurry, "Two Faces"; Edwards, *Gendered Strife*, 7–10; Stanley, *From Bondage to Contract*, 1–28; Bynum, *Unruly Women*; Bardaglio, *Reconstructing the Household*.

16. Roediger, *The Wages of Whiteness* and *Abolition of Whiteness*; Lipsitz, *Possessive Investment in Whiteness*; Haney López, *White by Law*.

17. Edwards, *Gendered Strife*; Gilfoyle, "Hearts of Nineteenth-Century Men," 135, 151;

Dubler, "Governing Through Contract"; Grossberg, *Governing the Hearth*; Stansell, *City of Women*; Bynum, *Unruly Women*.

18. Frankel, *Freedom's Women*, 79–145.

19. Deposition M, Lewis Williams, May 9, 1905, Samuel Hayden claim, Wid. App. 729789, Pensions, RG 15.

20. T. F. Maurin, Special Examiner, Vicksburg, to Honorable Commissioner of Pensions, April 16, 1895, Jefferson Boose claim, App. 400738, Pensions, RG 15.

21. Deposition A, Anna Hayden, May 6, 1905, Samuel Hayden claim, Wid. App. 729789, Pensions, RG 15. For a sample of similar claims, see Deposition E, Clara Boose, April 11, 1895, Jefferson Boose claim, B. App. 400738; Deposition A, Belle Harris, November 15, 1899, Samuel Bugg claim, Wid. Cert. 527482; Deposition B, Taylor Young, August 17, 1894, Daniel Bell claim, Cert. 421529, Pensions, RG 15.

22. Deposition, Isabella Harris, May 22, 1901, Samuel Bugg claim, Wid. Cert. 527482; Deposition K, Dock Townshend, May 8, 1905, Samuel Hayden claim, Wid. App. 729789, Pensions, RG 15. Also see Deposition M, Lewis Williams, May 9, 1905, Samuel Hayden claim, Wid. App. 729789; Deposition B, Haynes Sharkey, April 11, 1895, Jefferson Boose claim, B. App. 400738, Pensions, RG 15.

23. Deposition, Isabella Harris, May 22, 1901, Samuel Bugg claim, Wid. Cert. 527482, Pensions, RG 15. Under the 1864 law, women applying for a military widow's pension had to prove that they had been married to the soldier and never remarried after his death. Suspicious pension examiners went to great lengths to ferret out common-law marriages, interviewing every friend, enemy, and mere acquaintance of the applicant. Yet out of hundreds of interviews, very few examples of equivocation or contradictory evidence exist. The community shared a common understanding of what constituted marriage and what did not. A couple was perceived as married by the community if they let themselves be referred to as husband and wife, or if a woman casually called herself by her boyfriend's name. See Frankel, *Freedom's Women*, 94. See also, in Pensions, RG 15: Deposition, Charles Byas, February 21, 1876, John Anderson claim, B. Cert. 632823; Deposition A, Mary J. Clear, August 28, 1903, Silas Clear claim, Wid. Cert. 560243; Deposition M, Lewis Williams, May 9, 1905, Samuel Hayden claim, Wid. App. 729789; Deposition B, Silas Clear, October 3, 1890, Silas Clear claim, Wid. Cert. 560243; Deposition K, Dock Townsend, May 8, 1905, Samuel Hayden claim, Wid. App. 729789; Deposition K, Jane Reed, July 27, 1894, Daniel Bell claim, Cert. 421529; Deposition A, Maria Bell, September 23, 1890, Daniel Bell claim, Cert. 421529.

24. Deposition B, Taylor Young, July 17, 1894, Daniel Bell claim, Cert. 421529, Pensions, RG 15.

25. Affidavit, Robert Hudson, February 4, 1920, Robert Hudson claim, X.C.2.656–260, Pensions, RG 15.

26. Deposition, Charles Byas, February 21, 1876, John Anderson claim, B. Cert. 632823, Pensions, RG 15. For other examples, see in Pensions, RG15: Deposition M, Lewis

Williams, May 9, 1905, Samuel Hayden claim, Wid. App. 729789; Deposition B, Silas Clear, October 3, 1890, Silas Clear claim, Wid. Cert. 560243; Deposition K, Dock Townsend, May 8, 1905, Samuel Hayden claim, Wid. App. 729789; Deposition K, Jane Reed, July 27, 1894, Daniel Bell claim, Cert. 421529; and Deposition A, Maria Bell, September 23, 1890, Daniel Bell claim, Cert. 421529.

27. Affidavit, Charles Mitchell, May 31, 1897, John Hunter claim, Wid. App. 566309; Commissioner of Pensions to Mrs. Georgia Hunter, April 3, 1908, John Hunter claim, Wid. App. 566309; Deposition A, Edward Brown, November 7, 1904, Edward Brown claim, C. 2507843; Deposition, Nealy Graham, January 27, 1919, Nealy Graham claim, Wid. Cert. 931872; Deposition, Amanda Bell, March (Mark) Bell claim, Wid. App. 707670; Deposition B, Taylor Young, August 17, 1894, Daniel Bell claim, Cert. 421529; Deposition A, Hattie Willis, June 27, 1899, Charles Willis claim, Wid. Cert. 438850, Pensions, RG 15.

28. "Report of the Operations of the Bureau of Refugees, Freedmen, and Abandoned Lands for the State of Mississippi," November 28, 1867, AC, RG 105; "Report Upon the Conduct of Affairs Concerning the Freedmen in Mississippi," October 14, 1868, AC, RG 105.

For an interesting analysis of the role of regulation, see Franke, "Becoming a Citizen."

29. Quoted in Franke, "Becoming a Citizen," 289.

30. *Congressional Globe*, 38th Cong., 1st sess., 1864, p. 3233, cited in Franke, "Becoming a Citizen," 268; "Civil Rights Act of November 25, 1865," chap. 4, pt. 2, in *Laws of the State of Mississippi, . . . 1865*; McClintock, "Civil War Pensions," 473; Frankel, *Freedom's Women*, 82–83.

31. In Pensions, RG 15, see: Affidavit, Sallie Gillespie, November 14, 1905; Affidavit, Phoeby Broady, October 28, 1905; Deposition L, Iverson Granderson, May 10, 1905, Samuel Hayden claim, Wid. App. 729789; Deposition D, Perry Tillman, November 7, 1890, Thomas Alexander claim, Wid. App. 668360.

32. Deposition N, Anna Hayden, May 15, 1905, Samuel Hayden claim, Wid. App. 729789, Pensions, RG 15.

33. In RC, SFO–Yazoo City, AC, RG 105, see: Harriet Bordan, October 16, 1867; Caroline Denby, October 15, 1867; *Mrs. Garrett v. Oliver Garrett*, August 18, 1868; also see *Rose McClellan v. Randolph McClellan*, January 28, 1868, RC, SFO–Rosedale, AC, RG 105. Also see Schwalm, *Hard Fight*, 260–66.

34. In RC, SFO–Yazoo City, AC, RG 105, see: Caroline Denby, October 15, 1867; Susan Griffin, October 2, 1867; Harriet Bordan, October 16, 1867. Also, in RC, SFO–Yazoo City, SAC, RG 105, see: *Mrs. Garrett v. Oliver Garrett*, August 8, 1868; *Lucy Patterson v. Robert Patterson*, August 19, 1868; *Kitty Pale v. Isaac Pale*, August 24, 1868.

35. Glen Edwards, October 1, 1867, RC, SFO–Yazoo City, AC, RG 105; *Aura Dunlap v. U.S*, January 27, 1868, RC, SFO–Rosedale, AC, RG 105; *Capt. Gentry and Col. William*

Brown v. Willis Maddox, n.d., RC, SFO–Rosedale, SAC, RG 105; Susan Griffin, October 2, 1867, RC, SFO–Vicksburg, SAC, RG 105. Also, from Pensions, RG 15, see sources in note 21.

36. This changed in 1871, when the Mississippi Revised Code granted a married woman the rights to the "fruits of her personal service." See "Property of the Wife," Article 5, Section 1778, *Laws of the State of Mississippi, . . . 1871.* For a husband's right to his wife's wages more generally, see Siegel, "Marital Status Law"; Clark, "Matrimonial Bonds"; Dubler, "Governing Through Contract"; Speth, "Married Women's Property Acts."

37. In Pensions, RG 15, see: Deposition, Jane Graham, December 7, 1922, Nealy Graham claim, Wid. Cert. 931872; Deposition, Winnie Plummer, February 21, 1876, John Anderson claim, B. Cert. 632823; Deposition, John Ash, December 7, 1922, Nealy Graham claim, Wid. Cert. 931872; Deposition, J. L. Love, Stephen Anderson claim, Wid. Cert. 328874; Deposition, Minnie W. Asberry, March 26, 1925, William Asberry claim, B. Cert. 960729; Deposition A, Frances Bush, December 30, 1902, Henry Bush claim, Invalid Cert. 745220.

38. In Pensions, RG 15, under Henry Bush claim, Invalid Cert. 745220, see: Deposition A, Frances Bush, July 15, 1901; Deposition B, Laura Dickerson, July 16, 1901; Deposition F, David Bush, July 16, 1901; Deposition A, Frances Bush, December 30, 1902; Deposition K, Armstead Davis, March 15, 1902; Deposition K, Gray Cooper, March 15, 1902; Deposition, Samuel Roper, May 16, 1900; Affidavit, Sallie Ware, September 14, 1896.

39. Deposition A, Frances Bush, July 15, 1901; Deposition F, David Bush, July 16, 1901, Henry Bush claim, Invalid Cert. 745220, Pensions, RG 15.

40. See, for example, *Sidney Ann Carter v. City of Vicksburg,* August 23, 1868, RC, SFO–Vicksburg, SAC, RG 105. See also Miller et al., "Between Emancipation and Enfranchisement," 1069–71.

41. Hunter, *To 'Joy My Freedom*; Forbes, *African American Women*; Malcolmson, *English Laundresses*; Tucker, *Telling Memories.*

42. Deposition A, Frances Bush, July 15, 1901, and Deposition A, Frances Bush, December 30, 1902, Henry Bush claim, Invalid Cert. 745220, Pensions, RG 15.

43. Stansell, *City of Women*; Walkowitz, *Prostitution and Victorian Society*; Hill, *Their Sisters' Keepers*; Bell, *Prostitute Body.*

Chapter 5. Rights and Obligations: Marriage, Alternative Households, and the Reconstruction of Plantation Labor

1. George C. Corliss, SAC, Friars Point, to Acting Asst. Adj. Gen. Stuart Eldridge, April 9, 1866, RLR, AC, RG 105.

2. T. Sargent Free used the phrase "in a violent heat" in his "Report of Tour of Northern Mississippi," September 9, 1865, RLR, AC, RG 105.

3. Genovese, "'Our Family, White and Black.'" See also Father to Dear Child, June 23,

1861, Chamberlain-Hyland-Gould Family Papers, UT; John C. Burrus Family Papers, MDAH.

4. *Congressional Globe,* 38th Cong., 1st sess., p. 3233, cited in Franke, "Becoming a Citizen," 268; McClintock, "Civil War Pensions," 473.

5. Gutman, *Black Family*; Woodman, "Sequel to Slavery"; R. Davis, *Good and Faithful Labor*; Wayne, *Reshaping of Plantation Society*; Mann, "Slavery, Sharecropping, and Sexual Inequality"; Litwack, *Been in the Storm So Long*; Jacqueline Jones, *Labor of Love*; Saville, *The Work of Reconstruction*; Malone, *Sweet Chariot*; E. Brown, "Uncle Ned's Children"; Frankel, *Freedom's Women*; Edwards, *Gendered Strife*; Kolchin, *First Freedom*, 32–33, 62–63; L. Rowland, *Conference Group on Women's Historians Newsletter*, 22 (October 1991): 21–22; Schwalm, *Hard Fight*.

6. See Frankel *Freedom's Women*; Stevenson, *Life in Black and White*, and "Black Family Structure." For the Delta see Exhibit, Courtney Burton, November 9, 1883, Philip Burton claim, Mothers Appl. 203450; Deposition C, Roxie Passmon, June 30, 1899, Charles Willis claim, Wid. Cert. 483850; Deposition A, Maria Bell, September 9, 1890, Daniel Bell claim, Cert. 421529; Deposition, Martha Willis, December 12, 1922, George Willis claim, Wid. Cert. 928295; Deposition E, Emiline Farley, April 8, 1898, Gabriel Davis claim, Pensions, RG 15.

7. T. Sargent Free, "Report of Tour of Northern Mississippi," September 9, 1865, RLR, AC, RG 105.

8. T. P. Anderson to J. H. Weber, Acting Asst Comr, September 23, 1865, ULR, AC, WDM, RG, 105; C. A. Montross, "Statement of Plantations," March 1, 1864; Plantation leased March 1864, Vicksburg, Second Special Agency, RG 366, and in Report of the Court of Inquiry on the Proceeding for the Sale of Cotton, RG 159: vol. 1, 8–22, 69–71; Testimony of Maj. Gen. Samuel R. Curtis, March 19, 1863, Testimony of Lt. John Guilee, March 23, 1863, vol. 1, 37–39; Testimony of Willis Scott, June 27, 1863, vol. 2, 562–63; and Testimony of Gideon Pillow, July 2, 1863, vol. 2, 580–81, 683–84.

9. Charles W. Clark to J. H. Weber, October 10, 1865, WDM, RG 105.

10. *Harriet Murray v. Dick Porter,* November 1867, RC, SFO–Sardis, SAC, RG 105. The reports of beatings are too numerous to mention. See, in SAC, RG 105, the Registers of Complaints from SFOs in Yazoo City, Sardis, Greenville, and Rosedale; also, in AC, RG 105, M826, roll 30, the Narrative Reports, Sub Districts of Skipwith's Landing, Sardis, Greenville, Washington and Issaquena Counties, Tunica Co., Bolivar Co., Grenada, Yazoo Co., Rosedale, Greenwood, Sunflower Co., McNutt, Coahoma Co., and Carroll Co.

11. Fifty-eight percent of the labor contracts registered with the Bureau permitted workers land for gardens and livestock in the Delta. See Labor Contracts, Washington, Issaquena, Tunica, Yazoo, Sunflower, and DeSoto Counties, AC, RG 105, M826.

12. For examples of labor contracts stating people could "cultivate as much land as they desire," in Labor Contracts, AC, RG 105, M826, roll 43, see: William A. Fulgate and

Freedmen, January 1, 1865; J. P. Wilson and Freedmen, June 30, 1865; M. B. Lamb and Freedmen, July 1, 1865; Ben Roach and Freedmen, July 24, 1865; Eveline Purvis and Freedmen, July 7, 1865; Mrs. M. C. Vanderling and Freedmen, July 10, 1865; John H. Woolfolk, June 26, 1865.

13. For example, in the *Coahomian,* "Our Labor System," November 3, 1865; "We clip the following sensible remarks," November 10, 1865; in the *Weekly Panola Star,* "White Laborers," December 23, 1865; "The Question of Labor," January 20, 1866; "Free Negro Labor—Will It Pay Next Year," December 11, 1867.

14. In 1865, nuclear families made up only 25 percent of all labor contracts. By 1866, 53 percent of the contracts represented nuclear families. See Labor Contracts, Washington, Issaquena, Tunica, Yazoo, Sunflower, and DeSoto Counties, AC, RG 105, M826.

15. In Pensions, RG 15, see: Affidavit, Robert Hudson, February 4, 1920, Robert Hudson claim, X.C.2.656–260; Lucy Calhoun to J. L. Davenport, March 26, 1912, Jeff Washington (John C. Calhoun) claim, WO 931–744; Deposition A, Belle Harris, November 15, 1899, Samuel Bugg claim, Wid. Cert. 527482; Deposition, Jane Graham, December 7, 1922, Nealy Graham claim, Wid. Cert. 931872; Deposition, Dorcas Anderson, February 3, 1892, Isaac Anderson claim, Wid. Cert. 327211; Deposition A, Jane Boose, April 10, 1895, Jefferson Boose Claim, B. App. 400738.

16. In 1865, 25 percent of the contracts were signed by nuclear families. By 1866, the number had increased to 53 percent. See Labor Contracts, Washington, Issaquena, Tunica, Yazoo, Sunflower, and DeSoto Counties, AC, RG 105, M826.

17. Edwards, "Marriage Covenant" and "Politics of Marriage"; Dailey, *Before Jim Crow,* 89–94; Franke, "Becoming a Citizen."

18. For the Mississippi Valley, see Frankel, *Freedom's Women*; Powell, *New Masters*; R. Davis, *Good and Faithful Labor*; Wayne, *Reshaping of Plantation Society*; Malone, *Sweet Chariot.*

19. In 1865, 84 percent of all contracts in the Delta provided food, rations, and medicine. By 1866, only 47 percent provided such services, and of those, only 27 percent provided them for family members not working on the landowner's crop. See Labor Contracts, Washington, Issaquena, Tunica, Yazoo, Sunflower, and DeSoto Counties, AC, RG 105, M826.

20. Jerry Lightwood and James Rowe, January 19, 1866, Labor Contracts, AC, RG 105, M826, roll 49.

21. Agreement with Freedmen, Marietta Heard and Freedmen, January 1, 1866, Labor Contracts, AC, RG 105, M826, roll 49.

22. See note 19. Examples, in Labor Contracts, AC, RG 105, M826, include: A. T. Carson and Freedmen, January 1, 1866, Yazoo Co.; C. A. Gilman and Freedmen, January 8, 1866, Yazoo Co.; J. B. O'Reilly and Freedmen, January 1, 1866, Yazoo Co.; P. M. Black and Edward Burrell, January 15, 1866, DeSoto Co.; J. M. Vickers and Freedmen, January 8, 1866, Tunica Co.

23. Thos. Smith to Capt. J. H. Weber, AAAG, November 3, 1865, RLR, AC, RG 105. Also see J. L. Haynes to Capt. B. F. Morey, AAG, and Jno. A. McDonough to Gen. Thomas, June 17, 1865, RLR, RC, RG 105. Also see Frankel, *Freedom's Women,* 72–78; Schwalm, *Hard Fight,* 257–60.

24. *Amanda Williams v. John Griffin,* September 6, 1867, RC, SFO–Greenville, SAC, RG 105. Williams earned $37.20 in wages and $29.50 from poultry. Also see *Isaac Harris v. E. Warfield,* n.d., RC, SFO–Rosedale, SAC, RG 105. Also see L. Jones, "Gender, Race, and Itinerant Commerce"; S. Holt, "A Time to Plant."

25. In Labor Contracts, RG 105, M826, see, for example, Louisa Reid and Freedmen, January 4, 1866, Yazoo Co.; W. G. Caruthers et al. and King Solomon et al., January 23, 1866, DeSoto Co.; J. E. Grant and Lipton Lewis et al., January 6, 1866, DeSoto Co.; Silas Turner and Wells Turner, January 15, 1866, DeSoto Co.; P. M. Black and Edward Burrell et al., January 15, 1866, DeSoto Co.; Andrew L. Shotwell and Freedmen, January 23, 1866, Tunica Co.; Nathaniel Bettis and Freedmen, January 4, 1866, Coahoma Co.; Charles M. Terry and Squire Terry and his wife, Amanda, February 6, 1866, DeSoto Co.; J. R. Powell and Freedmen, February 22, 1866, Washington Co.; A. J. Carter and Freedmen, January 23, 1866, Washington Co.

26. For examples of contracts limiting livestock and restricting chickens for consumption only, in Labor Contracts, RG 105, M826, Roll 49 see: W. G. Caruthers et al. and King Solomon et al., January 23, 1866, DeSoto Co.; P. M. Black and Edward Burrell et al., January 15, 1866, DeSoto Co.; E. W. Dale and Freedmen, January 20, 1866, Tunica Co. In Roll 50 see: Newton F. Anderson and Nelson Watkins and Sons, February 12, 1866; J. D. Vance and Co. and Freedmen, November 1, 1866, Bolivar Co.; J. R. Powell and Freedmen, February 22, 1866, Washington Co.; Mary Hord and Freedmen, September 7, 1868, Washington Co.

27. Garner, *Reconstruction in Mississippi,* 195; "State Law in Regard to Estrays," RC, SFO–Vicksburg, SAC, RG 105. For recent literature on common land or the use of the range, see McCurry, *Masters of Small Worlds*; Hahn, "Common Right and Commonwealth" and "A Response."

28. For complaints concerning stolen livestock (cows, mules, horses, and hogs) see, in RC, SFO–Rosedale, SAC, RG 105: *Benton Bowen v. Bollivar Bowen,* September 23, 1867; M. Lanthrop to Mr. James Upshaw, April 28, 1868; M. Lanthrop to Z. T. Nichols, May 4, 1868; *Ephraim White v. John G. Shuth,* n.d.; *Nelly v. N. G. Coulter,* n.d.; also, *Jacob Brown v. Charles Gonie,* n.d., RC, SFO–Friars Point; *Abram Esquire v. Robert Hord,* September 1867, and *Allen Walker v. John A. Miller,* September 7, 1867, RC, SFO–Greenville, SAC, RG 105. For complaints concerning stolen money and watches, see *Silas Avan v. Fuller Beal,* November 7, 1867, RC, SFO–Rosedale, and *George Hushman v. George Easton,* September 3, 1867, RC, SFO–Greenville, SAC, RG 105. For complaints concerning stolen firearms, see *Jack Meredith v. Mr. Robinson,* November 14, 1867, and *F. Campion, R. Henderson, J. Williams v. R. M. Wilson, sheriff,* August 26, 1867, RC, SFO–

Rosedale; *Charles Coldwell v. Mr. Cressmon, Justice of the Peace,* n.d., RC, SFO–Friars Point; *George Hushman v. George Easton,* September 3, 1867, RC, SFO–Greenville, SAC, RG 105.

29. See stolen-livestock complaints in note 28.

30. "Negro Equality," *Coahomian,* September 22, 1865; "The Situation—Negro Testimony" and "Counsel From an Old Man," October 27, 1865.

31. "White Labor v. Black," *Coahomian,* December 8, 1865.

32. Lt. Sub-Comm. Charles W. Clarke to Capt. J. Weber, Acting Asst. Comm., November 28, 1865, ULR, WDM, RG 105; Clarke to Weber, October 28, 1865, ULR, WDM, RG 105.

33. James A. Hawley, Chaplain and Sub Commissioner of the State of Mississippi, to Capt. J. H. Weber, Acting Asst. Adj. Gen., October 28, 1865, RLR, AC, RG 105.

34. "An Act to Confer Civil Rights on the Freedmen, and for other purposes," *Laws of the State of Mississippi . . . 1865.* For discussion of Mississippi's Black Codes, see Wharton, *The Negro in Mississippi,* 80–96; Harris, *Presidential Reconstruction in Mississippi,* 129–32; Garner, *Reconstruction in Mississippi,* 113–21; J. Williams, "Civil War and Reconstruction," 118–25.

35. Edwards, "The Problem of Dependency."

36. "An Act to Regulate the Relation of Master and Apprentice," *Weekly Panola Star,* December 2, 1865. Also see Fields, *Middle Ground*; Saville, *The Work of Reconstruction*; Frankel, *Freedom's Women*; Edwards, *Gendered Strife.*

37. "Another Important Order from the Freedmen's Bureau Regarding Apprenticeship, & Vagrancy," *Coahomian,* October 20, 1865.

38. H. F. McWilliams to Capt. A. W. Allyn, December 21, 1867, Labor Contracts, AC, RG 105, M826, roll 49.

39. In RC, SFO–Greenville, SAC, RG 105, examples include *Albert McGee v. H. W. Anderson,* September 5, 1867; *Sidney Lamkins v. B. F. Connegyr,* October 31, 1868; *Wat Lewis v. Champion Bradley,* September 4, 1867; *Celia Smith v. William Hardin,* September 4, 1867; *Ann Bruton v. D. J. Wetherby,* September 7, 1867. In RC, SFO–Sardis, SAC, RG 105, see: *John Thomas v. C. S. Burkhalter,* October 15, 1867; *Prior Mitchell v. Sidney Mitchell,* September 7, 1867; *Bob Wilburn v. John Maddox,* September 28, 1867; *Esau Thweat v. Polly Newsom,* September 30, 1867; *Oscar Fowler, Buck Middleton v. Rufus Beard,* September 30, 1867.

40. Violence was extremely widespread. In one month the following complaints were registered in RC, SFO–Greenville, SAC, RG 105, just one office out of ten in the Delta: *Tom Williams v. Potts; Silas Gibson v. employer; James Marshall v. Samuel Frederick; Emily Holmes v. Charity Green; Mary Brown v. Haywood Barr; Henry Davis v. Benjamin Shaw; Harrison Hendricks v. Richard Saunders; Mary Johnson v. John H. Evans; Mary Tanner v. Robert Chew; Henry Collins v. James Shanks.*

41. *Mary Johnson v. John H. Evans,* September 1867, RC, SFO–Greenville, SAC, RG

105; Capt. *Gentry and Col. William Brown v. Willis Maddox,* n.d., RC, SFO–Rosedale, SAC, RG 105.

42. A. T. Morgan to Gov. Ames, September 9, 1874, Administration of Adelbert Ames, MGP.

Chapter 6. Going to Court and Claiming Citizenship: Property, Patriarchy, and Alternative Households

1. George W. Corliss, Friars Point, to Stuart Eldridge, April 9, 1866, RLR, AC, RG 105.

2. George W. Corliss to Stuart Eldridge, April 8, 1866, RLR, AC, RG 105.

3. Pvt. Calvin Holly to Maj. Gen. O. O. Howard, December 16, 1865, RLR, AC, RG 105.

4. Marshall, "Citizenship and Social Class."

5. Fraser and Gordon, "Contract versus Charity," 56–60. Also see Somers, "Public Sphere"; Franke, "Becoming a Citizen"; Cooper, Holt, and Scott, *Beyond Slavery,* 13–32.

6. Harris, *Presidential Reconstruction in Mississippi,* 37–60; Garner, *Reconstruction in Mississippi,* 75–95; Wharton, *The Negro in Mississippi,* 80–96, 131–36; J. Williams, "Civil War and Reconstruction," 110–30.

7. Edwards, "The Problem of Dependency"; Tomlins, *Law, Labor, and Ideology*; Stanley, "Beggars Can't Be Choosers"; Woodman, *New South, New Law.*

8. *Laws of the State of Mississippi . . . 1866 and . . . 1867*; Harris, *Presidential Reconstruction in Mississippi,* 173; R. Davis, *Good and Faithful Labor*; Woodman, *New South, New Law.*

9. Freedpeople did not let the matter drop. In 1867 and 1868 many freedpeople filed complaints with the Bureau asking to be paid for the work they performed in 1866. See, for example, *Willis Keyes et al. v. T. E. Barnwell,* October 13, 1867, RC, SFO–Friars Point, SAC, RG 105; Capt. Lain Tidball to Lt. Merritt Barber, February 11, 1868, and Agt. Thad. K. Preuss to Capt. S. C. Green, April 4, 1868, SFO–Greenville, SAC, RG 105; and, in RC, SFO–Yazoo City, SAC, RG 105: Eli Hudson, August 14, 1867; Lee Wilson, August 17, 1867; *J. Jackson v. Dan Munson,* November 6, 1867.

10. George Torrey to Gov. Humphreys, March 29, 1866, Administration of Benjamin G. Humphreys, MGP.

11. Speth, "Married Women's Property Acts"; Siegel, "Home as Work," 1075–86; Boydston, *Home and Work.*

12. Lebsock, "Property Rights," 197; Boswell, "Married Women's Property Rights," 99; Speth, "Married Women's Property Acts"; Moncrief, "Property Act of 1839."

13. Chap. 496, sections 1 and 2, *Laws of the State of Mississippi . . . 1866 and . . . 1867,* 725–26.

14. The four cases in which a wife sued a husband were *Thoms v. Thoms,* 45 Miss. 263 (1871); *Garland v. Garland,* 50 Miss. 694 (1874); *Collins v. Collins,* 51 Miss. 229 (1875); and *Garland v. Garland,* 51 Miss. 16 (1875). The other 141 cases involving married women's property rights between 1865 and 1880 were identified in "Mississippi Supreme Court

Case Law, 1818–2001," LexisNexis Academic Universe, Eastland Law Library, University of Mississippi.

15. *Lucy E. Wright and Husband v. Sarah J. Walton and Husband,* 56 Miss. 1 (1878).

16. Boswell, "Married Women's Property Rights," 99; Lebsock, "Property Rights"; Speth, "Married Women's Property Acts"; Moncrief, "Property Act of 1839."

17. Dr. Samuel Theobald to Mrs. H. B. Theobald, February 8, 1866, Blanton-Smith Letters, MDAH.

18. See note 14.

19. Jeanie to My dear Sisters, January 12, 1870, Blanton-Smith Letters, MDAH. Also see Amanda Worthington Journal, July 28, September 8 and 11, and October 8, 1865, Worthington-Stone Family Papers, MDAH.

20. Mother to My Dear Son, October 4, 1868, Kiger Family Papers, UT; Mother to My Dear Son, March 1, 1868; November 17, 1869; January 10, February 10, and November 2, 1870, Kiger Family Papers, UT.

21. Miller et al., "Between Emancipation and Enfranchisement."

22. O. B. Foster to Maj. T. S. Free, December 15, 1865, Narrative Reports, AC, RG 105, M826, Roll 30; W. S. Myers to Maj. A. W. Preston, December 31, 1866, RLR, AC, RG 105.

23. R. S. Donaldson to Capt. J. H. Weber, November 6, 1865, RLR, AC, RG 105. Also see D. W. White, April 23, 1867, LS, SFO–Yazoo City, SAC, RG 105; O. B. Foster to Maj. T. S. Free, Narrative Reports, AC, RG 105, M826, roll 30; T. Sargent Free, "Report of Tour of Northern Mississippi," September 9, 1865, RLR, AC, RG 105.

24. Miller et al., "Between Emancipation and Enfranchisement"; Zipf, "Reconstructing 'Free Woman'"; Rosen, "Not That Sort"; Franke, "Becoming a Citizen."

25. T. Sargent Free, "Report of Tour of Northern Mississippi," September 9, 1865, RLR, AC, RG 105.

26. General Order 10, March 11, 1867, U.S. Army Commands, 4th Military District, Orders, 1867–70, United States Military Records, RG 58, MDAH.

27. E. Foner, *Freedom's Lawmakers,* s.v. "Montgomery, William Thornton" and "Lewis, William"; Garner, *Reconstruction in Mississippi,* 164.

28. In RLR, SFO–Greenville, SAC, RG 105, see: William Lain Tidball to Lt. Merritt Barber, November 20, 1867; Thad K. Pruess to S. C. Green, April 14, 1868; S. G. French to Capt. Wm. L. Tidball, November 27, 1867; M. S. Lanthrop to Dear Sir, November 5, 1867; James R. Cox to Sir, August 29, 1867; see also D. M. White to H. W. Smith, August 31, 1867, and Geo. W. Corliss to Lt. Merritt Barber, November 13, 1867, AC, RG 105; Garner, *Reconstruction in Mississippi,* 166; Woodman, *New South, New Law.*

29. In the works of Harold D. Woodman, see: "Economic Reconstruction"; *New South, New Law;* "Agriculture and the Law"; "Sequel to Slavery."

30. In RC, SFO–Greenville, SAC, RG 105, see: *Nathan Garrett v. H. E. Keep,* September 7, 1867; *John Terrell v. H. E. Keep,* September 7, 1867; *Laborers on Peru and Lake Island Plantation v. Thos. H. Johnibes,* 1867; *Laborers v. John Estill,* 1867; *Laborers v. Z. C. Offutt,*

1867; *Laborers v. Victor Montgomery,* 1867; *Laborers v. Robert Carter,* 1867; *Laborers v. John Griffin,* 1867; *Gus Davis and his squad v. Dr. Thomas Geddis,* 1867. In RC, SFO–Yazoo City, SAC, RG 105, see: *Charles Hunter v. J. W. Stiles,* December 19, 1867; *G. D. Humphries v. J. Clanden,* December 19, 1867; *Newsom v. J. W. Watson,* December 20, 1867.

31. D. M. White to Bvt. Maj. Jno. Tyler, September 21, 1868, LS, SFO–Yazoo City, SAC, RG 105.

32. Harry Yerger to Capt. Tidball, November 14, 1867, LR, SFO–Greenville; *Harry Yerger v. Richard Coleman,* November 1867, RC, SFO–Greenville, SAC, RG 105.

33. D. M. White to Lt. Barber, December 12, 1867, LS, SFO–Yazoo City, RG 105.

34. *Willis Keyes et al. v. T. E. Barnwell,* October 31, 1867, RC, SFO–Greenville, SAC, RG 105. Also see *Jacob Epting v. A. G. Anderson,* October 31, 1867, RC, SFO–Greenville, SAC, RG 105; and, in RC, SFO–Yazoo City, SAC, RG 105, see: *Charles Hunter v. J. W. Stiles,* December 19, 1867; *G. D. Humphries v. J. Clanden,* December 19, 1867; *Newsom v. J. W. Watson,* December 20, 1867. Certainly action was possible in 1865 and 1866, but workers remained relatively quiet during those years. The former Confederates' control of the Mississippi legislature made state government hostile at best, and at the local level, freedpeople faced bloody reprisals if they challenged white authority. The structure for registering complaints was in place as early as 1865 in Greenville and Yazoo City, and by 1866 workers on extremely isolated plantations deep in the Delta swamps used the Bureau to challenge planters' hegemony.

35. H. F. McWilliams to Capt. A. W. Allyn, December 21, 1867, Labor Contracts, AC, BRFAL, RG 105, M826, roll 49, frame 950–53.

36. For examples in RC, SFO–Sardis, SAC, RG 105, see: *Fred Cromwell v. David Morton,* September 30, 1867; *William Link & Kinney Link, Philis Maddox v. R. T. Walton et al.,* September 20, 1867. For examples in RC, SFO–Yazoo City, SAC, RG 105, see: *Pleasant Mitchel v. Wm. Gale,* December 1, 1867; *Richard Clark v. Wm. Russman,* March 25, 1868; *Amanda Wilson v. J. B. Davenport,* March 4, 1868; *Wm. Middleton v. Wm. Goosey,* October 31, 1868; *Ugene Martin v. J. R. Mosley,* November 14, 1868; *Jane Dabney v. H. N. Hannah.* For examples in RC, SFO–Greenville, SAC, RG 105, see: *William Wright v. William Campbell,* September 4, 1867; *Albert McGee v. H. W. Anderson,* September 5, 1867; *Floyd Buckley v. A. V. Pearcefield,* September 6, 1867; *Amelia Williams v. John Griffin,* September 6, 1867; *Dennis Howard v. John Griffin,* September 6, 1867; *Moses Curd v. S. B. Alexander,* September 7, 1867; *Peter Holmes v. S. B. Alexander,* September 7, 1867; *James Hall v. S. M. Hunter,* September 7, 1867; *James Johnson v. S. M. Hunter,* September 7, 1867; *John H. Tyler v. Robert Chew,* September 7, 1867; *Edward Ness v. William Hunt,* September 7, 1867; *John Eaton v. Geo. T. Blackburn,* December 31, 1867; *Jim Travis v. Stephen Archer,* September 11, 1867.

37. W. Harper, Isaac Bryant, and Mark Tony, November 11, 1867, RC, SFO–Friars Point, SAC, RG 105. For a reference to a similar claim, see T. Wiseman to Sir, January 2, 1868, LR, SFO–Sardis, SAC, RG 105.

38. O'Donovan, "Transforming Work."

39. Fraser and Gordon, "Contract versus Charity," 56.

40. As historians Amy Dru Stanley and Nancy Cott argue, by the mid-nineteenth century, men relied on the marriage relationship to prove their independence. Cott and Stanley argue that as more men became wage workers, they lost control over productive property. Without property, men became like women and children. They were dependent on another man for their living. Until the 1820s, this lack of property disqualified men from voting in many states. To maintain men's status as independent people—who thereby deserved the right to vote—many states began to change the marriage laws. Common-law marriages became more accepted because, as Nancy Cott states, "having and supporting dependents was *evidence* of independence." Legal historian Katherine Franke concludes, "To be a husband necessarily entailed the status of head of household, while to be a wife rendered one structurally dependent upon the husband's support." Men's independence, as secured by marriage, won them full rights of citizenship: men alone had the right to vote. See Franke, "Becoming a Citizen"; Stanley, "Home Life and Morality"; Cott, "Marriage and Women's Citizenship"; Dubler, "Governing Through Contract."

41. Married women represented only 2 percent of all the individuals filing cases. Women, single and married, made up 11 percent of all complainants.

42. Elsa Barkley Brown counters the theory, demonstrating that in Richmond freedwomen played an active role in politics; see "Uncle Ned's Children" and "Public Sphere."

43. In the works of Harold D. Woodman, see: "Agriculture and the Law"; *New South, New Law*; "Economic Reconstruction"; "How New was the New South?"; "Class, Race, Politics"; "Sequel to Slavery."

44. *May Edwards v. Mrs. F. G. Boyd*, November 1868, 44–45, RC, SFO–Friars Point, SAC, RG 105.

45. *Jane Davis v. Mrs. H. H. Camp*, October 14, 1867, and *Chloe Taylor v. Jarvis Keith*, n.d., RC, SFO–Friars Point, SAC, RG 105; also see *Harriet Murray v. Dick Porter*, November 1867, RC, SFO–Sardis, SAC, RG 105.

46. For example, see Julia Gibson, April 25, 1868, RC, SFO–Vicksburg, SAC, RG 105; *Sarah Floyd v. A. Martin*, November 18, 1867, RC, SFO–Friars Point, SAC, RG 105; *Rebecca Thompson v. Julia Johnson*, March 5, 1868, and *Ann Washington v. Austin Ragsdale and John McMerchant*, March 10, 1868, RC, SFO–Yazoo City, SAC, RG 105; and, in RC, SFO–Greenville, SAC, RG 105: *Harriett Williams v. Jane Collins*, September 7, 1867; *Emily Holmes v. Charity Green and Berry Green*, September 1867; *Mary Brown v. Haywood Barr*, September 1867; *Mary Tanner v. Robt. Chew*, September 1867; *Ann Brown v. Bernard Doyle*, October 1867; *Rose Scott v. Robt. Carter*, October 1867; *Aura Dunlap v. U.S.*, January 27, 1868.

47. *Nancy Ann Mead v. Joseph Bloodson*, December 1867, RC, SFO–Greenville, SAC, RG 105.

48. Of course, one cannot be certain whether these women had husbands. Perhaps they were simply unmarried women defending their households. Yet, according to the 1870 census, only 7 to 8 percent of African-American women lived in female-headed households in the countryside. It stands to reason that single women would more aggressively defend their children, but it seems unlikely that 7 percent of the population would file 22 percent of all complaints. It seems reasonable to conclude that women in male-headed households took the responsibility to represent their children's interests in public.

49. For examples from RC, SFO–Friars Point, SAC, RG 105, see: *Pleasant Wright v. Cass Kirby,* June 29, 1868; *Mahala v. Emery S. Williams,* October 26, 1867; *Vina Flowers v. Hardy Flowers,* December 12, 1867; see also W. H. Eldridge to Mrs. C Montgomery, November 4, 1868, LS, SFO–Yazoo City, SAC, RG 105; *Major Wiley v. T. B. Allen,* September 30, 1867, RC, SFO–Sardis, SAC, RG 105; and, in RC, SFO–Greenville, SAC, RG 105: *Nancy Ann Ward v. Joseph Bloodsaw,* n.d.; *Emily Holmes v. Charity Green and Berry Green,* September 1867; *Ann Brown v. Bernard Doyle,* October 1867; *Harriett Williams v. Jane Collins,* June 7, 1867; Rachel Dodds, May 2, 1868.

50. *Mary Johnson v. John H. Evans,* September 1867, RC, SFO–Greenville, SAC, RG 105; *Charles Rivers v. Mary Lee,* March 17, 1868, RC, SFO–Vicksburg, SAC, RG 105; *Juliann Eaton v. Mrs. L. Montgomery,* November 4, 1868, RC, SFO–Yazoo City, SAC, RG 105.

51. See note 50.

52. Testimony of Jacob Wentworth, June 27, 1866, RLR, AC, RG 105; George W. Corliss to Stuart Eldridge, April 4, 1866; F. A. Harrow to Col. Saml. Thomas, March 24, 1866, RLR, AC, RG 105.

53. E. Brown, "Public Sphere"; also "Uncle Ned's Children."

54. Fraser and Gordon, "Contract Versus Charity"; Somers, "Public Sphere"; Cooper, Holt, and Scott, *Beyond Slavery,* 13–32.

Chapter 7. Legislating Rights: Citizens, "Legal Voters," and the Boundaries of the Household

1. *Susan Dickerson et al. v. W. N. Brown,* 49 Miss. 357 (1873); 1868 Constitution of Mississippi, art. 12, sec. 22, in *Journal of the Proceedings,* 739.

2. *Dickerson v. Brown,* 49 Miss. 357 (1873).

3. "A Strange Case with a Moral," *Jackson (Miss.) Weekly Clarion,* March 19, 1874.

4. Bynum, *Unruly Women;* Bardaglio, *Reconstructing the Household,* 37–78; Edwards, *Gendered Strife,* 25–31; Stevenson, *Life in Black and White,* 3–15; Dailey, *Before Jim Crow,* 77–102; Stanley, *From Bondage to Contract,* 228–37.

5. Fraser and Gordon, "Contract versus Charity." Also see Somers, "Public Sphere"; Franke, "Becoming a Citizen"; Cooper, Holt, and Scott, *Beyond Slavery,* 13–32.

6. General Order 10, March 11, 1867, U.S. Army Commands, 4th Military District, Orders, 1867–70, United State Military Records, RG 58, MDAH.

7. In Narrative Reports, AC, RG 105, M826, roll 30, see: Wm. Shields to Lt. M. Barber, December 31, 1867; J. R. Webster to Merritt Barber, February 1, 1868; Allen P. Huggins to Merritt Barber, March 31, 1868. In RLR, AC, RG 105, see: H. R. Williams to General Gillem, March 30, 1868; Nancy L. Lindsley to Capt. Tidball, August 12, 1867; Edward P. Jones to General, May 17, 1867; Dan B. Humphreys to Gen. A. C. Gillem, February 13, 1868.

8. In RLR, AC, RG 105, see: C. T. Lawson to Capt. J. Sunderland, June 23, 1867; W. S. Myers, Subcomm., Greenville, to Maj. Gen. Thos. J. Wood, January 17, 1867; O. O. Howard to A. C. Gillem, February 5, 1867; D. M. White, Subcomm., Yazoo City, to A. W. Preston, May 6, 1867; William Price to Lt. Shepley, December 17, 1866; James H. Shepley to A. W. Preston, June 30, 1867.

9. "Statement of Freedmen who are in the employ of Henry Gilmore of Yazoo Co Miss," July 22, 1867, RLR, AC, RG 105. Also in RC, SFO–Vicksburg, SAC, RG 105, see: R. S. Scott, October 2, 1867; Harrison Williams, October 9, 1867; *Richard Fletcher v. Oliver Bradford,* October 24, 1867; see also *Peter Pickens v. A. K. Vance,* December 22, 1867, RC, SFO–Yazoo City, SAC, RG 105; *James Howard v. Capt Gentry,* November 10, 1867, and *Chas. Amos, Henry Franklin v. James Harper,* n.d., RC, SFO–Rosedale, SAC, RG 105.

10. William Lain Tidball, August 31, 1867, SFO–Lake Station, Narrative Reports, AC, RG 105, M 826, roll 30; Dominick Olin, Burton Moses, Richard Williams, John Mathews, Jackson Woodland, and Oliver Taylor to Maj. Gen. Ord, December 20, 1867, LR, SFO–Yazoo City, RG 105; registration statistics from Wharton, *The Negro in Mississippi,* 146.

11. Wharton, *The Negro in Mississippi,* 137–50. Both Warren and Washington Counties had contributed many black men to the Union army and had been garrisoned with black troops. No doubt freedmen's military experience taught them the importance of having black representatives.

12. *Journal of the Proceedings,* 333, 739.

13. Jarrit Ware to Pension Examiner, June 13, 1890, William Brooks claim, Wid. App. 417996, Pensions, RG 15; H. M. Stovall to Commissioner of Pensions, July 23, 1910, Judson Burris claim, Wid. Cert. 706569. See Frankel, *Freedom's Women,* 80–84, 40–44.

14. E. Foner, *Freedom's Lawmakers,* s.v. "Stringer, Thomas W."

15. J. R. Webster, November 1867, Narrative Reports, AC, RG 105; also Narrative Reports for August 1867 for the subdistricts of Grenada and Tupelo, and for September 1867 for the subdistrict of Greenville, AC, RG 105. See also Franke, "Becoming a Citizen," 279–84.

16. *Journal of the Proceedings,* 199.

17. *Journal of the Proceedings,* 212. Also see Wharton, *The Negro in Mississippi,* 150–51.

18. For the Newsom and Stites amendments and the roll calls, see *Journal of the Proceedings,* 199, 211–12.

19. *Journal of the Proceedings,* 314–15.

20. *Journal of the Proceedings,* 403, 533. Exemptions from debts and taxes are also discussed on pp. 185, 461.

21. *Journal of the Proceedings,* 315–16. Also see Dailey, *Before Jim Crow,* 77–102.

22. McCurry, *Masters of Small Worlds* and "Two Faces"; Edwards, *Scarlett Doesn't Live Here,* 32–47; Stanley, *From Bondage to Contract;* Bynum, *Unruly Women;* Stevenson, *Life in Black and White;* Bardaglio, *Reconstructing the Household.*

23. *New York Herald,* August 18, 1868, quoted in Garner, *Reconstruction in Mississippi,* 209.

24. 1868 Constitution of Mississippi, art. 7, sec. 5, in *Journal of the Proceedings,* 732.

25. *New York Herald,* August 18, 1868, quoted in Garner, *Reconstruction in Mississippi,* 209.

26. Garner, *Reconstruction in Mississippi,* 210–12; *Appleton's Cyclopedia* (1868) as cited in Wharton, *The Negro in Mississippi,* 152.

27. D. N. Quinn, Sunflower Co., to Maj. John Tyler, June 12, 1868, RLR, AC, RG 105.

28. L. Galinger to Gen. Gillem, May 25, 1868, and Allen P. Huggins to Maj. S. C. Greene, May 12 and September 5, 1868, RLR, AC, RG 105. Also see T. N. Bowles & J. F. Kempton to Gillem, March 12, 1868; Huggins to Greene, April 12, 1868; Huggins to Major, July 20, 1868; Galinger to Gillem, May 5, 1868, RLR, AC, RG 105; July Report, Friars Point, July 31, 1868, SFO–Friars Point, SAC, RG 105; Thad. K. Pruess to Greene, March 28 and April 8, 1868, LS, SFO–Greenville, SAC, RG 105.

29. William Wedemeyer to Greene, July 25, 1868, RLR, AC, RG 105.

30. A. Morgan, *Yazoo,* 230–33; E. Brown, "Public Sphere."

31. J. Williams, "Civil War and Reconstruction," 151.

32. Wharton, *The Negro in Mississippi,* 156.

33. *Revised Code,* art. 5, sec. 1778.

34. *Revised Code,* art. 17, "Hawkers and Peddlers." Also see Miller et al., "Between Emancipation and Enfranchisement."

35. *Revised Code,* art. 8, "Bigamy," and art. 3, "Unlawful Marriages."

36. *Josephine Thoms v. Henry A. Thoms et al.,* 45 Miss. 63 (1871).

37. See "Mississippi" in "Index by Office during Reconstruction" and in "Index by State" in E. Foner, *Freedom's Lawmakers.*

38. *Laws of the State . . . 1873,* chap. 74, sec. 1.

39. *Laws of the State . . . 1873,* chap. 73, sec. 1.

40. *Laws of the State . . . 1874,* chap. 24, sec. 1.

41. "The New Temperance Law. What Outside Papers Say of It," *Weekly Clarion,* April 16, 1874.

42. Ibid.; in *Weekly Clarion,* see: "The Temperance Law," May 21, 1874; "East Mississippi, May 20, 1874," June 4, 1874.

43. *Journal of the Senate . . . 1874,* 502; *Journal of the House . . . 1874,* 756.

44. *John J. Rohrbacher v. Mayor and Aldermen of the City of Jackson*, 5 Miss. 735 (1875).

45. Ibid.

46. *W. H. Garland v. Mary Garland*, 50 Miss. 694 (1874); *W. H. Garland v. Mary Garland*, 61 Miss. 16 (1875).

47. The Mississippi Supreme Court waited until 1963 to loosen its definition of women's virtue. In *King v. King* the justices stated that a wife did not have to be blameless. However, lawyers still focus on the woman's role in marital discord to dismiss a wife's claim for support. See *King v. King*, 246 Miss. 798, 152 So. 2d 889 (1963); *Cox v. Cox*, 279 So. 2d 612 (Miss. 1973); *Rodgers v. Rodgers*, 349 So. 2d 540 (Miss. 1977).

48. *Ambrick Maples v. Violet Maples*, 49 Miss. 393 (1873); *Bettie Moore v. Thomas F. Christian*, 56 Miss. 408 (1879).

49. "Passage of the Social Equality Bill in the House," *Weekly Clarion*, February 6, 1873.

50. "Lee County," *Tupelo Standard*, June 7, 1873.

51. "The Civil Rights Bill and our Public School System," June 4, 1874, and "The Civil Rights Bill," June 11, 1874, *Weekly Clarion*. Also see Dailey, *Before Jim Crow*, 77–102.

52. Edmonia G. Highgate to My highly esteemed friend, September 2, 1870, in Sterling, *We Are Your Sisters*, 303–5; Powell, *New Masters*, 95, 127–35.

53. A. T. Morgan to Gov. Ames, January 11 and February 11, 1874, Administration of Adelbert Ames, MGP.

54. "Mississippi *Weekly Pilot*," in *Banner*, (Yazoo City, Miss.) July 31, 1875.

55. A. T. Morgan to Gov. Ames, January 11, 1874. For Meridian riots, see "A Resolution in Relation to the Riot at Meridian," in *Journal of the Senate . . . 1871*, 1129–81; Garner, *Reconstruction in Mississippi*, 349–53; Wharton, *The Negro in Mississippi*, 188–91. Violence also broke out in Tunica County. See A. G. Packer to Gov. Ames, August 10, 1874 and J. W. Brownlee to Ames, November 17, 1874, Administration of Adelbert Ames, MGP; "Riot in Austin," *Greenville Times*, August 15, 1874; Willis, *Forgotten Time*, 132–33; J. Williams, "Civil War and Reconstruction," 204–5.

56. J. Allen Ross to Gov. Ames, February 18, 1874, Administration of Adelbert Ames, MGP. Ross later came under attack in August 1874 when acting as part of the sheriff's department. He was arrested for kidnapping when he entered Issaquena County to capture a suspect. His many supporters attended his trial, setting white conservatives' nerves on edge. In *Greenville Times*, see "Crime in Issaquena," August 15, 1874; "Plundering and Murder in Issaquena and Washington Counties" and "Issaquena County," August 22, 1874.

57. Lynch, *Reminiscences*, 122. In Washington County, Democrats launched impeachment proceedings against Judge C. C. Shackleford to push him from the bench. "Two Wars—An Autobiography of General Samuel G. French," 457, French Papers, MDAH; in *Greenville Times* see "A Signal Gun of Distress!" and "Proceedings of a Public

Meeting," April 17, 1875; "Greenville, April 18" and "To the Ed. Times," April 24, 1875; C. P. Huntington to Gov. Ames, February 7, 1874, Administration of Adelbert Ames, MGP.

58. *Hinds County Gazette*, December 30, 1874, as cited in Wharton, *The Negro in Mississippi*, 185.

59. Adelbert Ames to my dear Frank, August 4, 1874, Administration of Adelbert Ames, MGP.

60. Whites were 36 percent of the population in Tallahatchie County in 1860 and 41 percent by 1870. In contrast, whites were only 23 percent of the population in Coahoma in 1860 and 25 percent in 1870. Moreover, the economy of Coahoma centered on cotton, whereas Tallahatchie's centered on livestock and corn. See *Ninth Census*.

61. W. A. Alcorn to Gov. Ames, September 15, 1875, Administration of Adelbert Ames, MGP.

62. Houston Burris to Ames, November 1, 1875, A. T. Morgan to Gov. Ames, September 4 and 24, 1875, Administration of Adelbert Ames, MGP.

63. Ames Executive Journal, January 4, 1876, Administration of Adelbert Ames, MGP.

64. Foner, *Freedom's Lawmakers*, s.v. "Dixon, James M.," "Parker, Noah," "Harris, Major," and "Patterson, James G."

65. *W. F. Hamilton, Sheriff, etc., v. N. E. Booth*, 55 Miss. 60 (1877). Also see *James Bowden v. Thomas Gray et Ux.*, 49 Miss. 547 (1873), and *Applegate & Sons v. H. M. Taylor, Garnishee*, 56 Miss. 685 (1879).

66. *Laws of the State . . . 1878*, chap. 79, sec. 1. For the earlier law, see *Laws of the State . . . 1872*, chap. 58, art. 3, secs. 2486 and 2487.

67. *H. W. Kinard v. The State*, 57 Miss. 1879.

68. Frederick A. Metcalfe Diary, November 2 and 4, 1875; August 22, 1876; November 7 and 9, 1876, Metcalfe Collection, MDAH.

69. Ibid., November 2, 1875; October 18, 1876; November 7 and 9, 1876.

70. Ibid., November 6, 1877; November 5, 1880; November 7, 1882.

71. Ibid., October 14 and 18, 1876; June 12, 1880; August 5, 1880; Wharton, *The Negro in Mississippi*, 203; Willis, *Forgotten Time*, 116–18; Sillers, *History of Bolivar County*, 33–37, 162–63, 337, 594.

72. S. M. Cole to Gov. Anthony, May 8, 1877, quoted in Painter, *Exodusters*, 155.

73. Frederick A. Metcalfe Diary, May 19, 1879, Metcalfe Collection, MDAH; Deposition, Dorcas Anderson, February 3, 1892, Isaac Anderson claim, Wid. Cert. 327211, Pensions, RG 15. Also in Pensions, RG 15, see: Deposition C, William Fletcher, July 21, 1894, and Deposition K, Jane Reed, July 27, 1894, Daniel Bell claim, Cert. 421529; Deposition A, Frances Bush, July 15, 1901, Henry Bush claim, Invalid Cert. 745220; Deposition AA, Ada Burton, January 19, 1904, Peter Burton claim, Wid. Cert. 572446.

74. Metcalfe Diaries, May 28, September 24, and December 8, 1878; May 19 and November 19, 1879; August 11 and September 3 and 4, 1880; May 6 and July 8, 1881.

Afterword

1. Green, "'I *AM* A MAN'" and "Battling the Plantation Mentality."

2. For the household as the cornerstone of planter-class hegemony, see, for example, McCurry, *Masters of Small Worlds*; Fox-Genovese, *Within the Plantation Household*; Bardaglio, *Reconstructing the Household*; K. Brown, *Good Wives*; MacLean, *Behind the Mask*; Stanley, *From Bondage to Contract*; Stansell, *City of Women*.

For resistance to the household, see, for example, Edwards, *Gendered Strife*; Bynum, *Unruly Women*; Hunter, *To 'Joy My Freedom*.

3. S. Hall, "Signification, Representation, Ideology"; Eagleton, *Aesthetic*.

Bibliography

Abrahams, Roger D. *Singing the Master: The Emergence of African-American Culture in the Plantation South.* New York: Pantheon, 1992.

Alcorn, James Lusk. *Views of the Honorable J. L. Alcorn on the Political Situation of Mississippi.* Friars Point, Miss.: n.p., 1867.

Alexander, Adele Logan. *Ambiguous Lives: Free Women of Color in Rural Georgia, 1789–1879.* Fayetteville: University of Arkansas Press, 1991.

Alexander, Sally. "Women, Class, and Sexual Differences in the 1830s and 1840s: Some Reflections on the Writing of a Feminist History." *History Workshop Journal* 17 (spring 1984): 125–49.

Andaya, Barbara Watson. "From Temporary Wife to Prostitute: Sexuality and Economic Change in Early Modern Southeast Asia." *Journal of Women's History* 9 (winter 1998): 11–34.

Appiah, Kwame Anthony. *In My Father's House: Africa in the Philosophy of Culture.* New York: Oxford University Press, 1992.

Appleby, Joyce, Lynn Hunt, and Margaret Jacob. *Telling the Truth about History.* New York: Norton, 1994.

Armstrong, Thomas F. "From Task Labor to Free Labor: The Transition Along Georgia's Rice Coast, 1820–1880." *Georgia Historical Quarterly* 64 (winter 1980): 432–47.

Ash, Stephen V. *Middle Tennessee Society Transformed, 1860–1870: War and Peace in the Upper South.* Baton Rouge: Louisiana State University Press, 1988.

———. *When the Yankees Came: Conflict and Chaos in the Occupied South, 1861–1865.* Chapel Hill: University of North Carolina Press, 1995.

Austin-Broos, Diane J. "Redefining the Moral Order: Interpretations of Christianity in Postemancipation Jamaica." In *The Meaning of Freedom: Economics, Politics, and Culture After Slavery,* edited by Frank McGlynn and Seymour Drescher, 221–43. Pittsburgh: University of Pittsburgh Press, 1992.

Ayers, Edward L. *Vengeance and Justice: Crime and Punishment in the 19th-Century American South.* New York: Oxford University Press, 1984.

Back, Les, and John Solomos, eds. *Theories of Race and Racism: A Reader.* London: Routledge, 2000.

Bardaglio, Peter W. "'An Outrage upon Nature': Incest and the Law in the Nineteenth-

Century South." In *In Joy and in Sorrow: Women, Family, and Marriage in the Victorian South, 1830–1900,* edited by Carol Bleser, 32–51. New York: Oxford University Press, 1991.

———. "Rape and the Law in the Old South: 'Calculated to Excite Indignation in Every Heart.'" *Journal of Southern History* 60 (November 1994): 749–72.

———. *Reconstructing the Household: Families, Sex, and the Law in the Nineteenth-Century South.* Chapel Hill: University of North Carolina Press, 1995.

Baron, Ava, ed. *Work Engendered: Toward a New History of American Labor.* Ithaca: Cornell University Press, 1991.

Bell, Shannon. *Reading, Writing, and Rewriting the Prostitute Body.* Bloomington: Indiana University Press, 1994.

Bennett, Judith M. "Feminism and History." *Gender and History* 1 (autumn 1989): 251–72.

Bercaw, Nancy, ed. *Gender and the Southern Body Politic.* Jackson: University Press of Mississippi, 2000.

Beringer, Richard E., Herman Hattaway, Archer Jones, and William N. Still Jr. *Why the South Lost the Civil War.* Athens: University of Georgia Press, 1986.

Berlin, Ira. *Many Thousands Gone: The First Two Centuries of Slavery in North America.* Cambridge: Harvard University Press, Belknap Press, 1998.

Berlin, Ira, Barbara J. Fields, Thavolia Glymph, Joseph P. Reidy, and Leslie S. Rowland, eds. *The Destruction of Slavery.* Ser. 1, vol. 1 of *Freedom: A Documentary History of Emancipation, 1861–1867.* Cambridge: Cambridge University Press, 1985.

Berlin, Ira, Thavolia Glymph, Steven F. Miller, Joseph P. Reidy, Leslie S. Rowland, and Julie Saville, eds. *The Wartime Genesis of Free Labor: The Lower South.* Ser. 1, vol. 3 of *Freedom: A Documentary History of Emancipation, 1861–1867.* Cambridge: Cambridge University Press, 1990.

Berlin, Ira, Joseph P. Reidy, and Leslie S. Rowland, eds. *The Black Military Experience.* Ser. 2 of *Freedom: A Documentary History of Emancipation, 1861–1867.* Cambridge: Cambridge University Press, 1982.

Besson, Jean. "Freedom and Community: The British West Indies." In *The Meaning of Freedom: Economics, Politics, and Culture After Slavery,* edited by Frank McGlynn and Seymour Drescher, 183–219. Pittsburgh: University of Pittsburgh Press, 1992.

Bettersworth, John K. *Confederate Mississippi: The People and Policies of a Cotton State in Wartime.* Baton Rouge: Louisiana State University Press, 1943.

———. *Mississippi: A History.* Austin, Tex.: Steck, 1959.

Bhabha, Homi K. "'Race,' Time and the Revision of Modernity." In *Postcolonial Criticism,* edited by Bart Moore-Gilbert, Gareth Stanton, and Willy Maley, 166–90. New York: Longman, 1997.

Biographical and Historical Memoirs of Mississippi Embracing an Authentic and Comprehensive Account of the Chief Events in the History of the State; and a Record of the

Lives of Many of the Most Worthy and Illustrious Families and Individuals. Chicago: Goodspeed, 1891.

Blair, Cynthia Marie. "Vicious Commerce: African-American Women's Sex Work and the Transformation of Urban Space in Chicago, 1850–1915." Ph.D. diss., Harvard University, 1999.

Blassingame, John W. *The Slave Community: Plantation Life in the Antebellum South.* New York: Oxford University Press, 1972.

Bleser, Carol, ed. *In Joy and in Sorrow: Women, Family, and Marriage in the Victorian South, 1830–1900.* New York: Oxford University Press, 1991.

Blewett, Mary H. *Constant Turmoil: The Politics of Industrial Life in Nineteenth-Century New England.* Amherst: University of Massachusetts Press, 2000.

———. *Men, Women, and Work: Class, Gender, and Protest in the New England Shoe Industry, 1780–1910.* Urbana: University of Illinois Press, 1988.

Bolton, Charles C. *Poor Whites of the Antebellum South: Tenants and Laborers in Central North Carolina and Northeast Mississippi.* Durham: Duke University Press, 1994.

Bolton, Charles C., and Scott P. Culclasure, eds. *The Confessions of Edward Isham: A Poor White Life of the Old South.* Athens: University of Georgia Press, 1998.

Bond, Bradley G. *Political Culture in the Nineteenth-Century South: Mississippi, 1830–1900.* Baton Rouge: Louisiana State University Press, 1995.

Boswell, Angela. "Married Women's Property Rights and the Challenge to Patriarchal Order: Colorado County, Texas." In *Negotiating Boundaries of Southern Womanhood: Dealing With the Powers That Be,* edited by Janet L. Coryell et al., 89–109. Columbia: University of Missouri Press, 2000.

Boydston, Jeanne. *Home and Work: Housework, Wages, and the Ideology of Labor in the Early Republic.* New York: Oxford University Press, 1990.

Brandfon, Robert L. *Cotton Kingdom of the New South: A History of the Yazoo Mississippi Delta from Reconstruction to the Twentieth Century.* Cambridge: Harvard University Press, 1967.

Brattain, Michelle. *The Politics of Whiteness: Race, Workers, and Culture in the Modern South.* Princeton: Princeton University Press, 2001.

Brown, Elsa Barkley. "African-American Women's Quilting: A Framework for Conceptualizing and Teaching African-American Women's History." *Signs* 14 (summer 1989): 921–29.

———. "Negotiating and Transforming the Public Sphere: African-American Political Life in the Transition from Slavery to Freedom." In *The Black Public Sphere: A Public Culture Book,* edited by The Black Public Sphere Collective, 107–46. Chicago: University of Chicago Press, 1995.

———. "Uncle Ned's Children: Negotiating Community and Freedom in Postemancipation Richmond, Virginia." Ph.D. diss., Kent State University, 1994.

———. "'What Has Happened Here': The Politics of Difference in Women's History and Feminist Politics." *Feminist Studies* 18 (summer 1992): 295–312.

———. "Womanist Consciousness: Maggie Lena Walker and the Independent Order of Saint Luke." *Signs* 14 (spring 1989): 610–33.

Brown, Kathleen M. *Good Wives, Nasty Wenches, and Anxious Patriarchs: Gender, Race, and Power in Colonial Virginia.* Chapel Hill: University of North Carolina Press, 1996.

Burke, Peter. *Popular Culture in Early Modern Europe.* New York: Harper and Row, 1978.

Burton, Orville Vernon. *In My Father's House Are Many Mansions: Family and Community in Edgefield, South Carolina.* Chapel Hill: University of North Carolina, 1985.

Bush, Barbara. "Hard Labor: Women, Childbirth, and Resistance in British Caribbean Slave Societies." In *More than Chattel: Black Women and Slavery in the Americas,* edited by David Barry Gaspar and Darlene Clark Hine, 193–217. Bloomington: Indiana University Press, 1996.

———. *Slave Women in Caribbean Society, 1650–1838.* Bloomington: Indiana University Press, 1990.

Butler, Judith. *Gender Trouble: Feminism and the Subversion of Identity.* London: Routledge, 1990.

Bynum, Victoria E. *The Free State of Jones: Mississippi's Longest Civil War.* Chapel Hill: University of North Carolina Press, 2001.

———. *Unruly Women: The Politics of Social and Sexual Control in the Old South.* Chapel Hill: University of North Carolina Press, 1992.

———. "War Within a War: Women's Participation in the Revolt of the North Carolina Piedmont, 1863–65." *Frontiers: A Journal of Women's Studies* 9:3 (1987): 43–49.

Campbell, Edward D. C., Jr., and Kym S. Rice, eds. *A Woman's War: Southern Women, Civil War, and the Confederate Legacy.* Charlottesville: University Press of Virginia, 1996.

Carby, Hazel V. *Reconstructing Womanhood: The Emergence of the Afro-American Woman Novelist.* New York: Oxford University Press, 1987.

Carter, Samuel, III. *The Final Fortress: The Campaign for Vicksburg, 1862–1863.* New York: St. Martin's Press, 1980.

Cashin, Joan E. *A Family Venture: Men and Women on the Southern Frontier.* New York: Oxford University Press, 1991.

Censer, Jane Turner. *North Carolina Planters and Their Children, 1800–1860.* Baton Rouge: Louisiana State University Press, 1984.

Chambers, William Pitt. *Blood and Sacrifice: The Civil War Journal of a Confederate Soldier.* Edited by Richard A. Baumgartner. Huntington, W.Va.: Blue Alcorn Press, 1994.

Cheatham, Edgar Jones. "Washington County, Mississippi: Its Ante-Bellum Generation." M.A. thesis, Tulane University, 1950.

Claiborne, J. F. H. *Mississippi as a Province, Territory and State, with Biographical Notices of Eminent Citizens.* Jackson, Miss.: Power and Barksdale, 1880.

Clark, Elizabeth B. "Matrimonial Bonds: Slavery and Divorce in Nineteenth-Century America." *Law and History Review* 8 (spring 1990): 25–54.

Clinton, Catherine. "Bloody Terrain: Freedwomen, Sexuality, and Violence During Reconstruction." *Georgia Historical Quarterly* 76 (summer 1992): 313–32.

———. *The Other Civil War: American Women in the Nineteenth Century.* New York: Hill and Wang, 1984.

———. *The Plantation Mistress: Woman's World in the Old South.* New York: Pantheon, 1982.

———. *Public Women and the Confederacy.* Milwaukee: Marquette University Press, 1999.

Clinton, Catherine, ed. *Southern Families at War: Loyalty and Conflict in the Civil War South.* New York: Oxford University Press, 2000.

Clinton, Catherine, and Nina Silber, eds. *Divided Houses: Gender and the Civil War.* Oxford: Oxford University Press, 1992.

Coahomian. Friars Point, Miss. September 1865–June 1866.

Cobb, James C. *The Most Southern Place on Earth: The Mississippi Delta and the Roots of Regional Identity.* New York: Oxford University Press, 1992.

Coclanis, Peter A. *The Shadow of a Dream: Economic Life and Death in the South Carolina Low Country, 1670–1920.* New York: Oxford University Press, 1989.

Cody, Cheryl Ann. "Cycles of Work and of Childbearing: Seasonality in Women's Lives on Low Country Plantations." In *More than Chattel: Black Women and Slavery in the Americas,* edited by David Barry Gaspar and Darlene Clark Hine, 61–78. Bloomington: Indiana University Press, 1996.

Cohen, William. *At Freedom's Edge: Black Mobility and the Southern White Quest for Racial Control, 1861–1915.* Baton Rouge: Louisiana State University Press, 1991.

Collins, Patricia Hill. *Black Feminist Thought: Knowledge, Consciousness, and the Politics of Empowerment.* London: Harper Collins Academic, 1990.

———. *Fighting Words: Black Women and the Search for Justice.* Minneapolis: University of Minnesota Press, 1998.

Connelly, Thomas Lawrence. *Army of the Heartland: The Army of Tennessee, 1861–1862.* Baton Rouge: Louisiana State University Press, 1967.

———. *Autumn of Glory: The Army of Tennessee, 1862–1865.* Baton Rouge: Louisiana State University Press, 1971.

Cooper, Frederick, Thomas C. Holt, and Rebecca J. Scott. *Beyond Slavery: Explorations of Race, Labor, and Citizenship in Postemancipation Societies.* Chapel Hill: University of North Carolina Press, 2000.

Cornish, Dudley Taylor. *The Sable Arm: Negro Troops in the Union Army, 1861–1865.* New York: Longmans, Green, 1956; New York: Norton, 1966.

Cott, Nancy F. *The Bonds of Womanhood: "Woman's Sphere" in New England, 1780–1835.* New Haven: Yale University Press, 1977.

———. "Giving Character to Our Whole Civil Polity: Marriage and the Public Order in the Late Nineteenth Century." In *U.S. History as Women's History: New Feminist Essays,* edited by Linda K. Kerber, Alice Kessler-Harris, and Kathryn Kish Sklar, 107–24. Chapel Hill: University of North Carolina Press, 1995.

———. "Marriage and Women's Citizenship in the United States, 1830–1934." *American Historical Review* 103 (December 1998): 1440–74.

Cotton, Gordon A. *The Murder of Minerva Cook.* Vicksburg, Miss.: n.p., 1993.

———. *Of Primitive Faith and Order: A History of the Mississippi Primitive Baptist Church, 1780–1974.* Raymond, Miss.: Keith Press, 1974.

Cotton, Gordon A., ed. *From the Pen of a She-Rebel: The Civil War Diary of Emilie Riley McKinley.* Columbia: University of South Carolina Press, 2001.

———. *Vicksburg Under Glass : A Collection of Early Photographs from the Glass Negatives of J. Mack Moore.* Vicksburg, Miss.: Vicksburg and Warren County Historical Society, 1975.

Crenshaw, Kimberlé, et al., eds. *Critical Race Theory: The Key Writings That Formed the Movement.* New York: New Press, 1995.

Cresswell, Stephen. *Multiparty Politics in Mississippi, 1877–1902.* Jackson: University Press of Mississippi, 1995.

Currie, James T. *Enclave: Vicksburg and Her Plantations, 1863–1870.* Jackson: University Press of Mississippi, 1980.

Dailey, Jane. *Before Jim Crow: The Politics of Race in Postemancipation Virginia.* Chapel Hill: University of North Carolina Press, 2000.

Dailey, Jane, Glenda Elizabeth Gilmore, and Bryant Simon, eds. *Jumpin' Jim Crow: Southern Politics from Civil War to Civil Rights.* Princeton: Princeton University Press, 2000.

Daniel, Pete. *The Shadow of Slavery: Peonage in the South, 1901–1969.* Urbana: University of Illinois Press, 1972.

Daniels, David Douglas. "The Cultural Renewal of Slave Religion: Charles Price Jones and the Emergence of the Holiness Movement in Mississippi." Ph.D. diss., Union Theological Seminary, 1992.

Davidoff, Leonore, and Catherine Hall. *Family Fortunes: Men and Women of the English Middle Class, 1780–1850.* Chicago: University of Chicago Press, 1987.

Davis, Angela Y. *Women, Culture, and Politics.* New York: Random House, 1989.

———. *Women, Race and Class.* New York: Random House, 1981.

Davis, Natalie Zemon. "Women on Top." In *Society and Culture in Early Modern France: Eight Essays.* Stanford: Stanford University Press, 1975.

Davis, Ronald L. F. *Good and Faithful Labor: From Slavery to Sharecropping in the Natchez District, 1860–1890.* Westport, Conn.: Greenwood Press, 1982.

Dean, Eric T., Jr. *Shook over Hell: Post-Traumatic Stress, Vietnam, and the Civil War.* Cambridge: Harvard University Press, 1997.

de Lauretis, Teresa. "Eccentric Subject: Feminist Theory and Historical Consciousness." *Feminist Studies* 16 (spring 1990): 115–50.

DeCanio, Stephen J. *Agriculture in the Postbellum South: The Economics of Production and Supply.* Cambridge: M.I.T. Press, 1974.

D'Emilio, John, and Estelle B. Freedman. *Intimate Matters: A History of Sexuality in America.* New York: Harper and Row, 1988.

Deupree, J. G. *Reminiscences of Service with the First Mississippi Cavalry.* N.p., 1903.

Dimond, E. Grey, and Herman Hattaway, eds. *Letters from Forest Place: A Plantation Family's Correspondence, 1846–1881.* Jackson: University Press of Mississippi, 1993.

Dollimore, Jonathan. *Sexual Dissidence: Augustine to Wilde, Freud to Foucault.* Oxford: Clarendon Press, 1991.

Donald, James, and Ali Rattansi. *"Race," Culture, and Difference.* London: Sage Publications, 1992.

Dong, Zhengkai. "From the Postbellum Plantation to Modern Agribusiness: A History of the Delta Pine and Land Company." Ph.D. diss., Purdue University, 1993.

Dubler, Ariela R. "Governing Through Contract: Common Law Marriage in the Nineteenth Century." *Yale Law Journal* 107 (1998): 1885–1920.

DuBois, W. E. B. *Black Reconstruction in America: An Essay Toward a History of the Part Which Black Folk Played in the Attempt to Reconstruct Democracy in America, 1860–1880.* 1935. Reprint, New York: Russell and Russell, 1962.

Durrill, Wayne K. *War of Another Kind: A Southern Community in the Great Rebellion.* New York: Oxford University Press, 1990.

Eagleton, Terry. *Ideology: An Introduction.* London: Verso, 1991.

———. *The Ideology of the Aesthetic.* Oxford: Blackwell, 1990.

Eaton, John. *Grant, Lincoln, and the Freedmen: Reminiscences of the Civil War with Special Reference to the Work for the Contrabands and Freedmen of the Mississippi Valley.* 1907. Reprint, New York: Negro Universities Press, 1969.

Edwards, Laura F. *"Gendered Strife and Confusion": The Political Culture of Reconstruction.* Urbana: University of Illinois Press, 1997.

———. "Law, Domestic Violence, and the Limits of Patriarchal Authority in the Antebellum South." In *Gender and the Southern Body Politic,* edited by Nancy Bercaw, 63–86. Jackson: University Press of Mississippi, 2000.

———. "'The Marriage Covenant Is at the Foundation of All Our Rights': The Politics of Slave Marriages in North Carolina After Emancipation." *Law and History Review* 14 (spring 1996): 81–124.

———. "The Politics of Marriage and Households in North Carolina during Reconstruction." In *Jumpin' Jim Crow: Southern Politics from Civil War to Civil Rights,* edited by Jane Dailey, Glenda Elizabeth Gilmore, and Bryant Simon, 7–27. Princeton: Princeton University Press, 2000.

———. "The Problem of Dependency: African-Americans, Labor Relations, and the Law in the Nineteenth-Century South." *Agricultural History* 72 (spring 1998): 313–340.

———. *Scarlett Doesn't Live Here Anymore: Southern Women in the Civil War Era.* Urbana: University of Illinois Press, 2000.

Encyclopedia of Mississippi History: A Definitive History from the Original Sources. Edited by Dunbar Rowland. Madison, Wis.: S. A. Brant, 1906.

Escott, Paul D. *After Secession: Jefferson Davis and the Failure of Confederate Nationalism.* Baton Rouge: Louisiana State University Press, 1978.

Evans, Augusta Jane. *Macaria; or, Altars of Sacrifice.* Edited by Drew Gilpin Faust. Baton Rouge: Louisiana State University Press, 1992.

Farnham, Christie Anne. *The Education of the Southern Belle: Higher Education and Student Socialization in the Antebellum South.* New York: New York University Press, 1994.

Farnham, Christie Anne, ed. *Women of the American South: A Multicultural Reader.* New York: New York University Press, 1997.

Faust, Drew Gilpin. "Altars of Sacrifice: Confederate Women and the Narratives of War." *Journal of American History* 74 (March 1990): 1200–1228.

———. "The Creation of Confederate Nationalism." Unpublished paper presented at the 1988 Southern Historical Association meeting in Charlotte, N.C.

———. *The Creation of Confederate Nationalism: Ideology and Identity in the Civil War South.* Baton Rouge: Louisiana State University Press, 1988.

———. *Mothers of Invention: Women of the Slaveholding South in the American Civil War.* Chapel Hill: University of North Carolina Press, 1996.

———. *Southern Stories: Slaveholders in Peace and War.* Columbia: University of Missouri Press, 1992.

———. "'Trying to Do a Man's Business': Slavery, Violence, and Gender in the American Civil War." *Gender and History* 4 (summer 1992): 197–214.

Fields, Barbara Jeanne. "The Advent of Capitalist Agriculture: The New South in a Bourgeois World." In *Essays on the Postbellum Southern Economy,* edited by Thavolia Glymph and John J. Kushma. College Station: Texas A&M University Press, 1985.

———. "Ideology and Race in American History." In *Region, Race, and Reconstruction: Essays in Honor of C. Vann Woodward,* edited by J. Morgan Kousser and James M. McPherson, 143–77. New York: Oxford University Press, 1982.

———. *Slavery and Freedom on the Middle Ground: Maryland During the Nineteenth Century.* New Haven: Yale University Press, 1985.

Findlay, Eileen J. "Decency and Democracy: The Politics of Prostitution in Ponce, Puerto Rico, 1890–1900." *Feminist Studies* 23 (fall 1997): 471–99.

Finkelman, Paul, ed. *Slavery and the Law*. Madison, Wis.: Madison House, 1996.

Finley, Randy. *From Slavery to Uncertain Freedom: The Freedmen's Bureau in Arkansas, 1865–1869*. Fayetteville: University of Arkansas Press, 1996.

Fiske, Claude E., ed. "Diary of James Oliver Hazard Perry Sessions of Rokeby Plantation on the Yazoo, January 1, 1862–June 1872." *Journal of Mississippi History* 39 (August 1977): 239–54.

Fitzgerald, Michael W. *The Union League Movement in the Deep South: Politics and Agricultural Change During Reconstruction*. Baton Rouge: Louisiana State University Press, 1989.

Flax, Jane. "Postmodernism and Gender Relations in Feminist Theory." In *Feminism/Postmodernism*, edited by Linda J. Nicholson, 39–62. New York: Routledge, 1990.

Flint, Timothy. *The History and Geography of the Mississippi Valley. To Which Is Appended a Condensed Physical Geography of the Atlantic United States, and the Whole American Continent*. Boston: Carter, Hendee, 1833.

Foner, Eric. *Free Soil, Free Labor, Free Men: The Ideology of the Republican Party Before the Civil War*. Oxford: Oxford University Press, 1970.

———. *Nothing but Freedom: Emancipation and Its Legacy*. Baton Rouge: Louisiana State University Press, 1983.

———. *Politics and Ideology in the Age of the Civil War*. Oxford: Oxford University Press, 1980.

———. *Reconstruction: America's Unfinished Revolution, 1863–1877*. New York: Harper and Row, 1988.

———. *The Story of American Freedom*. New York: Norton, 1998.

Foner, Eric, ed. *Freedom's Lawmakers: A Directory of Black Officeholders During Reconstruction*. Rev. ed. Baton Rouge: Louisiana State University Press, 1996.

Foner, Jack D. *Blacks and the Military in American History: A New Perspective*. New York: Praeger, 1974.

Forbes, Ella. *African American Women during the Civil War*. New York: Garland, 1998.

Ford, Lacy K., Jr. *Origins of Southern Radicalism: The South Carolina Upcountry, 1800–1860*. New York: Oxford University Press, 1988.

Foster, Gaines M. *Ghosts of the Confederacy: Defeat, the Lost Cause, and the Emergence of the New South, 1865 to 1913*. New York: Oxford University Press, 1987.

Fox-Genovese, Elizabeth. "Gender, Class, and Power: Some Theoretical Considerations." *History Teacher* 15 (February 1982): 255–76.

———. "Placing Women's History in History." *New Left Review* 133 (1982): 5–29.

———. "Property and Patriarchy in Classical Bourgeois Political Theory." *Radical History Review* 4 (spring/summer 1977): 36–59.

———. *Within the Plantation Household: Black and White Women of the Old South*. Chapel Hill: University of North Carolina Press, 1988.

Fox-Genovese, Elizabeth, and Eugene D. Genovese. *Fruits of Merchant Capital: Slavery and Bourgeois Property in the Rise and Expansion of Capitalism.* New York: Oxford University Press, 1983.

———. "Slavery, Economic Development and the Law: Dilemma of Southern Political Economists, 1800–1860." *Washington and Lee Law Review* 41 (winter 1984): 1–29.

Franke, Katherine M. "Becoming a Citizen: Reconstruction Era Regulation of African-American Marriages." *Yale Journal of Law and the Humanities* 11 (1999): 251–309.

Frankel, Noralee. *Freedom's Women: Black Women and Families in Civil War Era Mississippi.* Bloomington: Indiana University Press, 1999.

Frankenberg, Ruth. *White Women, Race Matters: The Social Construction of Whiteness.* Minneapolis: University of Minnesota Press, 1993.

Fraser, Nancy. "After the Family Wage: Gender Equity and the Welfare State." *Political Theory* 22 (November 1994): 591–618.

———. *Unruly Practices: Power, Discourse, and Gender in Contemporary Social Theory.* Minneapolis: University of Minnesota Press, 1989.

Fraser, Nancy, and Linda Gordon. "Contract versus Charity: Why Is There No Social Citizenship in the United States?" *Socialist Review* 22 (1992): 45–65.

———. "A Genealogy of Dependency: Tracing a Keyword of the U.S. Welfare State." *Signs* 19 (winter 1994): 309–36.

Fraser, Nancy, and Linda J. Nicholson. "Social Criticism without Philosophy: An Encounter between Feminism and Postmodernism." In *Feminism/Postmodernism,* edited by Linda J. Nicholson, 19–38. New York: Routledge, 1990.

Fraser, Walter J., Jr., R. Frank Saunders, Jr., and Jon L. Wakelyn, eds. *The Web of Southern Social Relations: Women, Family, and Education.* Athens: University of Georgia Press, 1985.

Frederickson, George. *The White Image in the Black Mind: The Debate on Afro-American Character and Destiny, 1817–1914.* New York: Harper and Row, 1971.

Frey, Sylvia. *Water From the Rock: Black Resistance in a Revolutionary Age.* Princeton: Princeton University Press, 1991.

Friedman, Jean E. *The Enclosed Garden: Women and Community in the Evangelical South, 1830–1900.* Chapel Hill: University of North Carolina Press, 1985.

Garber, Marjorie. *Vested Interests: Cross-Dressing and Cultural Anxiety.* New York: Routledge, 1992.

Garner, James Wilford. *Reconstruction in Mississippi.* 1901. Reprint, Baton Rouge: Louisiana State University Press, 1968.

Gaspar, David Barry, and Darlene Clark Hine, eds. *More than Chattel: Black Women and Slavery in the Americas.* Bloomington: Indiana University Press, 1996.

Genovese, Eugene D. "'Our Family, White and Black': Family and Household in the Southern Slaveholders' World View." In *In Joy and in Sorrow: Women, Family, and*

Marriage in the Victorian South, 1830–1900, edited by Carol Bleser, 69–87. New York: Oxford University Press, 1991.

———. *Roll, Jordan, Roll: The World the Slaves Made.* New York: Pantheon, 1974.

———. *The Slaveholders' Dilemma: Freedom and Progress in Southern Conservative Thought, 1820–1860.* Columbia: University of South Carolina Press, 1992.

———. *The World the Slaveholders Made: Two Essays in Interpretation.* New York: Pantheon, 1969.

———. "Yeoman Farmers in a Slaveholders' Democracy." *Agricultural History* 49 (April 1975): 331–42.

Gerteis, Louis S. *From Contraband to Freedman: Federal Policy Toward Southern Blacks, 1861–1865.* Westport, Conn.: Greenwood Press, 1973.

Gibson, James Monroe. *Memoirs of J. M. Gibson: Terrors of the Civil War and Reconstruction Days.* San Gabriel, Cal.: n.p., 1966.

Giggie, John Michael. "God's Long Journey: African-Americans, Religion and History in the Mississippi Delta, 1875–1915." Ph.D. diss., Princeton University, 1997.

Gilfoyle, Timothy J. "The Hearts of Nineteenth-Century Men: Bigamy and Working Class Marriage in New York City, 1800–1890." *Prospects* 19 (1994): 135–60.

———. "Prostitutes in History: From Parables of Pornography to Metaphors of Modernity." *American Historical Review* 104 (February 1999): 117–41.

Gillis, Irene, ed., *Mississippi 1850 Census: Surname Index.* Shreveport, La., n.p., 1972.

Glatthaar, Joseph T. *Forged in Battle: The Civil War Alliance of Black Soldiers and White Officers.* New York: Free Press, 1990.

Glenn, Evelyn Nakano. "From Servitude to Service Work: Historical Continuities in the Racial Division of Paid Reproductive Labor." *Signs* 18 (autumn 1992): 1–43.

Glymph, Thavolia. "Freedpeople and Ex-Masters: Shaping a New Order in the Postbellum South, 1865–1868." In *Essays on the Postbellum Southern Economy,* edited by Thavolia Glymph and John J. Kushma. College Station: Texas A&M University Press, 1985.

———. "'This Species of Property': Female Slave Contrabands in the Civil War." In *A Woman's War: Southern Women, Civil War, and the Confederate Legacy,* edited by Edward D. C. Campbell Jr. and Kym S. Rice, 55–71. Charlottesville: University Press of Virginia, 1996.

Glymph, Thavolia, and John J. Kushma, eds. *Essays on the Postbellum Southern Economy.* College Station: Texas A&M University Press, 1985.

Gordon, Linda. "The Trouble with Difference." *Dissent* 46 (spring 1999): 41–47.

Gordon, Linda, ed. *Women, the State, and Welfare.* Madison: University of Wisconsin Press, 1990.

Gramsci, Antonio. *Selections from the Prison Notebooks of Antonio Gramsci.* Edited and translated by Quintin Hoare and Geoffrey Nowell Smith. New York: International Publishers, 1971.

Gray, William F. *Imperial Bolivar.* Cleveland, Miss.: n.p., 1923.

Green, Laurie Beth. "Battling the Plantation Mentality: Consciousness, Culture, and the Politics of Race, Class, and Gender in Memphis, 1940–1968." Ph.D. diss., University of Chicago, 1999.

———. "Race, Gender, and Labor in 1960s Memphis: 'I *AM* A MAN' and the Meaning of Freedom." *Journal of Urban History,* forthcoming.

Grim, Valerie. "Black Farm Families in the Yazoo-Mississippi Delta: A Study of the Brooks Farm Community, 1920–1970." Ph.D. diss., Iowa State University, 1990.

Gross, Ariela J. *Double Character: Slavery and Mastery in the Antebellum Southern Court-room.* Princeton: Princeton University Press, 2000.

Grossberg, Michael. *Governing the Hearth: Law and the Family in Nineteenth-Century America.* Chapel Hill: University of North Carolina Press, 1985.

———. *A Judgment for Solomon: The d'Hauteville Case and Legal Experience in Antebellum America.* Cambridge: Cambridge University Press, 1996.

Gutman, Herbert G. *The Black Family in Slavery and Freedom, 1750–1925.* New York: Pantheon, 1976.

Hahn, Steven. "Class and State in Postemancipation Societies: Southern Planters in Comparative Perspective." *American Historical Review* 95 (February 1990): 75–98.

———. "Common Right and Commonwealth: The Stock-Law Struggle and the Roots of Southern Populism." In *Region, Race, and Reconstruction: Essays in Honor of C. Vann Woodward,* edited by J. Morgan Kousser and James M. McPherson, 51–88. New York: Oxford University Press, 1982.

———. "A Response: Common Cents or Historical Sense?" *Journal of Southern History* 59 (May 1993): 243–58.

———. *The Roots of Southern Populism: Yeoman Farmers and the Transformation of the Georgia Upcountry, 1850–1890.* New York: Oxford University Press, 1983.

Hale, Grace Elizabeth. *Making Whiteness: The Culture of Segregation in the South, 1890–1940.* New York: Pantheon, 1998.

Hall, Catherine. *White, Male, and Middle-Class: Explorations in Feminism and History.* New York: Routledge, 1992.

Hall, Kim F. *Things of Darkness: Economies of Race and Gender in Early Modern England.* Ithaca: Cornell University Press, 1995.

Hall, Stuart. "Signification, Representation, Ideology: Althusser and the Post-Structuralist Debates." *Critical Studies in Mass Communication* 2 (June 1985): 91–114.

Halperin, David M. "The Democratic Body: Prostitution and Citizenship in Classical Athens." *South Atlantic Quarterly* 88 (winter 1989): 149–60.

Haney López, Ian F. *White by Law: The Legal Construction of Race.* New York: New York University Press, 1996.

Harris, William C. *The Day of the Carpetbagger: Republican Reconstruction in Mississippi.* Baton Rouge: Louisiana State University Press, 1978.

———. *Presidential Reconstruction in Mississippi.* Baton Rouge: Louisiana State University Press, 1967.

Hawks, Joanne V. *Mississippi's Historical Heritage: A Guide to Women's Sources in Mississippi Repositories.* Hattiesburg: Society of Mississippi Archivists, 1993.

Hawks, Joanne V., and Sheila L. Skemp, eds. *Sex, Race, and the Role of Women in the South.* Jackson: University Press of Mississippi, 1983.

Helper, Laura. "A Whole Lot of Shakin' Going On: An Ethnography of Race Relations and Crossover Audiences for Rhythm and Blues and Rock and Roll in 1950s Memphis." Ph.D. diss., Rice University, 1997.

Hemphill, Marie H. *Fevers, Floods and Faith: A History of Sunflower County, Mississippi, 1844–1976.* Indianola, Miss.: Hemphill, 1980.

Hess, Earl J. "Confiscation and the Northern War Effort: The Army of the Southwest at Helena." *Arkansas Historical Quarterly* 44 (spring 1985): 55–75.

———. *Liberty, Virtue, and Progress: Northerners and their War for the Union.* New York: New York University Press, 1988.

Hewitt, Nancy. "Compounding Differences." *Feminist Studies* 18 (summer 1992): 313–26.

Heyrman, Christine Leigh. *Southern Cross: The Beginnings of the Bible Belt.* Chapel Hill: University of North Carolina, 1998.

Higginbotham, A. Leon, Jr. *In the Matter of Color: Race and the American Legal Process.* New York: Oxford University Press, 1978.

———. *Shades of Freedom: Racial Politics and Presumptions of the American Legal Process.* New York: Oxford University Press, 1996.

Higginbotham, Evelyn Brooks. "African-American Women's History and the Metalanguage of Race." *Signs* 17 (winter 1992): 251–74.

———. *Righteous Discontent: The Women's Movement in the Black Baptist Church, 1880–1920.* Cambridge: Harvard University Press, 1993.

Higgs, Robert. *Competition and Coercion: Blacks in the American Economy, 1865–1914.* Cambridge: Cambridge University Press, 1977.

Hill, Marilynn Wood. *Their Sisters' Keepers: Prostitution in New York City, 1830–1870.* Berkeley and Los Angeles: University of California Press, 1993.

Hine, Darlene Clark. *Hine Sight: Black Women and the Re-Construction of American History.* Brooklyn, N.Y.: Carlson, 1994.

———, ed. *Black Women's History: Theory and Practice.* Brooklyn, N.Y.: Carlson, 1990.

Hine, Darlene Clark, and Christie Anne Farnham. "Black Women's Culture of Resistance and the Right to Vote." In *Women of the American South: A Multicultural Reader,* edited by Christie Anne Farnham, 204–19. New York: New York University Press, 1997.

Hine, Darlene Clark, and Earnestine Jenkins. *A Question of Manhood: A Reader in U.S. Black Men's History and Masculinity.* Bloomington: Indiana University Press, 1999.

Hine, Darlene Clark, Wilma King, and Linda Reed. *"We Specialize in the Wholly Impossible": A Reader in Black Women's History.* Brooklyn, N.Y.: Carlson, 1995.

Hodes, Martha Elizabeth. *White Women, Black Men: Illicit Sex in the Nineteenth-Century South.* New Haven: Yale University Press, 1997.

Hodes, Martha Elizabeth, ed. *Sex, Love, Race: Crossing Boundaries in North American History.* New York: New York University Press, 1999.

Holt, Sharon Ann. *Making Freedom Pay: North Carolina Freedpeople Working for Themselves, 1865–1900.* Athens: University of Georgia Press, 2000.

———. "Symbol, Memory, and Service: Resistance and Family Formation in Nineteenth-Century African America." In *Working Toward Freedom: Slave Society and Domestic Economy in the American South,* edited by Larry E. Hudson Jr. Rochester, N.Y.: University of Rochester Press, 1994.

———. "A Time to Plant: The Economic Lives of Freedpeople in Granville County, North Carolina, 1865–1900." Ph.D. diss., University of Pennsylvania, 1991.

Holt, Thomas C. "Empire Over the Mind: Emancipation, Race, and Ideology in the British West Indies and the American South." In *Region, Race, and Reconstruction: Essays in Honor of C. Vann Woodward,* edited by J. Morgan Kousser and James M. McPherson. New York: Oxford University Press, 1982.

———. "Marking: Race, Race-making, and the Writing of History." *American Historical Review* 100 (February 1995): 1–20.

———. *The Problem of Freedom: Race, Labor, and Politics in Jamaica and Britain, 1832–1938.* Baltimore: Johns Hopkins University Press, 1992.

Holtzclaw, Robert Fulton. *Black Magnolias: A Brief History of the Afro-Mississippian, 1865–1980.* Shaker Heights, Ohio: Keeble Press, 1984.

hooks, bell. *Black Looks: Race and Representation.* Boston: South End Press, 1992.

———. *Feminist Theory from Margin to Center.* Boston: South End Press, 1984.

———. *Killing Rage: Ending Racism.* New York: Holt, 1996.

———. "Revolutionary Black Women: Making Ourselves Subject." In *Postcolonial Criticism,* edited by Bart Moore-Gilbert, Gareth Stanton, and Willy Maley. London: Longman, 1997.

Hudson, Larry E., Jr. *To Have and to Hold: Slave Work and Family Life in Antebellum South Carolina.* Athens: University of Georgia Press, 1997.

Hudson, Larry E., Jr., ed. *Working Toward Freedom: Slave Society and Domestic Economy in the American South.* Rochester, N.Y.: University of Rochester Press, 1994.

Hunt, Lynn. *The Family Romance of the French Revolution.* Berkeley and Los Angeles: University of California Press, 1992.

Hunter, Tera W. "Household Workers in the Making: Afro-American Women in Atlanta and the New South, 1861–1920." Ph.D. diss., Yale University, 1990.

———. *To 'Joy My Freedom: Southern Black Women's Lives and Labors after the Civil War.* Cambridge: Harvard University Press, 1997.

Hurtado, Aida. "Relating to Privilege: Seduction and Rejection in the Subordination of White Women and Women of Color." *Signs* 14 (winter 1989): 833–55.

Isenberg, Nancy. *Sex and Citizenship in Antebellum America.* Chapel Hill: University of North Carolina Press, 1998.

Jackson, Ronald Vern, and Gary Ronald Teeples, eds. *Mississippi 1850 Census Index.* Bountiful, Utah: Accelerated Indexing Systems, 1977.

Jacobson, Matthew Frye. *Whiteness of a Different Color: European Immigrants and the Alchemy of Race.* Cambridge: Harvard University Press, 1998.

Jaynes, Gerald David. *Branches Without Roots: Genesis of the Black Working Class in the American South, 1862–1882.* New York: Oxford University Press, 1986.

Jenkins, Wilbert L. *Seizing the New Day: African-Americans in Post–Civil War Charleston.* Bloomington: Indiana University Press, 1998.

Jensen, Joan M. *Loosening the Bonds: Mid-Atlantic Farm Women, 1750–1850.* New Haven: Yale University Press, 1986.

Johnson, Christopher Stephen. "Poverty and Dependency in Antebellum Mississippi." Ph.D. diss., University of California, Riverside, 1988.

Jones, Jacqueline. *Labor of Love, Labor of Sorrow: Black Women, Work, and the Family from Slavery to the Present.* New York: Basic Books, 1985.

Jones, James Boyd, Jr. "A Tale of Two Cities: The Hidden Battle Against Venereal Disease in Civil War Nashville and Memphis." *Civil War History* 31 (September 1985): 270–76.

Jones, Lu Ann. "Gender, Race, and Itinerant Commerce in the Rural New South." *Journal of Southern History* 66 (May 2000): 297–320.

Jordan, Winthrop D. *Tumult and Silence at Second Creek: An Inquiry into a Civil War Slave Conspiracy.* Baton Rouge: Louisiana State University Press, 1993.

———. *White Over Black: American Attitudes Toward the Negro, 1550–1812.* Chapel Hill: University of North Carolina Press, 1968.

Jordan, Winthrop D., and Sheila L. Skemp, eds. *Race and Family in the Colonial South: Essays.* Jackson: University Press of Mississippi, 1987.

Journal of the House of Representatives of the State of Mississippi at a Regular Session Thereof Convened in the City of Jackson, January 5, 1875. Jackson: Pilot Publishing, 1875.

Journal of the House of Representatives of the State of Mississippi at a Regular Session Thereof Held in the City of Jackson, 1874. Jackson: Kimball, Raymond, 1874.

Journal of the Proceedings of the Constitutional Convention of the State of Mississippi, 1868.
Jackson: E. Stafford, 1871.

Journal of the Senate of the State of Mississippi at a Regular Session Thereof Held in the City of Jackson, 1871. Jackson: Kimball, Raymond, 1871.

Journal of the Senate of the State of Mississippi at a Regular Session Thereof Held in the City of Jackson, 1874. Jackson: Kimball, Raymond, 1874.

Joyner, Charles W. *Down by the Riverside: A South Carolina Slave Community.* Urbana: University of Illinois Press, 1984.

Kane, Harnett Thomas. *Deep Delta Country.* New York: Duell, Sloan and Pearce, 1944.

Kantrowitz, Stephen. *Ben Tillman and the Reconstruction of White Supremacy.* Chapel Hill: University of North Carolina Press, 2000.

———. "One Man's Mob is Another Man's Militia: Violence, Manhood, and Authority in Reconstruction South Carolina." In *Jumpin' Jim Crow: Southern Politics From Civil War to Civil Rights,* edited by Jane Dailey, Glenda Elizabeth Gilmore, and Bryant Simon, 67–87. Princeton: Princeton University Press, 2000.

Kaye, Anthony E. "The Personality of Power: The Ideology of Slaves in the Natchez District and the Delta of Mississippi, 1830–1865." Ph.D. diss., Columbia University, 1999.

Keating, Bern. *A History of Washington County, Mississippi.* Greenville, Miss.: Greenville Junior Auxiliary, 1976.

Kelley, Robin D. G. "An Archaeology of Resistance." *American Quarterly* 44 (June 1992): 292–98.

———. *Hammer and Hoe: Alabama Communists during the Great Depression.* Chapel Hill: University of North Carolina Press, 1990.

———. *Race Rebels: Culture, Politics, and the Black Working Class.* New York: Free Press, 1994.

———. *Yo' Mama's Disfunktional!: Fighting the Culture Wars in Urban America.* Boston: Beacon Press, 1997.

Kerber, Linda K. "A Constitutional Right to Be Treated Like American Ladies: Women and the Obligations of Citizenship." In *U.S. History as Women's History: New Feminist Essays,* edited by Linda K. Kerber, Alice Kessler-Harris, and Kathryn Kish Sklar, 17–35. Chapel Hill: University of North Carolina Press, 1995.

———. *No Constitutional Right to Be Ladies: Women and the Obligations of Citizenship.* New York: Hill and Wang, 1998.

———. "Separate Spheres, Female Worlds, Women's Place: The Rhetoric of Women's History." *Journal of American History* 75 (June 1988): 9–39.

———. *Women of the Republic: Intellect and Ideology in Revolutionary America.* Chapel Hill: University of North Carolina Press, 1980.

rican Welfare State." In *Women, the State, and Welfare,* edited by Linda Gordon.
son: University of Wisconsin Press, 1990.

idney W. "Slavery and the Rise of Peasantries." *Historical Reflections/Réflexions
oriques* 6 (summer 1979): 213–42.

ppi Reports—Cases Argued and Determined in the High Court of Error and Appeals
he State of Mississippi. Vols. 39–45. Philadelphia: T. and T. W. Johnson, 1867.

Clarence L. *On the Threshold of Freedom: Masters and Slaves in Civil War Georgia.*
ens: University of Georgia Press, 1986.

ief, Sandra. "The Mississippi Married Women's Property Act of 1839." *Journal of
sissippi History* 47 (1985): 110–25.

hon, Carl H. *The Impact of the Civil War and Reconstruction on Arkansas: Persis-
ce in the Midst of Ruin.* Baton Rouge: Louisiana State University Press, 1994.

omery, David. *Beyond Equality: Labor and the Radical Republicans, 1862–1872.*
w York: Knopf, 1967.

—. *The Fall of the House of Labor: The Workplace, the State, and American Labor
tivism, 1865–1925.* Cambridge: Cambridge University Press, 1987.

gomery, Frank A. *Reminiscences of a Mississippian in Peace and War.* Cincinnati:
bert Clarke, 1901.

e, John Hebron. *The Emergence of the Cotton Kingdom in the Old Southwest: Mis-
ssippi, 1770–1860.* Baton Rouge: Louisiana State University Press, 1988.

an, A. T. *Yazoo; or, On the Picket Line of Freedom in the South: A Personal Narrative.*
ew York: Russell and Russell, 1884; reprint, 1968.

an, Edmund S. *American Slavery, American Freedom: The Ordeal of Colonial Vir-
nia.* New York: Norton, 1975.

an, Philip D. "Work and Culture: The Task System and the World of Lowcountry
lacks, 1700 to 1880." *William and Mary Quarterly* 39 (October 1982): 563–99.

ris, Thomas D. *Southern Slavery and the Law, 1619–1860.* Chapel Hill: University of
orth Carolina Press, 1996.

rison, Toni. *Playing in the Dark: Whiteness and the Literary Imagination.* Cambridge:
Harvard University Press, 1992.

h, Gary B. *Race and Revolution.* Madison, Wis.: Madison House, 1990.

man, Louise Michele. *White Women's Rights: The Racial Origins of Feminism in the
United States.* New York: Oxford University Press, 1999.

holson, Linda J. *Gender and History: The Limits of Social Theory in the Age of the
Family.* New York: Columbia University Press, 1986.

——. *The Play of Reason: From the Modern to the Postmodern.* Ithaca: Cornell University Press, 1999.

holson, Linda J., ed. *Feminism/Postmodernism.* New York: Routledge, 1990.

Kerr-Ritchie, Jeffrey R. *Freedpeople in the Tobacco South: Virginia, 1860–1900.* Chapel
Hill: University of North Carolina Press, 1999.

Kierner, Cynthia A. *Beyond the Household: Women's Place in the Early South, 1700–1835.*
Ithaca: Cornell University Press, 1998.

King, Deborah K. "Multiple Jeopardy, Multiple Consciousness: The Context of a Black
Feminist Ideology." *Signs* 14 (autumn 1988): 42–72.

Kolchin, Peter. *First Freedom: The Responses of Alabama's Blacks to Emancipation and
Reconstruction.* Westport, Conn.: Greenwood Press, 1972.

Laclau, Ernesto, and Chantal Mouffe. *Hegemony and Socialist Strategy: Towards a Radical Democratic Politics.* Translated by Winston Moore and Paul Commack. London:
Verso, 1985.

Landes, Joan B. *Women and the Public Sphere in the Age of the French Revolution.* Ithaca:
Cornell University Press, 1988.

*Laws of Mississippi, Passed at the Regular Session of the Mississippi Legislature Held in
Jackson, July 1861.* Jackson: E. Barksdale, 1861.

*Laws of Mississippi, Passed at the Regular Session of the Mississippi Legislature Held in
Macon, August 1864.* Jackson: J. J. Shannon, 1864.

*Laws of Mississippi, Passed at the Regular Session of the Mississippi Legislature Held in
October, November and December, 1865.* Jackson: J. J. Shannon, 1866.

*Laws of Mississippi, Passed at the Regular Session of the Mississippi Legislature Held in the
City of Jackson, November and December, 1861 and January, 1862.* Jackson: Cooper and
Kimball, 1862.

*Laws of the State of Mississippi, Passed at a Called and Regular Session of the Mississippi
Legislature Held in Jackson and Columbus, December 1862 and January 1863.* Selma,
Ala.: Cooper and Kimball, 1864.

*Laws of the State of Mississippi, Passed at a Called Session of the Mississippi Legislature,
Held in the City of Jackson, October, 1866 and January and February, 1867.* Jackson: J.
J. Shannon, 1867.

*Laws of the State of Mississippi, Passed at a Regular Session of the Mississippi Legislature,
Held in the City of Jackson, Commencing Jan. 1st and Ending May 13th, 1871.* Jackson:
Alcorn and Fisher, 1871.

*Laws of the State of Mississippi, Passed at the Regular Session of the Mississippi Legislature,
1865.* Jackson: J. J. Shannon, 1865.

*Laws of the State of Mississippi, Passed at the Regular Session of the Mississippi Legislature
Convened in the City of Jackson, January 20, 1874.* Jackson: Pilot Publishing, 1874.

*Laws of the State of Mississippi, Passed at the Regular Session of the Mississippi Legislature,
Held in the City of Jackson, Commencing Jan. 2, 1872 and Ending April 5, 1872.* Jackson:
Kimball, Raymond, 1872.

Laws of the State of Mississippi, Passed at the Regular Session of the Mississippi Legislature, Held in the City of Jackson, Commencing Jan 8th, 1878 and Ending March 5th, 1878. Jackson: Power and Barksdale, 1878.

Laws of the State of Mississippi, Passed at the Regular Session of the Mississippi Legislature Held in the City of Jackson, Commencing January 21, 1873 and Ending April 19, 1873. Jackson: Kimball, Raymond, 1873.

Lebsock, Suzanne. *The Free Women of Petersburg: Status and Culture in a Southern Town, 1784–1860.* New York: Norton, 1984.

———. "Radical Reconstruction and the Property Rights of Southern Women." *Journal of Southern History* 43 (May 1977): 195–216.

Lipsitz, George. *The Possessive Investment in Whiteness: How White People Profit from Identity Politics.* Philadelphia: Temple University Press, 1998.

Litwack, Leon F. *Been in the Storm So Long: The Aftermath of Slavery.* New York: Knopf, 1979.

Lohrenz, Mary Edna, and Anita Miller Stamper. *Mississippi Homespun: Nineteenth-Century Textiles and the Women Who Made Them.* Jackson: Mississippi Department of Archives and History, 1989.

Lott, Eric. *Love and Theft: Blackface Minstrelsy and the American Working Class.* New York: Oxford University Press, 1993.

Lynch, John R. *The Facts of Reconstruction.* 1913. Reprint, New York: Arno Press, 1968.

———. *Reminiscences of an Active Life: The Autobiography of John Roy Lynch.* Chicago: University of Chicago Press, 1970.

MacCabe, Colin. Foreword to *In Other Worlds: Essays in Cultural Politics,* edited by Gayatri Chatravorty Spivak, ix–xix. New York: Methuen, 1987.

MacLean, Nancy. *Behind the Mask of Chivalry: The Making of the Second Ku Klux Klan.* New York: Oxford University Press, 1994.

———. "The Leo Frank Case Reconsidered: Gender and Sexual Politics in the Making of Reactionary Populism." *Journal of American History* 78 (December 1991): 917–48.

Main, Edwin M. *The Story of the Marches, Battles, and Incidents of the Third United States Colored Cavalry: A Fighting Regiment in the War of the Rebellion, 1861–5.* 1908. Reprint, New York: Negro Universities Press, 1970.

Malcolmson, Patricia E. *English Laundresses: A Social History, 1850–1930.* Urbana: University of Illinois Press, 1986.

Malone, Ann Patton. *Sweet Chariot: Slave Family and Household Structure in Nineteenth-Century Louisiana.* Chapel Hill: University of North Carolina, 1992.

Mandel, Bernard. *Labor, Free and Slave: Workingmen and the Anti-slavery Movement in the United States.* New York: Associated Authors, 1955.

Manderson, Lenore. "Colonial Desires: Sexuality, Race, and Gender in British Malaya." *Journal of the History of Sexuality* 7 (January 1997): 372–88.

Mann, Susan Archer. "Slavery, Sharecropping, and Se[...] 1989): 774–98.

Marshall, T. H. "Citizenship and Social Class." In *Clas[...] ment: Essays,* 78–113. Garden City, N.Y.: Doubleda[...]

Mathews, Donald G. *Religion in the Old South.* Chicago: [...]

McCain, William D., and Charlotte Capers, eds. *Me[...] Papers of the Washington County Historical Society[...] Department of Archives and History, 1954.

McClintock, Megan. "Civil War Pensions and the Rec[...] *Journal of American History* 83 (September 1996): 4[...]

McCurry, Stephanie. "Citizens, Soldiers' Wives, and 'Hile[...] of Political Obligation in the Civil War South." In [...] *Politic,* edited by Nancy Bercaw, 95–124. Jackson: U[...] 2000.

———. "In Defense of Their World: Gender, Class, an[...] Carolina Low Country, 1820–1860." Ph.D. diss., State U[...] hamton, 1988.

———. *Masters of Small Worlds: Yeoman Households, Gen[...] Culture of the Antebellum South Carolina Low Country.*[...] Press, 1995.

———. "The Politics of Yeoman Households in South C[...] *Gender and the Civil War,* edited by Catherine Clinton[...] Oxford University Press, 1992.

———. "The Two Faces of Republicanism: Gender and Pr[...] lum South Carolina." *Journal of American History* 78 (N[...]

McGlynn, Frank, and Seymour Drescher, eds. *The Meaning [...] tics, and Culture After Slavery.* Pittsburgh: University of [...]

McMillen, Sally G. *Motherhood in the Old South: Pregnancy, [...] ing.* Baton Rouge: Louisiana State University Press, 1990[...]

McNeily, John Seymore. *Climax and Collapse of Reconstructio[...] N.p., n.d.

McPherson, James M. *Ordeal by Fire: The Civil War and R[...] Knopf, 1982.

Memphis Daily Appeal. March 1863–September 1886.

Miers, Earl Schenck. *Web of Victory: Grant at Vicksburg.* New[...]

Miller, Steven F., et al. "Between Emancipation and Enfranchi[...] litical Mobilization of Black Southerners During President[...] 1867." *Chicago-Kent Law Review* 70 (summer 1995): 1059–7[...]

Mink, Gwendolyn. "The Lady and the Tramp: Gender, Race, [...]

Oakes, James. *The Ruling Race: A History of American Slaveholders.* New York: Knopf, 1982.

————. *Slavery and Freedom: An Interpretation of the Old South.* New York: Knopf, 1990.

O'Donovan, Susan Eva. "Transforming Work: Slavery, Free Labor, and the Household in Southwest Georgia, 1850–1880." Ph.D. diss., University of California, San Diego, 1997.

O'Hanlon, Rosalind. "Recovering the Subject: Subaltern Studies and the Histories of Resistance in Colonial South Asia." *Modern Asian Studies* 22 (February 1988): 189–224.

Olmsted, Frederick Law. *A Journey in the Back Country.* 1860. Reprint, New York: Schocken, 1970.

Olwell, Robert. "'Loose, Idle, and Disorderly': Slave Women in the Eighteenth-Century Charleston Marketplace." In *More than Chattel: Black Women and Slavery in the Americas,* edited by David Barry Gaspar and Darlene Clark Hine, 97–110. Bloomington: Indiana University Press, 1996.

————. *Masters, Slaves, and Subjects: The Culture of Power in the South Carolina Low Country, 1740–1790.* Ithaca: Cornell University Press, 1998.

————. "'A Reckoning of Accounts': Patriarchy, Market Relations, and Control on Henry Laurens's Lowcountry Plantations, 1762–1785." In *Working Toward Freedom: Slave Society and Domestic Economy in the American South,* edited by Larry E. Hudson Jr. Rochester, N.Y.: University of Rochester Press, 1994.

Owens, Harry P. *Steamboats and the Cotton Economy: River Trade in the Yazoo-Mississippi Delta.* Jackson: University Press of Mississippi, 1990.

Owens, Harry P., and James J. Cooke, eds. *The Old South in the Crucible of War: Essays.* Jackson: University Press of Mississippi, 1983.

Ownby, Ted. "Patriarchy in the World Where There is No Parting? Power Relations in Confederate Heaven." In *Southern Families at War: Loyalty and Conflict in the Civil War South,* edited by Catherine Clinton, 229–44. New York: Oxford University Press, 2000.

Painter, Nell Irvin. *Exodusters: Black Migration to Kansas After Reconstruction.* New York: Knopf, 1977.

————. *Sojourner Truth: A Life, A Symbol.* New York: Norton, 1996.

Parks, Ken. *The Civil War in Mississippi, 1861–65.* Bolton, Miss.: Ken Parks Associates, 1959.

Pateman, Carole. *The Sexual Contract.* Stanford: Stanford University Press, 1988.

Penningroth, Dylan. "Slavery, Freedom, and Social Claims to Property Among African-Americans in Liberty County, Georgia, 1850–1880." *Journal of American History* 84 (September 1997): 405–35.

Powell, Lawrence N. *New Masters: Northern Planters During the Civil War and Recon-struction.* New Haven: Yale University Press, 1980.

Powell, Lawrence N., and Michael Wayne. "Self Interest and the Decline of Confederate Nationalism." In *The Old South in the Crucible of War,* edited by Harry P. Owens and James J. Cooke, 29–45. Jackson: University Press of Mississippi, 1983.

Pratt, Fletcher. *Civil War on Western Waters.* New York: Holt, 1956.

Rable, George C. *But There Was No Peace: The Role of Violence in the Politics of Reconstruc-tion.* Athens: University of Georgia Press, 1984.

———. *Civil Wars: Women and the Crisis of Southern Nationalism.* Urbana: University of Illinois Press, 1989.

———. *The Confederate Republic: A Revolution Against Politics.* Chapel Hill: University of North Carolina Press, 1994.

Raboteau, Albert J. *A Fire in the Bones: Reflections on African-American Religious History.* Boston: Beacon Press, 1995.

———. *Slave Religion: The "Invisible Institution" in the Antebellum South.* New York: Oxford University Press, 1978.

Ransom, Roger L., and Richard Sutch. *One Kind of Freedom: The Economic Consequences of Emancipation.* Cambridge: Cambridge University Press, 1977.

Rawick, George P., ed. *The American Slave: A Composite Autobiography.* v.7, Westport, Conn.: Greenwood Press, 1972.

"Reconstruction in the Northern Counties of Mississippi." Unpublished manuscript, Department of History, University of Mississippi, 1907–11.

Reidy, Joseph P. *From Slavery to Agrarian Capitalism in the Cotton Plantation South: Central Georgia, 1800–1880.* Chapel Hill: University of North Carolina Press, 1991.

———. "Slavery, Emancipation, and the Capitalist Transformation of Southern Agri-culture, 1850–1910." In *Agriculture and National Development: Views of the Nineteenth Century,* edited by Lou Ferlenger. Ames: Iowa State University Press, 1990.

Revised Code of the Statute Laws of the State of Mississippi, as Adopted at the January Session, A.D. 1871. Jackson: Alcorn and Fisher, n.d.

Roark, James L. *Masters Without Slaves: Southern Planters in the Civil War and Recon-struction.* New York: Norton, 1977.

Robertson, Claire. "Africa into the Americas?: Slavery and Women, the Family, and the Gender Division of Labor." In *More than Chattel: Black Women and Slavery in the Americas,* edited by David Barry Gaspar and Darlene Clark Hine, 3–40. Bloom-ington: Indiana University Press, 1996.

Robinson, Armstead L. "Day of Jubilo: Civil War and the Demise of Slavery in the Mis-sissippi Valley, 1861–65." Ph.D. diss., University of Rochester, 1977.

———. "'Worser Dan Jeff Davis': The Coming of Free Labor During the Civil War, 1861–

65." In *Essays on the Postbellum Southern Economy,* edited by Thavolia Glymph and John J. Kushma. College Station: Texas A&M University Press, 1985.

Roediger, David R. *Towards the Abolition of Whiteness: Essays on Race, Politics, and Working Class History.* New York: Verso, 1994.

———. *The Wages of Whiteness: Race and the Making of the American Working Class.* London: Verso, 1991.

Rose, Willie Lee. *Rehearsal for Reconstruction: The Port Royal Experiment.* Indianapolis: Bobbs-Merrill, 1964.

Rosen, Hannah. "The Gender of Reconstruction: Rape, Race, and Citizenship in the Postemancipation South." Ph.D. diss., University of Chicago, 1999.

———. "'Not That Sort of Women': Race, Gender, and Sexual Violence during the Memphis Riot of 1866." In *Sex, Love, Race: Crossing Boundaries In North American History,* edited by Martha Elizabeth Hodes, 267–93. New York: New York University Press, 1999.

Rowland, Dunbar. *Courts, Judges, and Lawyers of Mississippi, 1798–1935.* Jackson: Mississippi Department of Archives and History, 1935.

———. *History of Mississippi, the Heart of the South.* Chicago: S. J. Clarke, 1925.

———. *Military History of Mississippi, 1803–1898.* Jackson: n.p., 1908.

Rowland, Dunbar, ed. *Mississippi: Comprising Sketches of Counties, Towns, Events, Institutions, and Persons, Arranged in Cyclopedic Form.* Atlanta: Southern Historical Publishing Association, 1907.

Rowland, Leslie. Essay. *Conference Group on Women's Historians Newsletter* 22 (October 1991): 21–22.

Ryan, Mary P. *Civic Wars: Democracy and Public Life in the American City during the Nineteenth Century.* Berkeley and Los Angeles: University of California Press, 1997.

———. *Cradle of the Middle Class: The Family in Oneida County, New York, 1790–1865.* New York: Cambridge University Press, 1981.

Saville, Julie. *The Work of Reconstruction: From Slave to Wage Laborer in South Carolina, 1860–1870.* New York: Cambridge University Press, 1994.

Saxton, Alexander. *The Rise and Fall of the White Republic: Class Politics and Mass Culture in Nineteenth-Century America.* London: Verso, 1990.

Schwalm, Leslie A. *A Hard Fight for We: Women's Transition from Slavery to Freedom in South Carolina.* Urbana: University of Illinois Press, 1997.

———. "The Meaning of Freedom: African-American Women and Their Transition from Slavery to Freedom in Lowcountry South Carolina." Ph.D. diss., University of Wisconsin, 1991.

———. "'Sweet Dreams of Freedom': Freedwomen's Reconstruction of Life and Labor in Lowcountry South Carolina." *Journal of Women's History* 9 (spring 1997): 9–38.

Scott, Anne Firor. *The Southern Lady: From Pedestal to Politics, 1830–1930.* Chicago: University of Chicago Press, 1970.

Scott, James C. *Domination and the Arts of Resistance: Hidden Transcripts.* New Haven: Yale University Press, 1990.

———. *Weapons of the Weak: Everyday Forms of Peasant Resistance.* New Haven: Yale University Press, 1985.

Scott, Joan Wallach. *Gender and the Politics of History.* New York: Columbia University Press, 1988.

Scott, Rebecca J. "Exploring the Meaning of Freedom: Postemancipation Societies in Comparative Perspective." *Hispanic American Historical Review* 68 (August 1988): 407–28.

Scott, Robert N., ed. *Official Records of the Union and Confederate Armies.* Washington, D.C.: Government Printing Office, 1885.

Siegel, Reva B. "Home as Work: The First Woman's Rights Claims Concerning Wives' Household Labor, 1850–1880." *Yale Law Journal* 103 (March 1994): 1073–1217.

———. "The Modernization of Marital Status Law: Adjudicating Wives' Rights to Earnings, 1860–1930." *Georgetown Law Review* 82 (September 1994): 2127–2212.

———. "'The Rule of Love': Wife Beating as Prerogative and Privacy." *Yale Law Journal* 105 (June 1996): 2117–2207.

Silber, Nina. *The Romance of Reunion: Northerners and the South, 1865–1900.* Chapel Hill: University of North Carolina Press, 1993.

Sillers, Florence Warfield, et al. *History of Bolivar County, Mississippi.* Jackson, Miss.: Hederman Brothers, 1948.

Silverblatt, Irene. *Moon, Sun, and Witches: Gender Ideologies and Class in Inca and Colonial Peru.* Princeton: Princeton University Press, 1987.

———. "Women in States." *Annual Reviews in Anthropology* 17 (1988): 427–60.

Smith, Dorothy Vick. "Black Reconstruction in Mississippi, 1862–1870." Ph.D. diss., University of Kansas, 1985.

Smith, Frank E. *The Yazoo River.* 1954. Reprint, Jackson: University Press of Mississippi, 1988.

Smith, Raymond T. "Race, Class, and Gender in the Transition to Freedom." In *The Meaning of Freedom: Economics, Politics, and Culture After Slavery,* edited by Frank McGlynn and Seymour Drescher, 257–90. Pittsburgh: University of Pittsburgh Press, 1992.

Smith-Rosenberg, Carroll. *Disorderly Conduct: Visions of Gender in Victorian America.* New York: Knopf, 1985.

Somers, Margaret R. "Bringing Marshall Back In: Rediscovering and Reinventing Citizenship." *Inchiesta* 28 (April-June 1998): 7–13.

———. "Citizenship and the Place of the Public Sphere: Law, Community, and Political

Culture in the Transition to Democracy." *American Sociological Review* 58 (October 1993): 587–620.

———. "Citizenship between State and Market. Civil Society and the Problem of the 'Third Sphere.'" *Berliner Journal für Soziologie* 8 (1998): 489–505.

———. "Narrating and Naturalizing Civil Society and Citizenship Theory: The Place of Political Culture and the Public Sphere." *Sociological Theory* 13 (November 1995): 229–274.

———. "The Privatization of Citizenship: How to Unthink a Knowledge Culture." In *Beyond the Cultural Turn: New Directions in the Study of Society and Culture,* edited by Victoria E. Bonnell and Lynn Hunt. Berkeley and Los Angeles: University of California Press, 1999.

———. "Rights, Relationality, and Membership: Rethinking the Making and Meaning of Citizenship." *Law and Social Inquiry* 19 (winter 1994): 63–112.

Sparks, Randy J. *On Jordan's Stormy Banks: Evangelicalism in Mississippi, 1773–1876.* Athens: University of Georgia Press, 1994.

Spear, Jennifer Michel. "'Whiteness and the Purity Of Blood': Race, Sexuality, and Social Order in Colonial Louisiana." Ph.D. diss., University of Minnesota, 1999.

Speth, Linda. "The Married Women's Property Acts, 1839–65: Reform, Reaction, or Revolution?" In *Women and the Law: A Social Historical Perspective,* edited by D. Kelly Weisberg, 2:69–91. Cambridge, Mass.: Schenkman, 1982.

Spivak, Gayatri Chakravorty. "Subaltern Studies: Deconstructing Historiography." In *In Other Worlds: Essays in Cultural Politics.* New York: Methuen, 1987.

Stallybrass, Peter, and Allon White. *The Politics and Poetics of Transgression.* Ithaca: Cornell University Press, 1986.

Stanley, Amy Dru. "Beggars Can't Be Choosers: Compulsion and Contract in Postbellum America." *Journal of American History* 78 (March 1992): 1265–93.

———. "Conjugal Bonds and Wage Labor: Rights of Contract in the Age of Emancipation." *Journal of American History* 75 (September 1988): 471–500.

———. *From Bondage to Contract: Wage Labor, Marriage, and the Market in the Age of Slave Emancipation.* Cambridge: Cambridge University Press, 1998.

———. "Home Life and Morality of the Market." In *The Market Revolution in America: Social, Political, and Religious Expressions, 1800–1880,* edited by Melvin Stokes and Stephen Conway, 74–86. Charlottesville: University Press of Virginia, 1996.

Stansell, Christine. *City of Women: Sex and Class in New York, 1789–1860.* New York: Knopf, 1986.

Statistics of the United States in 1860: Compiled from the Original Returns of the Eighth Census. New York: Arno Press, 1976.

Sterling, Dorothy, ed. *We Are Your Sisters: Black Women in the Nineteenth Century.* New York: Norton, 1984.

Stevenson, Brenda E. "Black Family Structure in Colonial and Antebellum Virginia: Amending the Revisionist Perspective." In *The Decline in Marriage Among African-Americans: Causes, Consequences, and Policy Implications,* edited by M. Belinda Tucker and Claudia Mitchell-Kernan. New York: Russell Sage Foundation, 1995.

———. "Distress and Discord in Virginia Slave Families, 1830–1860." In *In Joy and in Sorrow: Women, Family, and Marriage in the Victorian South, 1830–1900,* edited by Carol Bleser, 103–24. New York: Oxford University Press, 1991.

———. *Life in Black and White: Family and Community in the Slave South.* New York: Oxford University Press, 1996.

Stoler, Ann Laura. *Race and the Education of Desire: Foucault's History of Sexuality and the Colonial Order of Things.* Durham: Duke University Press, 1995.

Sydnor, Charles Sackett. *Slavery in Mississippi.* New York: D. Appleton–Century, 1933.

———. "The Southerner and the Laws." *Journal of Southern History* 6 (February 1940): 3–24.

Sydnor, Charles S., and Claude Bennett. *Mississippi History.* New York: Rand, McNally, 1930.

Thomas, Emory M. *The Confederacy as a Revolutionary Experience.* Englewood Cliffs, N.J.: Prentice-Hall, 1971.

———. *The Confederate Nation, 1861–1865.* New York: Harper and Row, 1979.

Tomlins, Christopher L. *Law, Labor, and Ideology in the Early American Republic.* Cambridge: Cambridge University Press, 1993.

Tomlins, Christopher L., and Andrew J. King, eds. *Labor Law in America: Historical and Critical Essays.* Baltimore: Johns Hopkins University Press, 1992.

Trelease, Allen W. *White Terror: The Ku Klux Klan Conspiracy and Southern Reconstruction.* New York: Harper and Row, 1971.

Tucker, Susan, ed. *Telling Memories Among Southern Women: Domestic Workers and Their Employers in the Segregated South.* Baton Rouge: Louisiana State University Press, 1988.

Tunnell, Ted. *Crucible of Reconstruction: War, Radicalism, and Race in Louisiana, 1862–1877.* Baton Rouge: Louisiana State University Press, 1984.

Tupelo (Miss.) Standard. January 1873–June 1874.

Tushnet, Mark V. *The American Law of Slavery, 1810–1860: Considerations of Humanity and Interest.* Princeton: Princeton University Press, 1981.

Ulrich, Laurel Thatcher. *Good Wives: Image and Reality in the Lives of Women in Northern New England, 1650–1750.* New York: Knopf, 1982.

U.S. Bureau of the Census. Seventh Census, 1850. NA.

———. Eighth Census, 1860, NA.

———. Ninth Census, 1870. NA.

U.S. Senate. *Conditions of Affairs in the Southern States* in *United States Senate Reports,* no. 1, pts. 11 and 12, 42d Cong., 2d sess., 1872, serials 1494 and 1495.

Van Tassel, Emily Field. "'Only the Law Would Rule Between Us': Antimiscegenation, the Moral Economy of Dependency, and the Debate Over Rights after the Civil War." *Chicago-Kent Law Review* 70 (summer 1995): 873–926.

Waldrep, Christopher. *Roots of Disorder: Race and Criminal Justice in the American South, 1817–80.* Urbana: University of Illinois Press, 1998.

Walkowitz, Judith R. *Prostitution and Victorian Society: Women, Class, and the State.* Cambridge: Cambridge University Press, 1980.

Wallace, Jesse Thomas. *A History of the Negroes in Mississippi from 1865–1890.* 1927. Reprint, New York: Johnson Reprint Corp., 1972.

Watkins, James Hull. "Locating the Self: Southern Identity, White Masculinity, and the Autobiographical 'I.'" Ph.D. diss., University of Florida, 1995.

Watts, Trent Alan. "Imagining a White South: Narratives of (B)order and Community, 1890–1920." Ph.D. diss., University of Chicago, 2000.

Wayne, Michael. *Death of an Overseer: Reopening a Murder Investigation from the Plantation South.* New York: Oxford University Press, 2001.

———. *The Reshaping of Plantation Society: The Natchez District, 1860–1880.* Baton Rouge: Louisiana State University Press, 1983.

Weekly Clarion. Jackson, Miss. March 1869–December 1882.

Weekly Panola (Miss.) Star. January 1857–March 1873.

Weiner, Marli F. *Mistresses and Slaves: Plantation Women in South Carolina, 1830–80.* Urbana: University of Illinois Press, 1998.

Wexler, Laura. *Tender Violence: Domestic Visions in an Age of U.S. Imperialism.* Chapel Hill: University of North Carolina Press, 2000.

Wharton, Vernon Lane. *The Negro in Mississippi, 1865–1890.* 1947. Reprint, New York: Harper Torchbooks, 1965.

Whayne, Jeannie M., ed. *Shadows Over Sunnyside: An Arkansas Plantation in Transition, 1830–1945.* Fayetteville: University of Arkansas Press, 1993.

Whayne, Jeannie M., and Willard B. Gatewood, eds. *The Arkansas Delta: Land of Paradox.* Fayetteville: University of Arkansas Press, 1993.

White, Deborah Gray. *Ar'n't I a Woman? Female Slaves in the Plantation South.* New York: Norton, 1985.

Whites, LeeAnn. "The Civil War as a Crisis in Gender." In *Divided Houses: Gender and the Civil War,* edited by Catherine Clinton and Nina Silber. Oxford: Oxford University Press, 1992.

———. *The Civil War as a Crisis in Gender: Augusta, Georgia, 1860–1890.* Athens: University of Georgia Press, 1995.

———. "'Stand by Your Man': The Ladies Memorial Association and the Reconstruction of Southern White Manhood." In *Women of the American South: A Multicultural Reader,* edited by Christie Anne Farnham, 133–49. New York: New York University Press, 1997.

Wiley, Bell Irvin. *Southern Negroes, 1861–1865.* New Haven: Yale University Press, 1938.

Williams, James Levon, Jr. "Civil War and Reconstruction in the Yazoo Mississippi Delta, 1863–1875." Ph.D. diss., University of Arizona, 1992.

Williams, William H. *Slavery and Freedom in Delaware, 1639–1865.* Wilmington, Del.: SR Books, 1996.

Willis, John C. *Forgotten Time: The Yazoo-Mississippi Delta after the Civil War.* Charlottesville: University Press of Virginia, 2000.

———. "On the New South Frontier: Life in the Yazoo-Mississippi Delta, 1865–1920." Ph.D. diss., University of Virginia, 1991.

Wilson, Charles Reagan. *Baptized in Blood: The Religion of the Lost Cause, 1865–1920.* Athens: University of Georgia Press, 1980.

Wood, Betty. *Gender, Race, and Rank in a Revolutionary Age: The Georgia Lowcountry, 1750–1820.* Athens: University of Georgia Press, 2000.

———. *Women's Work, Men's Work: The Informal Slave Economies of Lowcountry Georgia.* Athens: University of Georgia Press, 1995.

Wood, Kirsten Elizabeth. "Fictive Mastery: Slaveholding Widows in the American Southeast, 1790–1860." Ph.D. diss., University of Pennsylvania, 1998.

Woodman, Harold D. "Class, Race, Politics, and the Modernization of the Postbellum South." *Journal of Southern History* 63 (February 1997): 3–22.

———. "Economic Reconstruction and the Rise of the New South, 1865–1900." In *Interpreting Southern History: Historiographical Essays in Honor of Sanford W. Higginbotham,* edited by John B. Boles and Evelyn Thomas Nolen, 254–307. Baton Rouge: Louisiana State University Press, 1987.

———. "How New Was the New South?" *Agricultural History* 58 (October 1984): 529–45.

———. *King Cotton and His Retainers: Financing and Marketing the Cotton Crop of the South, 1800–1925.* Lexington: University of Kentucky Press, 1968.

———. *New South, New Law: The Legal Foundations of Credit and Labor Relations in the Postbellum Agricultural South.* Baton Rouge: Louisiana State University Press, 1995.

———. "One Kind of Freedom after Twenty Years." *Explorations in Economic History* 38 (January 2001): 48–57.

———. "Post–Civil War Southern Agriculture and the Law." *Agricultural History* 53 (January 1979): 319–37.

———. "Sequel to Slavery: The New History Views the Postbellum South." *Journal of Southern History* 43 (November 1977): 523–54.

Woodruff, Nan. "African-American Struggles for Citizenship in the Arkansas and Mississippi Deltas in the Age of Jim Crow." *Radical History Review* 55 (1993): 33–51.

———. "Pick or Fight: The Emergency Farm Labor Program in the Arkansas and Mississippi Deltas During World War II." *Agricultural History* 61 (1990): 74–85.

Woods, Clyde Adrian. *Development Arrested: The Blues and Plantation Power in the Mississippi Delta.* New York: Verso, 1998.

Wyatt-Brown, Bertram. *Southern Honor: Ethics and Behavior in the Old South.* New York: Oxford University Press, 1982.

Zipf, Karin L. "Reconstructing 'Free Woman': African-American Women, Apprenticeship, and Custody Rights During Reconstruction." *Journal of Women's History* 12 (spring 2000): 8–31.

Index

Nancy Bercaw is assistant professor of history at the University of Mississippi. She is the editor of *Gender and the Southern Body Politic.*